Liberty and Utility

LIBERTY
and
UTILITY

The French Idéologues and the Transformation of Liberalism

CHERYL B. WELCH

New York · Columbia University Press · *1984*

Library of Congress Cataloging in Publication Data

Welch, Cheryl B.
Liberty and utility.

Bibliography: p.
Includes index.
1. Social sciences—France—History—18th century.
2. Social sciences—France—History—19th century.
3. Liberalism—France—History 18th century.
4. Liberalism—France—History—19th century. I. Title.
H53.F7W44 1983 300′.944   83–14435
ISBN 0-231-05130-1

COLUMBIA UNIVERSITY PRESS
NEW YORK   GUILDFORD, SURREY

*Clothbound editions of Columbia University Press books are
Smyth-sewn and printed on permanent and durable acid-free paper.*

*To my father
and to the memory of
my mother*

CONTENTS

ACKNOWLEDGMENTS

THE IDEA for this book grew out of a seminar on eighteenth-century political thought given by Julian H. Franklin. I would like to thank him for his patience and critical judgment during the writing of what was originally a doctoral thesis. Herbert Deane also read the entire dissertation with scrupulous attention. To them both I am very grateful as well for their generous encouragement throughout my graduate studies.

Emmet Kennedy read a later version of the manuscript with meticulous care and made many useful suggestions and corrections. Robert Scanlan was kind enough to check most of the translations. I would also like to thank Eileen Sullivan, Isser Woloch, Robert D. Cumming, Shannon Stimson, Stephen Holmes, and Stanley Hoffman for helpful criticisms at various stages of the manuscript preparation. Most of all I thank my husband, John, for his faultless editorial judgment and his unfailing support throughout.

Introduction

I HAVE two principal aims in this book. One is to offer an interpretation of the social and political ideas associated with the Idéologues, the loosely defined group of theorists and publicists who dominated the intellectual life of France during the later stages of the Revolution and the early years of the nineteenth century. This group has been the object of increasing interest for its role as *intercesseur* between the Ancien Régime and post-Revolutionary France, and for its illumination of those changes in cultural sensibilities at the end of the eighteenth and beginning of the nineteenth centuries that are at the root of the elusive concept of modernity.[1] We have recently had, for example, a massive reconsideration of the "twilight of the Enlightenment" in the works of Sergio Moravia, as well as book-length studies of several individual figures of the period.[2]

My concerns, however, are somewhat different from those of other recent students of the Idéologues. I want to chart a significant change in political vocabulary associated with important members of this group, most notably Destutt de Tracy. In reconstructing this view of society and politics, I will also have something to say about other thinkers, in particular Pierre Daunou and J.B. Say, but also Sieyès, Condorcet, Volney and Cabanis. This is a selective reading among the Idéologues, but not, I hope, an arbitrary one. The works of Tracy and Daunou are of interest precisely because they were so important in transmitting a relatively coherent vision of politics to the post-Revolutionary generation.[3] My aim, then, is not to characterize the politics of the group as a whole. I suspect that would be a laborious and perhaps pointless task, since the Idéologues were more a disparate group of somewhat like-minded individuals than an organized sect. Rather, I wish to elucidate one influential view of the liberal polity and to argue that this was a self-consciously utilitarian view, in many ways analogous to that of Bentham and James Mill in England. Like their English counterparts, the theories of these Idéologues criticize existing political rhetoric and attempt to find a conciliatory political force in the notion of "utility" or general happiness. Moreover, like the theories of Bentham and Mill in England, the social and political perspective exemplified in the writings of Tracy and Daunou is adopted and adapted by various groups of followers to fashion a distinct rationale for democratic reform.[4]

The language of utility, of course, was spoken in one or another dialect by many eighteenth-century thinkers. In France the Abbé de Saint-Pierre, Holbach, and Helvétius developed explicitly utilitarian theories of society; moreover, Holbach and Helvétius concluded that a psychology based on self-interest and a morality based on the greatest happiness principle implied some form of political democracy. And Bentham's *An Introduction to the Principles of Morals and Legislation* was published considerably before the French Revolution. My focus, however, is less on these indisputable precursors than on the ways in which utilitarian ideas were adopted and transformed to address new problems, problems that make the terms of eighteenth century debate about democracy seem curiously anachronistic.

My second purpose, then, is to use the theory of the Idéologues to illuminate a more general issue: the problem of how and why the fusion of utility, liberty, and democracy developed in the language of political theorizing. The recent revival of interest in utilitarian theories and their relationship to theories of rights has focused attention anew on the nature of this connection and, consequently, on its historical roots. It might seem that the obvious place to begin such a study would be British "philosophical radicalism." Halévy's masterful and in many ways unsurpassed work is based on this assumption, and utilitarianism has often been viewed as an almost exclusively English phenomenon.[5] But the amalgam of sensationalist philosophy, moral theory based on self-interest, economic liberalism, and democratic politics brought to mind by the term "philosophical radicalism," was far from peculiarly English. I will argue not only that there were utilitarian "radicals" on the continent, but that the French version of the theory provides us with a unique critical perspective from which to assess the genesis and theoretical character of this sort of early-nineteenth-century radical reformism. Because of his need to make sense of his own revolutionary past, and his greater attention to philosophic method, a political thinker like Destutt de Tracy brings the theoretical character of early utilitarianism more clearly into focus. And because of the polarized and politically charged atmosphere in France—from the Revolution to the Restoration—the peculiar vulnerability of this position is revealed more sharply as well.

The notion that philosophical radicalism is the quintessential bourgeois philosophy, or at least that it is explicable only in relation to the needs of a people directly confronting the problems of industrial growth and dislocation, is still the prevailing view of this theory. There has even been a certain amount of speculation as to why utilitarianism, allegedly so expressive of the calculating mentality of the modern age, did not "take root" outside England.[6] My focus on early-nineteenth-century French liberalism suggests that this line of inquiry is somewhat misguided. I want to argue that political revolution and the social distrust bequeathed by civil war were the essential crises to which classic utilitarianism was a response. Instead of asking why utilitarianism was not exportable, then, we might better ask, what particular factors intensified the influence in England of a widespread but transitional movement in liberalism?

The first and last chapters of the following essay are largely historical. The first examines the revolutionary experience of the French "philosophical party," the milieu in which the ideas of the Idéologues took shape. The last focuses primarily on the splintering of *idéologie* in the 1820s and 1830s. The central sections of the book are more analytical. Chatpers 2, 3, and 4 examine the implications of the search for a scientific grounding of principles of action, the character of the Idéologues' enthusiastic embrace of political economy, and the nature of the theory of politics found in the works of Tracy and Daunou. In chapter 5 I attempt to make the insights of the preceding chapters sharper by an explicit comparison with some of the ideas of Bentham and Mill.

Finally, I would like to add a word about terminology and citations. Whenever I wished "ideology" to convey what Tracy meant when he coined the word, I have either used quotation marks or the French *idéo-*

logie. For the most part I have used *liberal* in the loose way in which it was used in the early nineteenth century, i.e., to connote a commitment to certain individual rights (specifically equality before the law, freedom of the press, and religious freedom), opposition to the policies of the mercantilist state, opposition to monarchical power if not to monarchical government, and a certain expansiveness of social sympathies. I have used *radical* as a description of those liberals who sought reform through wholesale changes in political institutions and a significant extension of the franchise. This was the sense in which it was understood in early-nineteenth-century England, i.e., as against Whigs or "trimmers." I have extrapolated this use to France, as did some French contemporary observers, but this use should not be confused with the *radicalisme* of the Third Republic.[7]

In quoting from French works, I have used English translations, if these were adequate and readily available, although these have been checked whenever possible against the originals. More often I have quoted from the French texts; all these translations are my own.

CHAPTER ONE

The Revolutionary Legacy

T HE VIEW of society and politics that was transmitted to the post-Revolutionary generation in the works of the Idéologues is incomprehensible apart from its particular revolutionary heritage. Those who came to be called Idéologues under the Directory, Consulate, and Empire continued the efforts of political moderates who attempted—and failed—to establish liberal representative government in France during the early years of the Revolution. Despite the toll taken by the guillotine and by emigration, there was a continuity both of personnel and ideas within this moderate faction, especially among those who have been called the "philosophical party,"[1] i.e., thinkers like Condorcet and Sieyès, who explicitly took on the task of clarifying the theoretical bases of the Revolution. The Idéologues came to political consciousness in this milieu: in the salon of Madame Helvétius, in the houses of Condorcet and Mirabeau, and at the Society of 1789.[2]

Because much of the literature on the Idéologues fails to note the significant evolution in the view of politics held by these "philosophical" republicans during the revolutionary decade, this chapter will trace in some detail their political opinions and fortunes. In particular, it is necessary to underline the gradual abandonment of the language of politics originally adopted to justify the Revolution. Even before the rise of Jacobinism, there were reservations about the ideology of natural rights among liberals. But since the legitimacy of the new constitutional settlement depended on this theory, the original defense of the Revolution was a defense of the Declaration of the Rights of Man and Citizen. After the Terror, doubts hardened into a rejection of "rhetorical" liberalism. Given their political objectives during the Directory, however, the moderates found it difficult to develop any acceptable alternative. It was only with Napoleon's subversion of the Republic, a subversion in which they unwittingly participated, that the Idéologues transformed the non-Jacobin republican consensus into a defense of liberal republicanism on utilitarian grounds.

The Philosophical Party and the Rights of Man

In the years just before the outbreak of the Revolution, a younger circle of literary men began to frequent the important salon of the widow of Helvétius at Auteuil.[3] Usually introduced by Condorcet, the newer faces included the poet André Chénier and his brother Marie-Joseph Chénier, a political dramatist soon to be famous as the lyricist of revolutionary songs. Political journalists and general men of letters like Dominique-Joseph Garat, Pierre-Louis Roederer, Pierre-Louis Ginguené, François Andrieux, and Jean-Baptiste Say, began to replace the more famous *philosophes*. Destutt de Tracy, who may have visited the salon during the period of the Constituent Assembly, moved to Auteuil in 1792. Pierre Cabanis had come to Paris as a medical student in 1778 and was virtually adopted by Madame Helvétius. Eventually he became physician and advisor to Mirabeau.

The most important of the revolutionary theorists who frequented the Auteuil salon were Condorcet and Sieyès. While often in disagreement on specific matters, the two shared a common philosophical orientation expressed in their collaboration on the short-lived *Journal d'instruction sociale*. The aim of the *Journal* was to popularize the methods of scientific reasoning in social and political affairs, primarily through the analysis of political vocabulary.[4] Like other heirs of the *philosophes*, Condorcet and Sieyès applied the eighteenth-century method of the "analysis of ideas" to current social and political issues in order to defend the reconstitution of authority in France. Above all they wished to clarify the theory of natural rights as expressed in the rallying cry of the new order, the *Déclaration des droits de l'homme et du citoyen*.

The primary justification for overturning the *Ancien Régime* was indisputably a theory of the natural rights of man. Burke's indictment of this theory as abstract and dangerously metaphysical, an indictment given classical form by Taine in the nineteenth century, has never really disappeared from theoretical discussions of French revolutionary ideology. Even those more sympathetic to the principles of the French revolutionaries, however, usually assert that these principles connoted something very different from what the "practical" utilitarians meant by the greatest happiness principle. Thus, in *The English Utilitarians,* Plamenatz accuses the English Whig James Mackintosh of a fundamental mistranslation of the French theory of the natural rights of man when the latter argued in 1791:

> When I assert that a man has a right to life, liberty, etc., I only mean to enunciate a MORAL MAXIM founded on *general interest*, which prohibits any attack on these possessions. In this primary and radical sense, all rights natural as well as civil, arise from expedience.[5]

On the contrary, I will argue that Mackintosh's deliberately utilitarian interpretation of natural rights in his *Vindiciae Gallicae* described the position of a considerable body of liberal opinion in France. Some French liberals, as well as conservatives, were ambivalent about using the language of natural rights to support revolution. And, in proportion to the radicalization of the Revolution, these "philosophic" liberals would increasingly favor the utilitarian side of the revolutionary legacy.

At first the predominant sentiment in the Assembly was that the new constitution would be a contract between the Assembly and the king, based on a reaffirmation of the fundamental laws of the kingdom according to which law was made *consensu populi et constitutione regis.* However, with the defeat of the nobility, and with continuing conflict between the Assembly and the crown, arguments based on an ancient French constitution quickly became associated with counterrevolution. An insistence that popular rights were based solely on universal reason and natural law, and that France's constitution was yet to be made, became the dominant justification for the Assembly's assumption of power. Arguments from "nature" and "natural right" were pervasive in eighteenth-century France and provided the deputies with a ready-made vocabulary of revolution.

The example of the American Revolution tended to confirm the French predilection for natural right theory. The American practice of prefacing state constitutions with declarations of rights was well-known in France, and to some extent was the immediate cause of the French Declaration of 1789.[6] The French *Déclaration des droits de l'homme et du citoyen,* however, was strongly marked by the particular circumstances surrounding its birth. It was at once a protest against the most resented abuses of the old order, an attempted legitimization of the power exercised by the National Assembly, and a setting of goals for the Revolution. Aulard has aptly called it the death certificate of the *Ancien Régime.*[7]

The debate over the formulation of a declaration of rights reflected an intense awareness of the revolutionary situation; the resulting document was, in part, a tactical move to gain support for the revolutionary leadership of the Third Estate. Caught between mistrust of the court and uneasiness at the growing influence of the Parisian populace, the Assembly needed urgently to consolidate its position, and to establish its authority *de jure.* Hence, those in favor of a declaration of rights offered no reasoned, theoretical defense of natural rights. They alluded to natural law in a vague and emotive fashion, and declared rights to be invariable and eternal. No one considered the origin and substance of rights systematically. Rather, the issue was the usefulness of producing some statement of principle as a rallying point against the forces of counterrevolution.[8] To this end, they sought to consolidate revolutionary consciousness among the people by a concise and simple declaration "fit to become a national catechism."[9]

That prudential considerations were at the center of the debate over the adoption of a declaration of rights becomes even clearer when the arguments against a declaration are considered. The primary objection, eloquently stated by Malouet, was that the language of natural right promised the common man more than the constitution could deliver: "Why then take him first to the mountaintop, and show him his boundless dominion, when he must descend to find obstacles at every step."[10] While not denying that the rights of man should be the guiding spirit of legislation, Malouet insisted that the primary task of the Assembly was to devise a beneficial constitution for France. It was dangerous to tell the suffering and unenlightened masses, deprived of ways to remedy their situation, that they were equal in rights to the most powerful. In support of Malouet, others argued that a declaration of rights would be both dangerous and useless, since laws alone could prescribe rights and determine the status of citizens.[11]

The Declaration that finally emerged from the Assembly debate, then, was both the product of immediate political concerns and the expression of natural law principles widely shared among the deputies. It is a document obviously capable of bearing a radically democratic interpretation. The majority in the Assembly, however, intended to maintain the monarchy and to organize a purely representative regime. Indeed, the Declaration of the Rights of Man and Citizen was translated into a clear mandate for the sovereign authority of the National Assembly, regarded as the sole legal representative of the nation.[12]

Once the Declaration was accepted as the basis of the new regime, many liberals attempted to interpret the document "philosophically."[13] Three of the most influential interpretations can be found in the revolutionary pamphlets of Volney, Condorcet, and Sieyès. Although these thinkers differed in emphasis, certain shared themes are strikingly apparent. The common ground of their efforts to construct a "scientific" theory of natural law was the sensationalist psychology drawn from Locke's *Essay on the Understanding*. Here they followed the lead of the Abbé de Condillac.[14] They also drew heavily on the works of the French Physiocrats, whose call for "property, liberty, and security" was one of the most important mediums through which deputies to the Estates General became familiar with natural rights language.[15]

Like Condillac, the Physiocrats reasoned that although a natural law governed men in society, this law could not be discovered through intuition, but only through factual evidence. Observation "indicated" that man was a physical being motivated by desires and selfish interests. His ultimate goal was happiness, which could be identified with physical pleasure, and which consisted in the enjoyment of an abundance of economic goods. Since men could be observed discovering and utilizing means to this end, the Physiocrats concluded it to be proved that human nature was defined by the search for pleasure. The apparent uniformity and order that the Physiocrats attributed to human behavior were analogous, they thought, to the laws governing the physical universe. But they further argued that the natural laws governing men's actions imposed moral obligations. According to the Physiocrats, God imposed a duty on man to satisfy his instincts; therefore, he has a natural right to those things necessary for human satisfaction. The rights and duties of man increase with the increasing complexity of the social order, resulting in a "concatenation of duties and rights."[16] For the Physiocrats, then, rights were clearly based on individual interests, and they attempted to show that these interests, properly understood, accorded with a system of natural justice.

The Physiocratic theory of natural law and rights had been used above all to urge economic reform on France, to advocate the freeing of the "natural" order from "unnatural" interference. In the political sphere, the Physiocrats supported absolute monarchical sovereignty. On the eve of revolution in France, however, the Physiocratic theory of rights based on interest was appropriated by those who wished to justify the destruction of absolutism and the adoption of representative institutions.

Volney, already famous for his historical and geographical studies of Egypt and Syria,[17] elaborated the bases for the rights of man in *La Loi naturelle* (1789). His view, reiterated in the better-known *Les Ruines, ou méditation sur les révolutions des empires* (1791), is perhaps the most simplistic attempt to explain the philosophical basis of rights. For that very reason, however, it clearly reveals the logic that also underlies the works of Condorcet and Sieyès.

In the tradition of the eighteenth-century materialists, Volney describes man as gradually civilized by self-love, the desire for happiness, and aversion from pain: the "essential and primary laws that nature herself imposed on man."[18] Besides deducing all the moral virtues and vices from these premises, Volney goes directly to his conception of man as a sensate creature to deduce the necessary civil rights that man must be accorded to ensure his happiness: equality, liberty, and property.

Volney insists that men are equal in a physical sense because their faculties are the same in kind. One must presume that all men have an equal right to preserve and nourish themselves. The fact that each man is created free and independent of other beings sufficiently indicates his right to liberty. And since every man controls the movements of his body, and thus his labor, he has a right to the results of this activity, i.e., to property. In sum, from the physical facts of similar sensory apparatus, discrete identity, and the need for individual exertion in order to survive, Volney asserts the value of equality, liberty, and property in society.[19]

Volney's efforts to explain natural rights by leaping from physical attributes to moral and legal claims is characteristic of all attempts to derive the rights of man from sensationalist psychology. Moreover, he employs the same kind of reasoning underlying most utilitarian theories of morals: every individual is so constituted as to desire pleasure; therefore, he ought to have as much pleasure as possible. The "fact-value" distinction was meaningless to most eighteenth-century thinkers, and is similarly ignored in the theory of Condorcet. For Condorcet, as for Volney, the psychological facts of human nature logically imply conceptions of universal rights and justice.[20] Although never explicitly stated, the logic of the connection between the fact of equality and equality as a right seemed to him obvious from the very definition of man as a sensate being endowed with reason.

> We want a constitution whose principles are uniquely based on the natural rights of man, anterior to social institutions.
>
> We call these rights *natural,* because they are derived from the nature of man; that is to say, once a sensitive being exists, capable of reasoning and of having moral ideas, it follows as an evident and necessary consequence, that he must enjoy these rights, that he cannot be deprived of them without injustice.[21]

Condorcet discusses the natural rights of man in a series of pamphlets appearing on the eve of the Revolution.[22] He consistently identifies them as security and liberty of person, security and liberty of property, and equality before the law. The right to participate in the formation of the law is sometimes listed as a separate right, sometimes subsumed under equality. In general, equality is the only right that he believes to require much explanation. He carefully defines it so as to exclude only that inequality that is the "arbitrary" work of social institutions, reasoning that inequality based on riches or function is not foreign to the nature of man and things.[23]

Although Condorcet always accepted the sovereignty of the people as the theoretical basis of government, he distinguished clearly between the preservation of the rights of man and the exercise of popular sovereignty. The former was of much greater importance than the latter. Nevertheless, a central and increasingly important theme in Condorcet's later political writings is the attempt to devise a constitution under which the people might safely exercise political power. The natural right to participate in the formation of the law, however, remained problematical.

In the *Essai sur l'application de l'analyse à la probabilité des décisions rendues à la pluralité des voix* (1785), Condorcet attempted through probability theory to discover the conditions under which a majority decision was likely to coincide with "truth," and concluded that the coincidence would be likely only among an elite of rational decision-makers. Both Condorcet's revolutionary experience and his search for theoretical consistency, however, led him to abandon this position. In the Girondin constitution, Condorcet rejects any limitation on universal male suffrage as theoretically untenable: "We did not think it would be legitimate to sacrifice a natural right, acknowledged by the most simple reason, to considerations whose reality is at least uncertain."[24]

For Condorcet recognition of rights is a matter of intellectual enlightenment. Enlightenment, however, is a social process and thus historically conditioned. In the *Esquisse d'un tableau historique des progrès de l'esprit humain* Condorcet traces the growth of human reason and its gradual triumph over error. Hindered by the stubborn tendency of the human mind to cleave to customary ideas, the progress of philosophy nevertheless steadily continues, and in turn fosters economic and political progress. Eventually, man's psychological capacity to receive and compare sensations, to order them by the use of language, and to combine them to his own advantage reveals the true rights of man, the key to real happiness in the social order.[25] Condorcet places this discovery in the ninth epoch of human history, i.e., in his own age.

Although Condorcet assigns a central role to man's psychological capacities in the development of society, his descriptions of man's progress through the hunting, pastoral, and agricultural stages to the modern commercial state, have much in common with the historians of the Scottish Enlightenment.[26] Like the Scots, Condorcet gives a functional explanation of the origin and growth of political authority. Furthermore, he does not discuss an original social compact, and he specifically rejects the notion of an original contract between the people and the government.[27] Nevertheless, in his revolutionary pamphlets, he continually refers to a voluntary social contract, by which men enter society to protect their rights, and which alone legitimizes political authority.

> Too weak, when they are isolated, to resist the evils that surround them [men] come together, and in order to profit from their union, they make an agreement; each one promises to the community that he will support it with his power; the community promises each of the members to defend him by employing all the forces of the association, and this contract is as obligatory

for the whole community as for each individual, since it is the effect of a unanimous will determined by the common interest.[28]

Condorcet's most characteristic expression can be found in the Declaration of Rights prefacing the proposed Girondin constitution. "The purpose of all joining of men into society being the preservation of their natural rights, civil and political, these rights are the basis of the social compact."[29]

Condorcet is supremely unconcerned by the apparent conflict between these approaches to rights because he regards the historical development of society and government as irrelevant to their logical foundations.[30] The use of the idea of a social contract is merely a convenient way to emphasize the fundamental importance of consent in political arrangements, given a certain level of enlightenment. Ultimately, the justification for men's rights lies not in the specific terms of a contract, but in the benefits conferred by a social and political order that recognizes such rights. Condorcet freely calls rights inalienable and urges the adoption of a solemn declaration enumerating them, but he also can state that the legitimacy of the new order lies as much in its advantages to the people as in formal consent.

> The nation did not establish the old regime and named none of its officials; the change was made without it and it still names no one. It has therefore lost nothing and gained nothing; the old regime and the new are equally legitimate; the only question is which of the two is more advantageous to the people.[31]

The new order, in which men's rights are recognized, is more advantageous because it is not committed to particular privileges and is more open to useful innovation.

It is obvious that Condorcet sees no important distinction between natural rights properly understood and social utility. He faces the problem squarely in his introduction to *De l'influence de la Révolution d'Amérique sur l'Europe* (1786), which deals with the measurement of different degrees of public happiness. Condorcet rejects the view that the happiness of a people can be considered as a kind of mean value of the happiness and unhappiness of all the individuals in society.[32] Rather, he proposes that the happiness of a people be measured in terms of the general capability a nation possesses to achieve happiness. This capability can be divided into two categories: 1) the extent to which the political constitution recognizes the universal rights of man, and 2) physical and economic factors, such as geographical location, resources, the level of industry, distribution of the means of production, and regulations governing foreign trade. The second category specifically concerns the means that a nation has to obtain the most satisfaction from the least output of labor. Natural rights and a favorable economic organization are, furthermore, closely interdependent variables: "As for the second category of means to achieve happiness, it can easily be seen that they still depend to a great extent on a wider and freer exercise of natural rights.[33] As Condorcet states in the *Esquisse,* "the guaranteeing to each man his rights is . . . the whole of social utility."[34]

The theoretical approach of the Abbé Sieyès to the reconstitution of political authority differs from that of Condorcet, but exhibits a similar ambiguity about the ultimate justification of the political order. Although Sieyès cultivated the reputation of an impartial philosopher, he was above all a polemicist for a certain constitutional settlement for France. In his influential pamphlets, he borrows and attempts to synthesize arguments from many disparate sources.[35]

The *Préliminaire de la constitution française* begins in the spirit of the framers of countless proposed declarations by stating that the only object of governing is the protection of the rights of man. Thus the political philosopher's task is to discover the precise outline of these rights.

> No social union, and consequently no political constitution can have any other object than to guarantee, to serve, and to extend the rights of men living in society; they [framers of constitutions] therefore conclude that they must begin by recognizing these rights.[36]

Sieyès does not discuss in detail the physical or psychological nature of man, but assumes the truth of an egoistic model of human nature.[37] Men are physical beings with certain basic needs and a desire for happiness. Their moral and physical faculties are developed in response to needs and desires, and are the means to attain happiness (*bien-être*). Very much like Volney or Hobbes, Sieyès asserts that equal natural rights are derived from universal needs: "Either all men have the right to dispose of their means, or no man has this right. Individual *means* are linked by nature to individual *needs*. Therefore, whoever must bear the needs must also freely dispose of the means.[38] The equal right to satisfy needs can also be defined as man's property in his person. From this primitive property right are derived the rights of property in one's actions (the right to come and go as one pleases, to think, to speak, to print, to produce, to exchange, to consume, etc.).[39]

Without speaking directly of a state of nature, Sieyès contrasts man's exercise of his rights toward the nonhuman environment with his behavior toward others of his kind. The first presents no problems; men simply take what they need from nature. The second situation, however, results in a dynamic interaction with two possible outcomes. Either men regard other men as obstacles to satisfaction and objects to be destroyed, or they recognize the reciprocal utility involved in a joint effort to procure satisfaction. The second kind of human interaction is the only one that Sieyès regards as legitimate; however, in explaining the development of cooperative society and its underlying rules, he proposes more than one criterion for political legitimacy.

One argument for the rightful authority of government begins from the description of natural rights as the exercise of individual power to satisfy wants and desires. Cooperative social relations allow men to fulfill their needs and desires much more efficiently, and "man, as we have said, strives constantly for this end; he surely did not intend to change this goal when he joined in association with his fellow men."[40] Society does not inhibit, but rather increases liberty: "it is true to say that liberty is fuller and more complete in the social order than it ever could be in the so-called *natural* state."[41] Thus, according to Sieyès, society based on cooperation is preferable because it increases both the possibilities for and the means of satisfaction. He then states that the object of social union is the happiness of the associated. He even extends his argument to assert that men have a right to all the benefits of association, which increase as time, experience, and reflection produce an enlightened public. The most important duty of society is to increase the amount of *bien* produced by society, for "an association devised for the greatest good of all will be the masterwork of intelligence and virtue."[42] In this argument, the protection of rights has disappeared as a defense of the legitimacy of society and government, except in the sense that men have a right to have their wants and desires fulfilled in the most efficient manner possible.

Concurrently with this utilitarian approach, however, Sieyès presents an argument couched in language more consistent with traditional natural law theories of the state, and with the current justifications for the French Revolution. This argument emphasizes the element of consent rather than the element of gain in cooperation. It stresses the particular rights derived from equal needs rather than the general human right to satisfaction.

In trying to explain the mechanisms through which social cooperation is achieved, Sieyès relies on convention and contract. Men perceived that their self-interest could be better served through agreements than force, and they gradually built up a set of conventions to regulate behavior. Sieyès does not limit himself, however, to basing social arrangements on self-interested bargains. He stresses that aspect of contract that had been the basis of obligation in older natural law theories: voluntary consent to the terms of a contract. An association is considered to be legitimate only if it is based on a reciprocal, voluntary, and free contract on the part of the associates.[43] From this vantage point Sieyès criticizes social relationships based on warfare and violence, not because they are inefficient, but because they are based on force rather than on free consent.

According to Sieyès, free consent involves a recognition of equal, reciprocal rights: the specific rights to personal freedom and property that are implied in man's nature. It follows that the right of each implies the duty of all others to respect it. The law has no right to establish any privileges that deny individual rights; when it does so, "the social pact is broken."[44]

Sieyès's second line of reasoning is similar to the classic argument of Locke's *Second Treatise*. Locke's theory, however, presupposes a natural moral law that commands a recognition of the rights of others and is perceptible to all men who will but consult "right reason." Sieyès recognizes no divine moral law, but tries to derive all human values from physical needs. How, then, can he posit a spontaneous recognition by individuals of the rights of others, or the illegitimacy of social arrangements that are not based on free consent?

Sieyès's "rights" model is consistent with his utilitarian theory only if the former is understood as an abbreviated expression for maximum social utility in advanced civil society. Experience has shown that, given a certain level of social development, certain legal principles are the necessary bases of any government consistent with man's happiness. In this sense, such principles are natural laws. Sieyès's constitutional theory thus presupposes a social situation in which cultivation of social utility assures good order in society.[45]

Sieyès only partially recognizes the premises of this position. He does see that the natural law upon which he bases his theory refers to a group of principles that have been gradually accepted by men in society because of their usefulness.[46] The function of the philosopher is to discover the useful principles inherent in practice, to clarify and state them, and thus to influence public opinion in a beneficial direction.[47] Furthermore, in his discussion of the proper limits of individual rights, Sieyès assumes the operation and efficacy of a system of repressive positive law. It is the law that recognizes and marks the boundaries of any natural right, and the law is only as good as its enforcement by the authorities.[48]

Sieyès rarely calls attention, however, to these presuppositions. In fact, he seems at times to obscure them, whether deliberately or inadvertently, by emphasizing the inflexible character of rights. His reliance on the traditional language of natural law facilitates this emphasis, since the great systems of natural law were supposed to be universally valid, independent of any particular historical development. The prestige of natural law was a potent source of support for Sieyès's constitutional theory. In *Qu'est-ce que le Tiers Etat?* he relies on it even more strongly, although he certainly does not abandon arguments based on the economic productivity of the Third Estate.

In *Qu'est-ce que le Tiers Etat?* Sieyès explicitly adopts the model of the state of nature and the contract origin of society, describing three periods in the development of political society. First, a considerable number of isolated individuals come together to form an association. "This first period is characterized by the activity of the *individual* wills. The association is their work and they are the origin of all power." Second, these individuals create a common will (*volonté commune*) through the mechanism of majority vote, affirming that "power exists only in the aggregate." Finally, when the people become too numerous to exercise their common will, they form a government and delegate to it that portion of their common will necessary to maintain order. This is "government by proxy," in which the delegates exercise a "representative general will" in trust for others.[49]

Sieyès's purpose here was to identify the Third Estate with the nation, and to assert its right to exercise the constituent power without the participation of the other two orders.

> In the previous chapter we demonstrated that the *common* will can be discovered only in the opinion of the majority. This lies beyond question. It follows that in France the representatives of the Third Estate are the authentic trustees of the national will. They may speak then without error, in the name of the whole nation.[50]

In this context, Sieyès borrows elements from the Lockean theory of constituent and constituted powers, and from Rousseau's theory of the general will, in order to underline the sovereign right of the nation, and thus of the National Assembly, to change its constitution.

There are, then, two predominant strands of argument about the fundamental basis of the political order in the theories of liberals of the French Revolution. At times the ultimate purpose of political arrangements is to protect rights; at other times it is to foster social utility, generally interpreted as national productivity and prosperity. Both Condorcet and Sieyès would, of course, have denied any incompatibility between these points of view. Indeed, the confounding of social usefulness with natural right was a central feature of eighteenth-century thought; one finds the same tendency in Paine, Price, and Priestley in England.[51] Approval of the French Revolution initially intensified this connection, as theorists attempted to draw on the moral suasion of "natural law." Furthermore, there was a significant renascence—both in England and France—of the contract model. Despite widespread familiarity with attacks on contract theory, the symbol of contract was thought to be crucial to the task of legitimizing the National Assembly's assumption of power in France. Priestley, for example, refutes Burke's attack on the French Revolution by citing the implicit compact between magistrates and people. If the compact is broken, men revert to the state of nature.[52]

An especially clear statement of the importance of natural rights and the contract model to revolutionaries can be found in James Mackintosh's *Vindiciae Gallicae*. Mackintosh, like Condorcet and Sieyès, stresses the benefits of the social and political state and condemns any theory that supposes the actual existence of a state antecedent to the social. Nevertheless, Mackintosh goes on to refer to a state of nature in which equality of right is potential, if not actual; to discuss man's entering society by resigning a portion of his natural sovereignty over his own actions; and to insist that all natural rights are not sacrificed to government. For Mackintosh, the doctrine of natural rights is both abstractly evident and practically important, because it alone provides redress for the oppressed.[53] Though rights are ultimately based on utility and expedience, it would be fatal to insist on expedience in politics. One should, on the contrary, stress the "immutable basis of natural rights."[54]

The efforts of Condorcet and Sieyès to explain and justify the principles underlying the Revolution are the best-known examples of the political thinking characteristic of those frequenting the Auteuil salon. The opinions of others in Madame Helvétius's circle (insofar as their opinions can be determined) indicate support for these efforts. Nevertheless, an examination of the general reaction to revolutionary rhetoric reveals an undercurrent of doubt concerning both the actual Declaration of Rights and the adequacy of natural rights as a foundation for the new political order.

Sieyès himself was primarily interested in the explanatory essay that prefaces his proposed declaration. His actual list of rights is presented in a somewhat disdainful manner, as if yielding to the current fashion. In later articles for the *Journal d'instruction sociale* he repeats the utilitarian, rather than the natural rights, themes of the *Préliminaire,* and manifests uneasiness that the representative system was being attacked in the name of liberty.[55]

Mirabeau, an important spokesman for moderate views in the Constituent Assembly, had presented the first committee report on a declaration of rights. It was clear from his presentation, however, that he personally opposed the idea of a declaration on prudential grounds. For this reason, his report was rejected in favor of that of the sixth bureau.[56]

Volney and Garat also initially opposed the proposal for a specific declaration of rights. Volney attempted to ground the theory of natural rights in sensationalist psychology; nevertheless, he believed that a catalogue of particular rights would place arbitrary limits on reason, and would not be a "philosophical and progressive" work.[57] Furthermore, he thought that the most important problem was to concentrate on the logical foundations of the new order in France so as to put an end to the administrative anarchy of the Old Regime. In the debate on the final articles of the Declaration, Volney abruptly proposed a new preamble that simply listed the most serious grievances against past royal government: the dissipation of tax revenues, bad fiscal management, and violations of security, liberty, and property. This speech created an uproar in the Assembly because of its "brutal frankness."[58]

Destutt de Tracy's attitude toward the theoretical justification of the Revolution was similarly cautious. At the outbreak of the Revolution, Tracy was Colonel of the Penthièvre regiment and a prominent member of the *nobilité de race* with close ties to the court.[59] After having helped to draft the *cahier* of the Bourbonnais nobility, he was elected as a delegate to the Estates General. During his career in the Constituent Assembly, Tracy associated with the members of the liberal nobility and with the moderates in the Society of 1789, though he deliberately attempted to remain independent of factional ties and personal obligations. But it proved to be impossible to steer a middle course between the court and the Assembly. Uncomfortable with the machinations of parliamentary politics, Tracy did not emerge as a real force in the Assembly.[60] Unlike many liberal nobles, however, he remained loyal to the Assembly and to the new army, and he refused to emigrate.

Tracy's view of the principles underlying the Revolution can be inferred from two early writings that he published while a member of the Assembly: a letter to Edmund Burke and a pamphlet on the colonial problem. In these works Tracy displays many of the characteristic opinions that he and others later to be called Idéologues maintained throughout their careers. These attitudes, however, are often expressed in language subsequently abandoned as imprecise and rhetorical.

The letter to Burke does not attempt to refute Burke's arguments in detail, for Tracy admits that he knows Burke's opinions only from excerpts of his speeches.[61] Rather, Tracy defends in a general way the aims and methods of the Revolution, in response to what he sees as Burke's major criticisms. The tone is that of an earnest patriot, confident that the Revolution represents the dawn of a new era of world peace, domestic prosperity, and human justice.

Tracy was perhaps the first to make arguments against Burke that countless defenders of the French Revolution have repeated. Tracy con-

cedes that the Glorious Revolution in England was only a restoration, but he argues that France required a complete political revolution. The political role of the French aristocracy was historically different from that of its English counterpart; compromised by the nature of its association with an absolutist monarchy, the French nobility was useless as a vehicle of general reform. Furthermore, according to Burke's own theory, the principles of the English Constitution could not be applied in France, since they had been developed in response to specifically English conditions. In addition to these arguments, Tracy notes the peaceful intentions of the National Assembly, and defends its policy regarding civil disturbances: "I see there on one part only praiseworthy motives in the people, and a prudent conduct in their representatives." [62]

Throughout the letter to Burke, Tracy praises moderate representative government "founded on morality and the desire of making mankind happy." [63] In a style that unmistakably dates from the early phase of the Revolution, he expresses faith in public education and in the ability of a liberal regime to foster economic prosperity. Tracy speaks continually of liberty, freedom, and patriotism in an easy rhetorical fashion, invoking those general phrases about rights and liberty that signify his approval of the liberal reforms of 1789.

> A profound politician [Burke] ought to have pointed out the astonishing patriotism by which every province of the French empire has hastened to renounce every privilege—feeling that there are none to be compared to liberty—nor any private distinction so valuable as general union. [64]

For the sake of argument, Tracy even entertains a defense of liberty that he will later abandon as inconsistent with his more pragmatic and utilitarian approach to these matters. He chides Burke for referring to the French "collapse," arguing that Burke has mistaken the restoration of liberty for its demise.

> Indeed, without going back to the fourteenth century, in which ignorance caused us to lose the assemblies of the nation, and the elements of a true constitution, which we had; it is the pride and even the glory of Lewis the XIVth which laid the foundation of our ruin, which caused us to take glitter for glory, which drove us from truth, the only source of good. [65]

Although the Declaration of Rights was a primary object of Burke's attack, Tracy undertakes no theoretical defense of the Declaration. How-

ever, neither does he disclaim it. His attitude seems to be close to that of the Declaration's framers: i.e., that such a document was a useful abridgement of political principles, a rallying point for men severely divided on practical issues.

> If our declaration of rights is nonsense, our conduct is an excellent commentary on it. It was at the instant in which America busied herself with such nonsense that she became invincible to the whole force of England.[66]

If Tracy were truly committed to defending the social and political reforms of the Revolution in terms of the natural rights of man, one would expect him to base his defense of the rights of the Santo Domingo blacks on the Declaration of Rights. The cause of the slaves and free blacks was defended in the Assembly by certain deputies, led by the *Société des amis des noirs,* on the basis of the need to fulfill the promises inherent in the proclamation of natural equality.[67] The colonial problem was the issue with which Tracy was most closely associated in the Constituent Assembly. However, although he did contend that "natural laws that are the same everywhere" should be applied in Santo Domingo,[68] his primary argument for the rights of blacks was not based on this contention.

In the *Opinion sur Saint-Domingue* Tracy takes issue with the policies of the colonial committee of the National Assembly (dominated by a coalition of white colonists and French business interests), but prefaces his remarks with the assertion that he is not a member of the *Société des amis des noirs.* Although Tracy is clearly in favor of recognizing the civil and political rights of all the free men of Santo Domingo, most of his reasoning is purely prudential. He asserts that there is no reason to exclude free blacks, other than the selfish interests of the white colonists who wish to dominate the colony totally. According to Tracy, the white colonists occupied a precarious position in their own society, and would be untrustworthy allies. On the other hand, the free blacks, saved by the Assembly from oppression, would be France's obvious allies. Furthermore, there were almost as many *gens de couleur* as whites in the colony, and their numbers were increasing more rapidly. With civil and political rights, the black population and its productivity would grow even faster. Tracy certainly notes approvingly that an alliance with the free blacks could be seen as consistent with the principles of the Declaration of Rights, but his polemical point here is that such a policy was in the

interest of the French people, as well as in the interest of the majority of those in Santo Domingo.[69]

For many of the French revolutionaries, the question of rights for the free blacks of Santo Domingo posed a dilemma. Most arguments for the new French constitutional theory claimed that this theory was both morally right and socially useful. But, in the case of the colonial issue, social utility was generally thought to preclude the application of the general principles embodied in the Declaration of Rights.[70] Tracy, however, managed to avoid the appearance of a confrontation between rights and utility by rhetorically supporting the claims of the blacks on prudential grounds.

> I maintain then, that even if the Assembly were not honor bound to keep its decrees and to preserve the civil and political rights of free and propertied men, it is in our most urgent interest to do so.[71]

In 1790–91, then, Tracy defended the Revolution in the manner of most of its supporters, i.e., by exploiting the perceived consonance between natural rights and social utility. But he was not particularly interested in discussing the Declaration of Rights as a serious philosophical basis for the new constitutional order. However, if his use of the language of natural rights was more cautious than that of Condorcet of Sieyès, he shared the belief that there was a practical need for such a revolutionary manifesto.

Disillusionment

Beginning with the period of Jacobin ascendancy, and especially after the publication of the Constitution of 1793, serious doubts emerged about the language of natural rights. We begin to find both an echo of the original objections to the Declaration, and a groping toward a new position that would avoid the language of natural rights and popular sovereignty, but would remain supportive of the liberal reforms of the Revolution.

Appeals to natural rights, as had been foreseen by some conservatives in the Constituent Assembly, could be used to justify not only the claims of the more privileged members of the Third Estate, but also the demands of the artisan class, and of the unpropertied in general. Conservatives had frequently warned of the dangers of providing "unscrupulous agitators" with intellectual weapons to arouse the populace. The popular revolution seemed to confirm these fears.[72] Furthermore, it was both apparent and frightening to moderates that the revolutionary crowds, beyond being merely passive instruments, absorbed and adopted the slogans and ideas of the political groups contending for power during the Revolution. A typical example is that of a journeyman gunsmith arrested at Versailles who supported his claim to a fair hearing with an appeal to *le droit de l'homme*.[73] The report of the police commissioner examining this incident illustrates the growing equation of appeals to natural rights with anarchy. "He talks continuously of liberty and the rights of man, which shows clearly enough that he is bent on sedition." [74]

For the sans-culottes, the principle of 1789 declaring that "men are born and remain free and equal in rights" implied political sovereignty. Furthermore, sovereignty had an immediate and concrete referent: it was the sans-culottes themselves exerting their rights in the sectional assemblies.[75] The politicization of the Parisian populace, particularly their willingness to take part in armed demonstrations in support of their demands, was crucial both to the success and the course of the Revolution. After the fall of the monarchy, when the Girondin and Jacobin factions contested for leadership of the newly proclaimed Republic, the Jacobins' ability to mobilize support in the sections helped to assure their victory. The Jacobins and the sans-culottes never shared identical world views, but they established a temporary working relationship that was crucial to the defense and maintenance of the Revolution of 1793–94. Robespierre contended that in order to remain stable, revolutionary authority should be exercised in the name of the Convention; but to remain strong, it had to act in concert with the sans-culottes.[76] The majority in the Convention came to agree with the Montagnard position, and thus acquiesced in the purge of the Girondins.

During the period of Jacobin domination the language of natural rights was increasingly associated with two phenomena: the demand for economic controls, and the justification of revolutionary terror. The first development can be seen very clearly in Robespierre's speech to the Convention concerning the declaration of rights to be prefixed to the new republican constitution. Robespierre proposed a clarification of the natural right to property that would affirm the power of the state to regulate property rights and to impose progressive taxation.

> You also talk about taxation in order to establish the incontestable principle that it can emanate only from the will of the people or of its representatives, but you forget a measure that the interests of humanity demand; you forget to sanction the principles of progressive taxation.[77]

Robespierre did not question the abstract right to property; however, the willingness of the Committee of Public Safety to accept some state regulation of the economy won the support of sans-culottes leaders. Robespierre's oratory echoed sans-culotte demands such as those in the petition *Liberté, égalité ou la mort* for wage and price fixing. The petition denied that economic regulation would infringe on property rights; "do they not know, those scoundrels, do they not know that property rights have no limits except people's physical needs?"[78] The demand is put more crudely and ominously by Jacques Roux.

> It is thus that, through fear of counterrevolution, they try to raise the price of commodities: but don't they know that the people want liberty or death? What other object do these speculators have than to appropriate industries, businesses, and the products of the soil in order to drive people to despair, in order to force them into the arms of despotism? How much longer will you permit these rich egotists to go on drinking from their golden goblets the purest blood of the people?[79]

The principle of popular sovereignty was also used to justify the Committee of Public Safety's policy of calculated revolutionary terror. In a remarkable statement of the principles underlying revolutionary government, Robespierre clearly distinguished between the principles of democracy in peacetime, and the necessities of a revolutionary regime at war.

> The theory of the revolutionary government is as new as the Revolution that led to it.
> The end of the constitutional government is to conserve the Republic; that of the revolutionary government is to found it.
> The Revolution is the war of liberty against its enemies, the Constitution is the regime of liberty in victory and peace.[80]

Terroristic revolutionary measures, however, were undertaken only as the expression of the "real" will of the French people. Although revolutionary government was more repressive, Robespierre did not consider it necessarily less just or less legitimate. It still drew its mandate from the general will.

> Terror . . . is less a particular principle, than a consequence of the general principle of democracy, applied to the most urgent needs of the nation (*patrie*).[81]

The moderates were increasingly alarmed about the course of the Revolution and about their own earlier espousals of revolutionary slogans. This anxiety can be seen in a series of pamphlets published by Pierre Daunou. In 1789 Daunou was a teacher of Latin, philosophy, and theology. He welcomed the Revolution, left the priesthood, and accepted the civil constitution of the clergy. Elected both to the Constituent Assembly and to the Convention, Daunou became one of the Revolution's most respected orators and would become one of the most visible Idéologues in the political life of the Directory and of the Restoration.

In a revolutionary pamphlet published in 1789, Daunou enthusiastically justifies the Revolution on the basis of natural rights. He divides constitutional laws into two classes, those deriving from the very essence of civil associations, and those depending on particular circumstances. The first should be set out in a declaration of rights, and should include the rights to life, liberty, and property, along with the principle of popular sovereignty. According to Daunou, it was impossible that people could have renounced these rights when they contracted to form societies in order to escape the evils inseparable from the state of nature.[82]

After the fall of the monarchy and the abrogation of the Constitution of 1791, Daunou begins to waver from this position. While retaining his theoretical division of constitutional laws into invariable and circumstantial, and while continuing to call the first a declaration of rights, he emphasizes that the proper task of the framers of a constitution is to focus on the particular circumstances of the state for which they legislate.[83] Furthermore, Daunou discusses the status of persons (i.e., their civil and political rights) and the guarantee of property as "intermediary dispositions" between a declaration of rights and the constitution proper.[84]

Finally, in his *Essai sur la Constitution* (1793), Daunou presents a full-blown critique of the 1789 Declaration of Rights, which he now calls obscure and equivocal. While disassociating himself from those who attack any declaration of rights out of aristocratic prejudice, he charges that the incoherence, ambiguity, and imprecision of the original Declaration led to feeble laws, constitutional humiliation, and "our long calamities."[85]

The initial conclusion that Daunou draws from this critique is that the French Republic requires a new declaration, more complete, more exact, and better-ordered. Its function should be to

> banish every obscure or equivocal term, and above all to beware of those vague and uncertain phrases that are thought to be clear because they are commonplace, and that, under a dangerous appearance of simplicity, actually express only familiar errors.[86]

It also becomes obvious that Daunou criticized the original Declaration of Rights partly in order to lend credence to his criticism of the Declaration prefixed to the Constitution of 1793. He charges that the new enumeration of rights is arbitrary and that there are still no concrete ideas attached to the words *natural, civil, political, citizen, constitution,* and *government.* Although he does not completely abandon the idea of a preamble to the constitution, Daunou begins to call such a document an "analysis of the establishment of political relations."[87]

Like Daunou, most of the intellectuals at Auteuil accepted the proclamation of the republic. They played no direct role, however, in the factional struggles of the Convention. Too much in favor of national unity to support the Girondins, but too "scrupulous" to support the Montagnards, they attempted to maintain a neutral position.[88] Nevertheless, their political opinions, especially on matters such as procedural justice, were much closer to those of the proscribed Girondins than to those of the victorious Montagnards. Consequently, they tended to share the formers' fate: exile, imprisonment, or death. Condorcet, who had eventually rallied to the Girondins, died while a fugitive from the Committee of Public Safety. Chamfort committed suicide in prison, and the poets Roucher and André Chénier were executed. Volney, Daunou, Ginguené, La Roche, and Destutt de Tracy were imprisoned, Tracy escaping the guillotine only because of the fall of Robespierre. After Condorcet's proscription, Cabanis, who was his closest friend at Auteuil, was under constant surveillance by revolutionary committees.[89]

The future Idéologues generally used the period of political oblivion for study and reflection. After the dissolution of the National Assembly,

Tracy had returned to the army as second in command of the cavalry in Lafayette's Army of the Center. He refused to emigrate with Lafayette, however, and returned to settle at Auteuil with his family. During this retirement he began reading extensively in the natural sciences, especially the works of Buffon, Lavoisier, and Fourcroy. Imprisoned from November 1793 to July 1794, he spent his time studying Condillac and Locke, and developing the outlines of *idéologie.*

While the circle at Auteuil may have approved some aspects of revolutionary Jacobinism,[90] for the most part, they would always associate the Terror with a perverted regime that had attempted to force society into an unnatural pattern. As the victims of extralegal revolutionary persecution, they emerged from the period with their belief in civil liberties and the rule of law strengthened, but with their faith in political rhetoric shaken.

New Beginnings

During the Thermidorian reaction and the rule of the Directory, the Idéologues emerged as a distinct group of thinkers, and "ideology" took on the connotations originally associated with the term. To the extent that the group ever achieved a corporate identity, it was during this brief period before the eclipse of public life under Napoleon. There is considerable scholarly debate over who should be included among the Idéologues and what criteria of membership should be applied.[91] There probably will never be complete agreement on the use of the term, since the Idéologues were not in any real sense a sect. The rough criteria of identification used here are three. First, they moved in a particular social orbit. Besides meeting in the Auteuil Salon, many were members of the newly organized *Institut national* and attended weekly dinners in the rue du Bac to discuss politics and current events.[92] Second, the Idéologues shared certain political convictions. Though they might disagree on specific policies, they were anti-Jacobin after 1793, but also antiroyalist and anticlerical. Most favored a republic with a considerable role for an educated secular elite. After 1801, they opposed Napoleon, though they made varying degrees of peace with his regime. These views were expressed in the new legislature and in numerous journals, the most important of which was the *Décade philosophique,* founded by Ginguené and J. B. Say in 1794.[93] Finally, and most importantly, the Idéologues continued the eighteenth-century belief in the necessity of a preliminary "science of man" for the reconstruction of society. Towards this end, they acknowledged the intellectual leadership of Destutt de Tracy and Pierre Cabanis, although they did not always agree with them. And, indeed, there were important differences between Tracy and Cabanis as well.

The Idéologues were close to the group that congregated around Madame de Staël, and many public figures moved freely in both circles.[94] Nevertheless, there were recognizable differences between the two groups. Madame de Staël and Constant remained Protestant Christians, and were disturbed by the atheistic implications of *idéologie.*[95] The liberalism associated with Coppet always had a more romantic, intuitionist basis than that of the rationalists of Auteuil. Furthermore, Madame de Staël based her constitutional theory on the English model, and was more comfortable with constitutional monarchy than with republican institutions. The Idéologues, on the other hand, tended to be strongly antiroyalist and increasingly looked to the United States as a model of successful representative government. The hopes of all the moderates, however, rested ultimately on the creation of government that was stable and favorable to reform.

At first the Convention had shown no real haste to propose a new constitution for France. The initial aim of Thermidor was to rid the Convention of Robespierre, not to dismantle the revolutionary government. Reaction developed rapidly, however, hastened by the popular uprisings of Germinal and Prairial, which inspired fears of renewed terroristic activity. The armed insurrections of Prairial, demanding "bread and the Constitution of 1793," were among the least organized of the Revolution, seemingly a spontaneous protest against the appalling food crisis of the winter of 1795. They were quickly and decisively crushed, marking the end of popular intervention in the course of the Revolution. Nevertheless, at the time, a majority of deputies perceived the demonstrations as a political threat. The disturbances thus served to detach the Convention further from Jacobin ideas.

A commission dominated by moderates and former Girondins was named to draw up a new constitution. Daunou emerged as the central figure of this commission, and is generally credited as the primary author of the Constitution of the Year III. The details of this constitutional scheme are complicated, and it eventually proved wholly inadequate to the needs of a nation still torn by civil and foreign war. In theory, however, it was meant to correct the most glaring deficiencies of earlier regimes, and to establish effective, yet liberal, government.

Like every previously adopted or proposed French constitution of the revolutionary period, the Constitution of 1795 began with a Declaration of Rights. In light of the growing doubts about the use of natural rights language in a political context, we might expect that such a declaration would have been suppressed altogether. Indeed, at the beginning of the debates on the adoption of the new constitution, the orator Rouzet angrily contested its usefulness. He argued that the French should have learned that to invest metaphysical principles with the character of law is disastrous.[96] Daunou argued against Rouzet, but only on practical grounds. He claimed that the elimination of a declaration of rights could be exploited by agitators representing the Assembly as "trampling on the Charter of the Rights of Man and Citizen."[97] Daunou himself, in his speeches from 1795 to 1799, continued to mistrust the revolutionary tendency to "exploit" the concept of popular sovereignty.

> To organize the downfall of the throne, the bounds of liberty were passed in a rush; the rigorous principles that, in a large state, can alone maintain the respect due to public law, and the moral authority of the social virtues, were deeply undermined.[98]

Rather than seeking the perfection of the Republic in terms of the realization of rights, Daunou stresses the need to penetrate the real secret of moral institutions and constitutional laws, a task upon which France "has barely begun."[99]

Moderate and conservative republican journalists also tried to avoid dwelling on natural rights. The events of Germinal and Prairial provoked an especially severe reaction against the lower classes. This reawakened fear of "popular democracy" influenced the social thought of the *Décade philosophique* in a permanent fashion.[100] While *Décade* editors continued to refer to the rights of man, the evocation was largely a matter of political cant. Indeed, editors would routinely condone arbitrary governmental policies, rationalized as necessary to the safety of the Republic.[101]

In general, moderate republicans found themselves in an extremely awkward position. They wished to maintain the Republic: "We have not, in the Revolution, made a habit of seeking our security outside of the security of the Republic." [102] Many moderates were also regicides, and thus had a great personal stake in preventing the return of the Bourbons. Yet they did not wish to call attention to the theoretical bases of the Republic for fear of giving too much support to resurgent Jacobinism. Throughout the Directory years, they would use the language of popular sovereignty and natural rights only when necessary to vindicate their claim to the "true" revolutionary mantle, i.e., to distinguish themselves from those who would reestablish the monarchy or from those hopelessly compromised by the Terror. Thus, concerning the deportation to Guiana of two former Jacobins, an anonymous writer in the *Conservateur* would write: "How, for example, can a people with the least humanity and the least idea of the rights of man deport the likes of Billaud-Varennes and Bourdon de l'Oise anywhere but to a desert?" [103]

Although an adherence to the language of rights was seen as an occasional political necessity, in Idéologue circles it became increasingly acceptable to criticize the proliferation of proposed and adopted declarations. J. B. Say wrote an especially strong indictment of this practice in the *Décade.* The article advocated a "positive" constitutional theory and questioned whether it was suitable to place a declaration "that establishes rights in their most extensive sense" at the head of a constitution "that must necessarily restrain them." [104] Furthermore, Say deplored such general maxims as "the law is the expression of the general will." While these exhortations had been useful in 1789 because they established principles that turned public opinion against the old government, they were now superfluous. Experience had shown that a usurper (Say referred to Robespierre) would not be curbed by such a declaration, but would manipulate it for his own purposes.

Even Volney backed away from his earlier passionate defense of the equality of rights. In his *Lectures on History* given at the short-lived Normal School in 1795, he reiterated his former position, but dealt with the matter only in passing. Furthermore, he expressed new doubts about the substance of rights. In the context of a discussion of scientific principles, he analyzed the "fundamental principle of the present political movements in Europe," i.e., that all men are born equal as to rights.

> What is this maxim, but a *collective and summary fact,* deduced from a multitude of particular facts? in this manner: Having compared all mankind, or at least an immense number of individuals, with each other, and finding

them all furnished with similar organs or faculties, we discover by way of *addition, the total fact,* that they are all *born equal as to rights.* What a *right* is, still remains to be defined; and that definition is more difficult than is generally imagined.[105]

Volney never went on to define a *right*.

The actual Declaration of Rights prefixed to the constitution of 1795 bears a strong resemblance to the 1789 declaration, with the addition of more explicit statements on religious liberty and liberty of the press. But there was also a significant omission. What Volney called the "fundamental principle of the present movements of Europe" was suppressed, and replaced by a more carefully defined notion of equality having subtle implications for the concept of sovereignty itself. The Declaration of 1789 stated that "men are born and remain free and equal in rights." In 1795 this article was omitted because it would have permitted a demand for universal suffrage. Although equality was mentioned along with the other rights of man in society (i.e., liberty and security), it was defined carefully as consisting only in the principle that "the law is the same for all, whether it punishes or protects." Any implication of political equality was avoided.

The suppression of universal suffrage was generally accepted as a clear necessity in order to avoid the recurrence of what was characterized as Jacobin demagoguery. In the plebiscite on the Constitution few Frenchmen rejected the Constitution because it was not sufficiently "democratic." The negative votes were those of counterrevolutionaries.[106] However, the retreat to limited voting rights was not just a retreat from the principles of 1793 to the principles of 1789. It denoted a growing suspicion of the very concepts that had inspired the Constituent reformers with their revolutionary élan.

In the Constitution of 1795, the sovereign is no longer synonymous with the nation (as in 1789), or with the people (as in 1793), but with the body of citizens, i.e., with specific individuals who are invested with special rights because they fill particular functions. The word "citizens" recurs in all the formulas relative to sovereignty, which has changed from a natural right to a function. Only those who fulfill express conditions are included in the category of citizens with sovereign rights. And, as in 1791, exercise of sovereign power was to be limited to the election of representatives (in two stages).

If the founders of the Directory showed distrust of the people in their definition of the sovereign, in their organization of the state power they manifested an even greater distrust of the governing bodies that were to exercise the sovereignty. In sharp departure from revolutionary precedent, the legislature was divided into two houses: the Council of Five Hundred, which was to present and debate proposed laws, and the Council of Elders, which would have the power of acceptance or rejection. All members of the judicial hierarchy were to be elected by various electoral assemblies. At the apex of the court system was a High Court of Justice that was to have jurisdiction over members of the legislative bodies and the Directory. Finally, the Constitution provided for a plural executive of five directors, to be chosen by, but not from, the legislature for five-year terms, with one member to be renewed every year. The Directory was nominally in charge of internal and external security, including the nomination of generals, ministers, and certain high functionaries. However, it had no legislative initiative, no veto, no control over the legislative bodies by adjournment or dissolution, and no means of participating in legislative debate.

The constitutional machinery of the second French republic has often been blamed, at least in part, for the regime's failure.[107] But this complicated and cumbersome system illustrates clearly the theoretical dilemma that plagued moderates like the Idéologues, a dilemma that worsened under Napoleon. At the beginning of the Revolution, even if the language of natural right and popular sovereignty was not essential to the moderate position, it provided a sense of certainty and righteousness and the illusion of a final appeal against despotism. Now this appeal seemed hopelessly tarnished. Yet, at the same time, there was an increased fear of despotism—indeed, of a new sort of despotism perceived to be more terrible than that of an absolute monarch. Hence, there was an effort to multiply, specialize, and complicate the governmental machinery in order to provide checks and limits on governmental power. The difficulty was that there was no obvious way to justify these limits; there was no longer a generally accepted final appeal.

For the Idéologues, the problem of finding an ultimate justification for political and social action intensified their search for "scientific" principles, and made more urgent the eighteenth-century project of a "science of man." This new direction can be seen in the intellectual program of the *Institut national.*

One of the first concerns of those Thermidorians who wished to suppress Jacobinism, but also to combat royalists and the Church, was to rehabilitate "sane" philosophy, and to implement the many revolutionary proposals for educational reform.[108] In April of 1795, the Committee of Public Instruction (led by Daunou, Chénier, Lakanal, and Sieyès) ordered that three thousand copies of Condorcet's *Esquisse* be distributed throughout France. In October of the same year, the Convention passed the organic decree known as the Law of Third Brumaire an IV, which represented the final realization of revolutionary planning in the field of education. It provided for primary schools in each canton, secondary schools (*écoles centrales*) in each department, a normal school to be established in Paris, and a National Institute of Arts and Sciences.[109]

The new Institute was meant to be more than a mere replacement for the academies that had been abolished during the course of the Revolution. It was intended to unite all of human knowledge, to create a living *Encyclopédie,* and to exorcise forever what was characterized as the Terror's elevation of virtue over reason.[110] The Institute was divided into three classes: the class of Physical and Mathematical Sciences (which resembled the old *Académie des sciences*), the Class of Moral and Political Sciences, and the Class of Literature and Fine Arts (which resembled the old *Académie française*). The newly conceived Second Class was subdivided into sections: Analysis of Sensations and Ideas, Morality, Social Science and Legislation, Political Economy, History, and Geography. Until its suppression in 1803, the Second Class of the Institute was the intellectual stronghold of the Idéologues.[111]

The method underlying Institute research and public instruction was of course to be analysis, i.e., the decomposition of all ideas into their basic elements and the recomposition of these elements into complex ideas. Inherited from the *philosophes,* and especially from Condillac, analysis was invoked as the universal method for achieving progress in the physical and social sciences. In 1795 Garat gave a course at the new *Ecole normale* on the analysis of the understanding based on the theories of Condillac, while Volney lectured on history, preaching the value of analyzing historical "facts" in order to construct general principles.

Methodology was to be the particular concern of the Section on the Analysis of Sensations and Ideas. The most important of the Institute *Mémoires* are the lectures of this Section dealing with the physiological and rational aspects of analysis, and delivered concurrently by Cabanis and Tracy.[112] To avoid the limited connotations of such words as "metaphysics" or "psychology," Tracy suggested the neologism *idéologie* to designate the science resulting from the analysis of sensations and ideas.[113] Tracy saw knowledge of the human understanding as the unique science, at once the foundation of the art of communicating ideas (grammar), of combining ideas to generate new truths (logic), of teaching and spreading acquired truths (instruction), of forming habits in men (education), of recognizing and regulating our desires (morality), and, finally, of regulating society in such a way that man finds the most help and least trouble from other men.[114] "Ideology" was thus to be the method of a normative social science that would both explain social and political organization, and transform it in the interests of human happiness. Committed to systematizing and correlating knowledge to serve as a guide to social reform, the Idéologues of the Institute were, in the words of one historian, "infatuated with utility."[115]

If the ultimate aim of the Idéologues was to transform both society and politics, their immediate objective was to stabilize the Republic. The basis of their hopes was the successful operation of the Constitution of 1795, optimistically seen as the triumph of reason founded on experience.[116] The search for a stable liberal government was a central preoccupation of the Idéologues during the Directory years; however, such a government remained a vainly sought chimera.

From Directory to Empire

The Constitution of the Year III was in operation from October 1795 to November 1799. During that entire period, domestic disorder and internal violence were more the norm than the exception. The sans-culottes had been disarmed after the events of Prairial, and were forbidden to travel freely. Their principal leaders were in prison, as were many of the ex-terrorists. These measures increased the vulnerability of former terrorists and Jacobins in general and facilitated the spread of a bloody reaction. Waves of violence asnd killings continued throughout 1795 and 1796. On the eve of the constitutional plebiscite, there was a royalist uprising to protest the "Two Thirds Decree" by which the Convention hoped to assure its initial dominance of the new dual legislature. Royalist intrigue, veiled or open, was a pervasive feature of Directorial politics. There was also agitation on the left. Babeuf's famous Conspiracy of Equals aroused panic among the ruling clique of conservative republicans and served as the justification for a host of repressive measures.

Moreover, the Jacobin movement was not completely dead. Democratic clubs enjoyed a marked resurgence in 1797–98. The ruling oligarchy never distinguished this resurgent democratic impulse from the earlier Jacobin-dominated Terror, although the neo-Jacobins had largely severed ties with the sans-culotte movement. The Directors equated dissent with subversion, thus intensifying their self-image as the moderate center, beleaguered by royalist treason on the right and terrorist subversion on the left.[117] Sporadically exercising dictatorial powers, first against emigrés, then against the constitutional clubs, the government retained a semirevolutionary character, periodically renewing itself through illegal coups d'état. The period known as the First Directory ended in the coup of 18 Fructidor, directed against the royalists. A year later the law of 22 Floréal effected a similar purge of newly elected deputies who, the Directors feared, were too pro-Jacobin.

The primary concern of the Idéologues was to reestablish order in the Republic. Since they saw no viable alternative to the Directory, they lent considerable support to the regime. Many, including Daunou, Cabanis, Garat, Chénier, and Ginguené, served in the legislative councils. The Institute maintained close ties to the Ministry of the Interior and provided the government with numerous departmental administrators, as well as ambassadors to the "sister republics." Maine de Biran, Tracy's foremost philosophical disciple, was an administrator in the department of the Dordogne; Ginguené was sent as minister plenipotentiary to Turin; Garat became ambassador to Naples; Lakanal was charged with reorganizing the four new departments of the Middle Rhine; Daunou headed the mission to organize a republic in Rome.[118]

Despite some reservations about the new Constitution, and growing concern over corruption and procedural irregularities, the editors of the *Décade* consistently supported the Directory's policies. J.B. Say, who had initially expressed doubts about the Declaration of Rights prefixed to the Constitution, also opposed the strict separation and division of government powers, finding it absurd that so much care should be lavished on organizing ways of disagreeing. Another editor, Duval, also opposed the separation of powers, foreseeing difficulties in execution.[119] Daunou, who bears responsibility for much of the constitutional organization of powers, would have preferred a presidential system, or at least a dual consulship.[120] Once the Constitution was voted by the Convention, however, the editors rallied to the Directory. Horace Say, brother of J.B. Say, became the new political editor of the *Décade*. He supported the laws of exception against emigrés and refractory priests, and, after the disclosure of the Babeuf plot, also encouraged government persecution of the Jacobins. The *Décade* supported the antiroyalist Fructidor coup in September 1797, and from then on was ready to accept many other controls the Directory thought necessary, even including surveillance of the press. Cabanis wrote to a friend during this period that "the government has saved the republic. . . . The Constitution has not been violated an instant, except in order to conserve it."[121]

When the Directory's fears of resurgent Jacobinism resulted in the purge of 121 newly elected deputies in May 1798 (the Floréal purge), the *Décade* again acquiesced, although with more reluctance. An anonymous editor reacted to the preparations for another coup with apprehension. He reproached the Directory for exciting the country with vague denunciations and threats, and dreaded another violation of the Constitution. Eventually this editor was replaced and J. B. Say wrote an apology for the Floréal purge.[122] After Floréal, however, the domestic political section, now headed by Andrieux, was more likely to underline the deficiencies and failures of the regime, particularly in financial matters. It was clear to many republicans that the Directory's primary motivation had been to assure a docile majority in the legislature. Evidence for a grand conspiracy was paltry, and many were uneasy about their acquiescence in a clearly unconstitutional maneuver.[123] The Directory began to be characterized as negligent and extravagant, and deputies were reproached for egotism and corruption.

In the spring of 1799 the war in Europe began to go badly. The combination of military defeat and the deplorable state of the Republic made the dictatorship of the Directory less and less tolerable. Many Idéologues began to lean toward a revisionist movement crystallizing around Sieyès, who had been elected to the Directory in May of 1799. The object of the conspiracy was to modify the Constitution in a conservative direction, strengthening and centralizing the government, but keeping the main outlines of a representative republic.

Except for an abortive attempt to influence the drafting of the Constitution of 1795, Sieyès had remained in the shadows since his great period of influence during the Constituent Assembly. He retained, however, a considerable reputation for constitutional expertise. His knack for patient and shrewd maneuvering now put him at the center of a complicated plot to overthrow the Directorial regime. Recognizing that military force was necessary, the "Brumairians" thought first of General Joubert. Joubert's death at the battle of Novi forced them to look elsewhere. Sieyès's second choice was Napoleon Bonaparte, preferred as the most "civil" of military men.

For the most part the Idéologues supported the Eighteenth Brumaire, and many were personally involved in its execution. Napoleon actively sought their support and made a symbolic trip to Auteuil to pay homage to Madame Helvétius. Volney prepared the way for Bonaparte with fulsome articles in the *Moniteur,* comparing the General to the wise Legislator of the *Ruines.*[124] Cabanis also put his respected name and character at the disposal of Napoleon. The intermediary legislative commission, a vestigial remnant of the Five Hundred, included Cabanis, J.B. Say, Daunou, and Chénier.

It is clear that the Idéologues supported Napoleon because they thought that the reestablishment of a strong central authority was necessary to the Republic. It is equally clear that they did not envision the development of a dictatorship, or the complete evisceration of representative government. Disillusionment came swiftly. Napoleon easily outmaneuvered the Sieyès faction, rejecting both Sieyès's constitutional proposals and the hastily conceived suggestions of Daunou.[125] Bonaparte, however, seized on Sieyès's notion of "power from above, authority from below" as the rationale of his dictatorship.

Cabanis wrote an apology for the new government, in which he put the most optimistic construction on Bonaparte's assumption of vast personal power, noting that liberty had never been placed in hands more anxious to defend it. The pamphlet defended Brumaire as a strike against an absurd system that was leading the Republic to inevitable ruin. The object of the coup was not to establish the domination of a few men, but to remove the obstacles preventing the complete and solid organization of a government capable of protecting its citizens effectively without impinging on public liberty.[126] Even in this overt apology for Brumaire, however, there was an undercurrent of doubt about the future course of the regime. But Cabanis plainly saw no other course than to hope for the best, and to defend the intentions and purposes of those involved. In private, he justified himself by insisting that those involved in Brumaire had hoped to found the republic at last on solid social bases. "At least, such was the intention of the men who were involved in this movement."[127]

Assiduously courted by Napoleon, a fellow member of the Institute, many of the "philosophers of Auteuil" had actively abetted the Brumaire coup. It was not long, however, before Napoleon had thoroughly repudiated his erstwhile philosophical masters and turned "Idéologue" into a word of scorn.

At the beginning of the Consulate, the liberals were clearly at a disadvantage. Sieyès was discredited by his acceptance from Bonaparte of a rich estate, an action widely regarded as the selling out of principle for personal gain. His Brumairian allies shared in the general disfavor. In contrast, Bonaparte's personal popularity was immense. Napoleon was careful to conciliate all factions, and to maintain a public attitude of dignified indifference to criticism. Public opinion saw him as a practical and realistic leader, opposed only by the intellectuals, philosophic liberals, and pedantic scholars who had ruined the nation through their support of a corrupt oligarchy.[128] The liberals, however, were not yet totally voiceless. Well-represented in the legislative bodies, and especially in the Tribunate, they attempted in a series of skirmishes to block many of Bonaparte's authoritarian moves. They protested restrictions on legislative debate, the setting up of special criminal courts, and parts of the *Code Napoléon* that were seen as regressions from legal gains made in the Revolution.[129]

The *Décade,* four of whose editors were members of the Tribunate, enthusiastically supported this protest, but there was no response from the revolution-weary country. Although the tribunes had little support among the general public, Napoleon was infuriated at their opposition. He began a campaign to discredit all "obstructionists" as dangerous metaphysicians.

> Metaphysicians are my *bêtes noires.* I have classed all that crowd under the denomination of *idéologues*. . . . The word has caught on, I believe, because it was my own. . . . Yes, they are obsessed with meddling in my govern-

ment, those windbags! My aversion for this race of *idéologues* amounts to disgust.[130]

With the growing support of Catholics and royalists, Bonaparte easily carried out a thorough purge of legislative dissenters in 1802.

After the purge of the Tribunate, the opposition was relatively powerless. Within a short time Bonaparte pushed through a series of measures disagreeable to the liberals, beginning with the Concordat.[131]

A particular blow to the Idéologues was the abolition of the *écoles centrales,* which had been the cornerstone of their educational system. The school system set up by the Law of Third Brumaire had long been under fire, both by the forces of resurgent religion, and by those who attacked it on the grounds of confusion and inefficiency. By 1801, however, the Idéologues could point to the success of certain central schools. A report of Ginguené, presented in the *Décade,*[132] stressed that the central schools would have a real chance to develop their potential, if the government would manifest a more sympathetic attitude.

Destutt de Tracy, who had been named to the Council of Public Instruction in 1799, was deeply involved in the battle over the central schools. With the approval of the Council, he sent out five circulars stressing the importance of "ideology" as the foundation of courses in general grammar and legislation, thus strengthening the connection between the Idéologues and the schools. With the growing campaign against "ideology" in the press after Brumaire, it appeared that some attempt would be made to change the curriculum. Tracy's pamphlet *Observations sur le système actuel d'instruction publique,* which appeared in the spring of 1801, was an attempt to arrest criticism of the educational system.

In order to salvage the spirit of "ideology" in education, Tracy was clearly willing to deemphasize any democratic implications of the system. He explains that men are divided into two great classes: those that draw their subsistence from manual labor (the *classe ouvrière*), and those who live off the revenue of properties or from the product of certain necessary functions (the *classe savante*).[133] These two classes have different needs that should be met by two different systems of education.

The *classe ouvrière* would be educated in numerous primary schools that would be open to everyone. These schools were not to provide the first elements of a coordinated system of education, but rather an abridged and simplified version of all general subjects. Following this would be an apprenticeship to trade. Elite schools, on the other hand, would be few and select. Most of Tracy's pamphlet discussed the curriculum of these elite schools, which were clearly modeled on the existing central schools. Above all, he underlined the role of "ideological" reasoning in the moral and political sciences.[134] However, the link between "ideology" and politics was precisely the notion to which Napoleon objected. Although Tracy's pamphlet was received enthusiastically by other Idéologues, it had no effect in arresting the abolition of the central schools in 1802.

In 1803 Napoleon reorganized the Institute, suppressing the Class of Moral and Political Sciences and thus completely eliminating the principal forum of the Idéologues. After 1802 the political section of the *Décade* became totally banal, but it continued to stress anticlericalism (in a prudent fashion), and to defend the philosophy of "ideology." It also opposed the reestablishment of the slave trade, advocated economic policies contrary to official policy, and combatted claims of French cultural hegemony.[135] Despite a few allusions to the growing despotism of the regime, the *Décade* became even more politically servile in its last years. It remained too much an organ of the Idéologues, however, to avoid suppression in 1807.

Napoleon's distrust of the Idéologues increased with his growing personal power. He tended to blame them for all manifestations of domestic unrest, but his suspicions were largely unfounded.[136] Although their private opinions remained very bitter toward the regime, especially after the establishment of the Empire, the Idéologues made no serious effort to overturn the government. Effectively isolated from political power, they traded public silence for the opportunity to remain in France.

> Rather than be exiled, rather than lose the tools of their trade, their libraries, these scholars were prepared to burn a pinch of incense at the altar of the Caesar whom they had called to power.[137]

Daunou became archivist of the Empire, while Volney, Cabanis, and Tracy remained in the largely decorative Napoleonic Senate, conspicuous only for their reticence, a few negative votes, and long periods of absence. The years from 1800 to 1815 were also years of increasing cultural isolation, as counterrevolutionary and religious attitudes became more fashionable.[138]

Nevertheless, the Idéologues met regularly at Auteuil. Madame Helvétius had died in 1800, leaving her property to Cabanis, who continued the salon. After Cabanis's death in 1808, Tracy moved the Idéologue salon to Paris. During the Restoration, Tracy's salon would become an important gathering place for the liberal opposition.

Throughout the later years of the Revolution, there had been a growing dissatisfaction with revolutionary ideology. It was exceedingly difficult, however, to criticize the bases of the Republic while at the same time defending it from counterrevolutionary attacks. François Furet has recently refocused attention on the power of this revolutionary ideology: a dynamic kaleidoscope of shifting democratic symbols in which men engaged in life and death struggles for the right to speak for *la nation*.[139] It was only after the republican experiment was over, then, that some of the Idéologues attempted a definitive break with revolutionary rhetoric and turned to a reformulation of the principles underlying their vision of a moderate republic. In the works of Destutt de Tracy and Pierre Daunou in particular, a new perspective on republican politics emerges, a view that self-consciously attempts to divest itself of the language of 1789.[140]

The language of revolution now appeared to these men a discredited vehicle for their ideas; sovereignty itself seemed a dangerously suggestive notion. This disillusionment can be partly explained by the Revolution's apparent confirmation of the fears that had haunted some of the "philosophical party" as early as 1789. The abstraction of a specific set of rights might be misunderstood, with fatal consequences for society. Indeed, equal political rights to participate in the formulation of the law were always problematical for liberals like Condorcet. But the revolutionary experience also brought deeper dissatisfactions with the initial defense of a "philosophized" theory of natural rights.

The arguments of Volney, Condorcet, and Sieyès had always been in part sincere efforts to set out the principles they believed ought to govern the "new France," partly accommodations to a rhetoric that they did not fully endorse, and partly attempts to mold that rhetoric to fit their conceptions of social science. This initial political articulation had proved inadequate. The derivation of governmental power from alleged natural rights appeared to place the government alternately in a weak and defensive and then in a despotic and arbitrary posture. The facile reduction of the "moral" to the physical order no longer seemed so easy. And the link between utility and right could no longer be accepted as patently obvious. Yet the quest for moral certainty was if anything more imperative for the Idéologues. They sought it in a particular theory of mind, that, they still believed, would dissipate linguistic confusions and allow men to reach a consensus on their true interests.

CHAPTER TWO

Idéologie and Social Science

L IKE THE English Utilitarians, the Idéologues projected the eighteenth-century philosophy of sensationalism and the association of ideas into the nineteenth century in yet another hopeful attempt to create a science of man. Persistent failures to influence the course of French revolutionary events did not discredit their conception of social science, but only produced a resolution to be more "positive," i.e., more exact and careful in their epistemology. Thus, the theorists of "ideology" deliberately attempted to follow the lead of the physical scientists in the French Institute, who displayed a careful attention to detail and to empirical investigation.[1] Yet the "ideologists" of the Institute's Second Class still believed in a unitary scientific method that eventually would unlock the mysteries of both the physical and social universes. The coexistence of this philosophic monism with a sensitivity to the intractability of specifically human phenomena brought to "ideology" a number of unresolved contradictions.

This chapter will explore some of these tensions in the works of Pierre Cabanis and Destutt de Tracy, in particular their ambivalent naturalism and their troubled attempts to find a certain standard for social science. Cabanis and Tracy thought of themselves as the joint architects of a new system based on the scientific analysis of sensations. But although they set out to establish a science of man, and hence of politics, the result of their work was to call into question the very possibility of such a science. The Idéologues themselves recognized the implications of their failed project only fitfully and imperfectly, and some of the subsequent neglect of these theorists is certainly due to the confusing and transitional nature of their work. But the lasting significance of this work lies in the way in which it at once undermines the existing epistemological bases of liberalism, and yet affirms the value of liberal procedures and institutions. The Idéologues' predicament is the peculiarly modern one of finding authoritative arguments for social action in the absence of religious or philosophical support.

The Dictates of "Nature"

In the *Rapports du physique et du moral de l'homme* Cabanis continually refers to the need to penetrate the secrets of nature. The term *nature*, however, functions at several different levels in his analysis, and often provides a sense of unity that is semantic rather than real.

Some of the ambiguity surrounding *nature* in Cabanis's thought is due to his effort to transcend the eighteenth-century argument between mechanists and vitalists over the character of human sensibility. The former, materialists like La Mettrie and D'Holbach, had subsumed the laws of human nature under universal natural laws governing the combination of all matter. The latter, physicians of the Faculty of Montpellier and later followers such as Barthez and Bichat, insisted that organic systems obey their own laws, and that there is something inexplicable and specifically "vital" in their operation.

Cabanis was certainly influenced in a fundamental way by vitalism.[2] He uses its language—*énergie vitale, irritabilité, mouvements vitaux*—and emphasizes the peculiar nature of living systems.

> Whatever idea one adopts about the nature of the cause that determines the organization of plants and animals, or about the necessary conditions for their production and their development, one cannot help but concede a principle, or a life-giving faculty, that nature fixes in the embryos.[3]

He also observes that precipitate applications of mechanistic theories should be avoided in favor of direct observation of human phenomena.[4]

Yet, Cabanis at times suggests that the physical laws governing human life may be subsumed under general laws of chemistry or physics.[5] He merely declines to discuss the precise nature of this interconnection. Nor does he deny that these general laws of the universe may be related to "first causes," although he also declines to speculate on these causes.[6] In fact, the concept of nature in Cabanis often refers to some underlying rational unity in the universe; it even evokes the anthropomorphic associations of a conscious plan or purpose.[7]

The implication that nature, and specifically human nature, has some underlying moral significance is also reflected in Cabanis's continuing faith in the exemplar of an ideally sympathetic and rational individual. Such a model of man is sometimes referred to as "human nature"; it implies for Cabanis maximum satisfaction of physical needs, "without, however, departing from the order of nature."[8] The *Rapports* never falters in its conviction that this conception of human nature is the proper objective of both doctors and moralists, who should strive to create intelligent, vigorous, sympathetic individuals capable of judging their own interests, i.e., to create *"des citoyens sages et bons."*[9] Although substantial differences among men will perhaps always remain, Cabanis is optimistic that a general mental and physical equality "that does not at all exist in primitive [physical] organization"[10] will eventually prevail among men in society.

Cabanis, then, continues to evoke a vague humanistic goal reminiscent of the predominant tendency in Enlightenment thought to seek out the "natural man" as a standard by which to judge human relations and institutions. He himself encourages this impression of continuity by placing himself in the tradition of those moral philosophers who have looked to physical sensibility for the source of all human ideas and habits, "for it is only by resting on the constant and universal nature of man that one can hope to make real progress in the sciences."[11]

It becomes clear in the course of Cabanis's discussion, however, that his effort to base the science of man on universal, "natural" human tendencies differs somewhat from that of his predecessors. Cabanis's primary concern was in fact to provide a basis for *modifying* existing human characteristics in a radical way, for changing human physiology itself. With this practical goal in mind, he urges that "primitive organization" be considered a variable concept.

> Actually, nature is for us the present state or order of things, however changed or altered they may have been in times past; it cannot be for us the primordial state, which is of necessity almost always unknown; it can be only the fixed order of things as transmitted to us by the past.[12]

Human nature is fixed only in a relative sense. Cabanis suggests that *régime* and *hygiène,* as well as improved education, can contribute to a progressively better being: "Nature brings forth man with fixed organs and faculties; but art can increase these faculties, change or direct their use, effectively create new *organs*."[13] Since Cabanis assumes that acquired characteristics are inherited, he predicts that the combined efforts of doctors and moralists can ameliorate both the nature of individuals and the nature of the human species.

This point of view in fact tends to dissolve the link between the "constant and universal nature of man" and specific ethical or political precepts. Primitive organization has lost much of the normative connotation that it still retained in the analyses of such theorists as Condorcet and Sieyès, for whom the fact of physical equality served as *prima facie* justification for equality as a right. For Cabanis primitive organization is a purely physiological concept. The laws of human nature are most often depicted as existing physiological regularities—infinitely complex, but theoretically subject to human manipulation.

If the laws of human nature are not ahistorical, man must be studied as he appears concretely and historically. Therefore, Cabanis's conception of the science of man is not Condorcet's vision of social mathematics based on an abstract model of human nature, but rather a methodical collection of facts for a history of human "nature." Cabanis himself eschews the direct study of morals and social theory. He claims only to perform "simple investigations of *physiology* but directed toward the particular study of a certain order of functions."[14] His *Rapports* was meant to begin the task of cataloguing the influences (including temperament, age, sex, disease, climate, and diet) upon individual sensibility in order to provide a factual basis for the creation of more equal individuals. Though Cabanis does not himself abandon this goal, the reader of the *Rapports* is likely to be left with the impression of overwhelming diversity and complexity in human nature.

Cabanis's most original contribution to sensationalist psychology was his revision of the model to allow for internal impressions caused by the bodily organs and the functioning of the nervous system. While agreeing that all human responses are responses to sense impressions, and that life is only a series of movements that take place in reaction to the impressions received by different organs, Cabanis defines sense impression so as to include internal activity or "instinct." In his view, both the reductionist psychology of Helvétius and the statue-man model of Condillac were naive and misleading because they lacked any real basis in human physiology. The activity of internal organs, as well as the reactions caused by outside impressions, affect thinking and morality. Cabanis understands sensibility as "active" in the peculiar sense of vitalist physicians.

Although Cabanis concedes that the effects of internal impressions are sometimes difficult to see in normal individuals, he argues that they are quite clear in abnormal cases. Changes in behavior due to madness or illness, in addition to the more regular manifestations of puberty and maternity, show that much of human character is formed without the rational participation of the will. This conclusion is strengthened by studying the development of the foetus, which Cabanis assumes to be cushioned from outside sense impressions. "It is the totality of these determinants that we call instinct." [15] Sympathy falls into this class of instinctual motivations that are analogous to animal attractions and repulsions. Although the most complex of reflective sentiments, sympathy is basically an innate organic impulse whose strength varies with the individual. Cabanis speculates that there are many unconscious physiological movements that affect behavior. Therefore, past accounts of human psychology have surely simplified human motivation. In the future, conclusions may have to be drawn "in a less general and absolute manner." [16]

The specific influences on sensibility discussed by Cabanis can be divided into those that have relatively unchanging effects (temperament, age, and sex), and those whose influence is more variable (climate, occupation, health, and diet). Natural temperament is fixed at birth as a pattern of affinities resulting from the strength or weakness of bodily systems, especially the reproductive, muscular, and nervous systems. The "best" temperament would be one in which all forces, organs, and functions are in equilibrium; however, such a model is a pure abstraction. [17] In general, people are more or less intelligent, energetic, courageous, phlegmatic, melancholic, irritable, etc. Furthermore, these predispositions are not constant, but are intensified or attenuated by age. Cabanis hypothesizes, for example, that youthful enthusiasms and melancholy are related to physiological changes induced by puberty. [18] The strength of sympathy and of religious feeling in the mature individual is probably related to passions unleashed in adolescence. [19]

According to Cabanis, sexual differences come under the heading of natural temperament. In his views on the nature of women, he explicitly acknowledges the influence of Rousseau and of Pierre Roussel, a fellow member of the Institute.[20] Cabanis assumes that major differences between the sexes develop at puberty, when the reproductive organs release distinctive substances that invigorate the male and induce passivity in the female. Cabanis thus finds physiological explanations for then current opinions about the special character of women. Furthermore, although women's natural tendencies, like sensitive nature in general, may be powerfully modified by habit, Cabanis argues that this modification ought not to be attempted: "Man must be strong, bold, enterprising; woman must be weak, timid, dissembling. Such is the law of nature."[21]

Cabanis's discussion of natural temperament was intended as a guide for the egalitarian social reformer. His emphasis on innate differences and unique capacities, however, actually serves to undermine earlier justifications of equality. His contemporary Bichat went even further in the direction of differentiating individuals on the basis of their natural endowments. According to Bichat, the interaction between environment and inherited "organs of animal life" cause three broad classes to emerge: sensory men, brain men, and motor men.[22] Since men are born only with a particular quantity of power or energy, universality of knowledge in the same individual is a chimera. Bichat, furthermore, did not share Cabanis's vision of using his knowledge to improve the human species. He believed that habit could perfect judgment, but could not really alter natural temperament and character.

Although temperament, age, and sex are relatively fixed influences on human development, Cabanis notes the vast influence of other factors that contribute to what he sometimes calls "acquired temperament."[23] Causes capable of changing or modifying temperament include illness, climate, diet, and habits of work.[24] The notion of acquired temperament would seem to hold out the promise of greater "management" of the formation of character. But in Cabanis's discussion, acquired temperament can be seen to increase, rather than to lessen, human diversity, since temperaments acquired through long exposure to the same climate and occupation can eventually become inherited physical modifications. Thus, characteristics acquired by people in similar environments ultimately determine the special character of that people.

> Discrete, but constant and unchanging impressions are thus capable of modifying organic dispositions, and making these modifications permanent in

any one race. . . . If, then, impressions differ sufficiently in different climates to act on the very state of the organs, temperaments will of necessity show marked variety.[25]

Cabanis does argue that the growth of commerce, communication, and enlightenment (particularly a clearer, more rational language) can break up and destroy habit and custom; nevertheless, his discussion leaves the distinct impression that human physiology is the product of a slow evolutionary process, a process that is still opaque to human reason.

Cabanis's physiological theory, then, had the paradoxical result of providing a basis for an attack on his own political ideals and of reorienting the thrust of social science. The *Rapports* in effect cast doubt on the existing arguments for liberty and equality by stressing that *sensibilité* itself was a very unequally distributed property. Utopians like Saint-Simon and Fourier would translate the physiological assumptions of Cabanis and Bichat into new schemes for universal happiness, based on the satisfaction and harmonization of different human types.[26] Indeed, in the area of sexual characteristics, Cabanis himself explicitly rejected the revolutionary argument for equality in favor of a functional view of social relations.

The rational "ideology" of Destutt de Tracy was primarily concerned with analyzing the development of ideas and language out of sense impressions. As Cabanis's closest friend and intellectual collaborator, Tracy made a real attempt to assimilate Cabanis's ideas about physiology. However, Tracy's concern with rational method inevitably led him away from Cabanis's preoccupation with human variations to a reaffirmation of the common, universal elements in human thinking. Nevertheless, Tracy's examination of the universal "facts" of human nature does not follow the path of earlier exponents of the sensationalist theory of mind. Like that of Cabanis, his work began to call into question the contemporary political implications of the theory.

After the enormous disruption and flux of the early revolutionary period, Tracy turned to the study of philosophy with a renewed sense of purpose. If irrefutable principles of thought could be established, men would be able to communicate, and might no longer shed blood in vain controversies.

> Once certain of the formation and genesis of our ideas, all that we subsequently say about the manner of expressing these ideas, of combining them,

of teaching them, of governing our sentiments and our actions, and directing those of others, will be but consequences of these preliminaries, and will have a constant and invariable foundation in the very nature of our being.[27]

At the same time, he knew thet there was a continuing campaign to discredit this philosophical point of view, precisely by linking it with revolutionary excesses. La Harpe's polemical *Du fanatisme dans la langue révolutionnaire,* for example, depicted revolutionary language as an "intolerable jargon" that used known words in a perverse sense, in order to legitimize the regime of the bayonet.[28] La Harpe seemed to equate Idéologue philosophy with this Jacobin "demagoguery" and impugned both at once.

> All the men of party, all the enemies of truth, whether enraged *Jacobins,* or *fanatics of philosophy,* or *revolutionary politicians,* always have only one language, and, defeated by the truth, attempt at least to destroy the testimony of those who dare to speak it.[29]

Tracy of course disputed such failures to discriminate among supporters of the Revolution. The dry, emotionless quality of his "ideology" was actually intended as an explicit antidote to revolutionary flamboyance. Tracy's desire to suppress useless signs and ellipses, and to banish hyperbole, illusion, and metaphor reflected his own conviction that language had been dangerously distorted during the Revolution.

> As for those [ways of speaking], and there are some, which cling to a certain verbal abuse that causes words to deviate from their natural meaning, they must surely be renounced . . . .
>   With regard to the means of eloquence, all those that do not contribute to the clarity and precision of the expression . . . appear to me no more than means of deception that would hardly be missed.[30]

Certainty in method and precision in expression were to be the fundamental goals of an ideologist.

Tracy's work demonstrates his initial acceptance of the by now familiar outlines of sensationalist philosophy, especially as articulated by his acknowledged master, Condillac: the basis of all knowledge in sense impressions; the central place of pleasure and pain in the development of complex ideas; the attempt to clarify and purify ideas by reconstructing the chain from simple perception to complex thought; and, finally, the conviction that philosophy is really only a well-made language.[31] Nevertheless, Tracy's desire to vindicate Condillac's philosophical method obscures some real differences. For example, he often approvingly quotes Condillac's theory that all human faculties are born of *sensation,* that thought is but transformed sensation. Yet he also sharply criticizes the famous expression "transformed sensation." Rather than having laboriously attempted to explain how sensation "turns into" memory or judgment, Condillac should have been satisfied to accept as given that all ideas are merely various kinds of sensations, with different characters and different effects.[32] Condillac's penchant for relating everything to "nature" led him astray.

> To want to divine or intuit it [nature], to conjecture its causes and origins, is very dangerous. It is an inexhaustible source of confusions and errors. The only useful thing is to study what is; this leads to knowing it and deriving from it all possible advantage.[33]

Furthermore, Tracy rejects Condillac's model of a purely passive subject as insufficient to explain the subtleties of human reasoning. He accepts Cabanis's theory of internal sensations, and goes so far as to call "ideology" a part of zoology.[34]

Tracy begins his discussion of sensibility with an explanation, derived from Cabanis, of the human nervous system—the mechanism through which we receive all sensation: "Every disturbance of one of our nerves, whether it is the effect of a vital movement, or the product of an outside cause, is the occasion for a sensation, and sets our sensibility to work."[35] He admits that he does not know precisely of what the *force vitale* consists, but, like Cabanis, speculates that it may be the result of the attraction and combination of chemical substances. He explains muscular movement by the flow and constriction of nervous fluids.[36]

Tracy never abandoned the attempt to accommodate the theories of Cabanis and other physiological ideologists; however, these speculations failed to become an integral part of his theory of mind.[37] Physiology remained an outside authority to which he referred in order to affirm the scientific "truth" of his analysis of the understanding. Cabanis's work had displaced attention from an abstract sentient individual to the actual uniqueness of sense impressions. Tracy was more apt to consider such differences as deviations. In practice, he assumed that original sense impressions are the same, or at least similar, in everyone. Temperament, occupation, or diet may greatly influence thinking, but there remained a "norm," and it was with this norm that Tracy was concerned.

If Tracy's appreciation of the contribution of physiology to "ideology" differed from that of Cabanis, he shared the latter's preoccupation with movement as the basic property of living matter. It was this idea of movement that led Tracy to his most distinctive philosophical innovation: the place of *motilité* in the development of consciousness.

Tracy first discussed what he originally termed the "faculty of motility" in his Institute *Mémoire sur la faculté de penser,* in the context of an attempt to explain how we can be certain of the reality of the external world. Tracy seems to have believed that a definitive answer to Bishop Berkeley, a proof of the correspondence between primitive sense experience and external reality, would give "ideology" a concrete, irrefutable basis in fact. Convinced of the inadequacy of Condillac's reliance on the sense of touch to account for knowledge of reality,[38] Tracy suggested that muscular activity interacts with nervous sensitivity in such a way as to give rise to a distinct sensation of movement. It is the general perception of movement against a resistant world that establishes a communication between the interior modifications of the self and the sensible universe. Recognition of movement is a kind of sixth sense that enables us to feel the relation between ourselves and exterior objects.[39] Tracy also explained the ideas of extent, space, and time as expressing certain quantities of movement.[40]

Tracy's conception of *motilité,* which accounted for knowledge of reality through the sense of movement in the perceiver, introduced a dynamic element implying a time factor into the sensationalist theory of mind. This element in Tracy was developed by his disciple Maine de Biran into an exploration of the autonomous aspects of consciousness. Tracy himself, however, never realized the potential of this aspect of his theory. He explained the "self" as a group of sensitive parts obeying the same will.[41] Though at first uncertain about the relationship of will to the consciousness of movement (i.e., whether some previous consciousness of movement is necessary for the perception of resistance), he eventually interpreted Cabanis's findings on instinctive determinations in infants to mean that sensation and movement are actually the same thing.

Thus, whereas his original account of the genealogy of human faculties had located the genesis of human faculties in the consciousness of movement, he later locates it in the general faculty of sensation.[42]

Although Tracy believed that he had found in the experience of frustrated movement a special sort of sensation that gives evidence of something beyond itself, he indirectly conceded the validity of the skeptical point of view by noting that it really makes no difference if we believe in the reality of other beings.[43] He moved to an emphasis on correct internal inference and reasoning as the decisive constituent of experience. Tracy wished above all to show men how they could clarify and rectify their thinking by following "reason, good sense, or common sense."[44]

Tracy's mature theory distinguishes four mental faculties: 1) sensing direct (simple) sensations, both internal and external; 2) sensing sensations of recall (memory); 3) sensing relations (judgments); and 4) sensing desires (will). The operations of these faculties constitute thinking:

> It is clear, when one reflects on it, that to think is to have perceptions or ideas; that our perceptions or our ideas (I will always use these two words synonymously) are things that we sense, and consequently, to *think* is to *sense.*[45]

Complex ideas are formed by generalizing from simple sense impressions. We develop the general notion of man, for example, by first forming the complex idea of a specific man. Tracy terms this operation *concraire*. Acquaintance with many specimens necessarily leads us to form the abstract and general idea of man, or "mankind." Tracy terms this operation *abstraire*. Thus, all knowledge is composed of a series of judgments that have no real validity beyond the concrete cases to which they originally referred.[46] Present associations must always be checked against the elementary perceptions being associated.

In his social and political analyses, Tracy begins by dissecting the important terms "ideologically." His discussion of *law* at the beginning of the *Commentaire sur l'Esprit des lois* is a good illustration of this approach. Objecting to Montesquieu's definition of law as the "necessary relationships arising from the nature of things," Tracy discovers in the word *law* three essential elements: 1) it is a rule governing human behavior, 2) it is ordered by an agent accepted as authoritative, and 3) there is punishment attached to its infraction, a tribunal that applies the punishment, and a physical force that produces submission.[47] These elements define *law* in its most primitive sense; hence, the notion could not have arisen until there were organized societies. "This word is necessarily relative to the social organization and could have been invented only in an already established society."[48] Indeed, properly speaking, there are no laws where there are no "coercive means to prevent [rules] from being infringed."[49]

What, then, is the significance of natural law? Tracy argues that when we observe the phenomena of nature, or of our own intelligence, we discover that things always happen in the same way, given the same circumstances. Extending the primitive meaning of law, we call such regularities natural laws because it seems to us as if some invincible authority had ordered them. The relationship between the two kinds of law is that positive laws ought to take account of natural laws in order to save men unnecessary suffering. "This is why our positive laws are either good or bad, just or unjust."[50] In a sense, just and unjust can be said to exist outside of positive law; these are judgments about the probable effects of positive laws on public happiness. Regardless of whether a particular law is just or unjust, however, it is still a binding rule. Thus, Tracy insists, "I call legal those [representatives] who are authorized by the existing law, and whose acts are valid, even when the law is not just."[51] The point is to distinguish questions of law from questions of morals.

Tracy's reconstruction of the associations in the term *law*, then, emphasizes certain elements in law—its source and its power to compel obedience—that will be characteristic of the command theory of law. He did so, however, not because he wished to deny the relevance of a higher law standard, but because he wished to put an end to the peculiar combination of legalism and incitation that was the distinguishing mark of French revolutionary discourse. He used "ideology" in the same way in his analysis of *right,* and rarely spoke of natural rights or the rights of man.[52]

Tracy's most extensive discussion of the basis of rights occurs in his *Traité sur la volonté,* the fourth part of the *Elémens d'idéologie.* It seemed as obvious to him as it had to earlier theorists that rights can come only from needs, and duties from the means to satisfy needs.[53] A need is triggered by a simple or pure sensation, resulting immediately from our organization, that affects us either agreeably or disagreeably. These sensations engender the need either to change a particular state of being (if the sensation is painful) or to maintain it (if the sensation is pleasurable). "Every pleasure or pain is a need and every perceived sensation is itself a need."[54] Needs precede all judgment, all perception of relation, and thus all knowledge. However, although needs are prior to all intellection, they are expressed only in terms of *desires,* which are not precedent to judgment and knowledge. When one primitive sensation is compared to another, the perception of some relationship between them necessarily follows. From this perception, which is a judgment, follows the desire to experience one or the other sensation, whichever gives the most pleasure. For example, hunger is merely a vague need to have the pain of hunger cease. The sensation of eating an apple engenders the need to have the pleasure of appeasing hunger continue. From the juxtaposition of these two sensations (hunger and appeasement of hunger) follows the judgment that the latter is preferable, and a desire is born to experience the preferable sensation. Thus desires are the only way in which we experience needs, and every desire represents a need.[55]

Whatever the failures of Tracy's analysis as psychology, his account enables him to subordinate the idea of need to the state of our knowledge. Since desires (the form in which needs are made known) come from judgments, they are always exactly proportioned to our true or false knowledge. Desires can be directed and regulated by the "rectification" of judgment.[56] But, for Tracy, this rectification is eminently a social process; hence, rights, which ultimately come from needs, are always modified by social experience.

To clarify his reasoning on rights and duties, Tracy analyzes the human will in four possible contexts. The first three are completely hypothetical and address the philosophical issue of whether rights and duties are absolutely correlative. Tracy admits that they seem to be so, since both rights and duties always have a positive content when referring to relationships among men. But he is here following his philosophical curiosity to determine whether there is any sense in which rights are prior to duties.

In the first situation, Tracy imagines an isolated "monad" that senses and wills but cannot act. This creature would have a right to satisfy its needs, but not a duty to do so, since it is incapable of action. The second hypothetical situation grants the capacity to act, but maintains the condition of isolation. In this state the subject's rights are coterminous with desires, but he also has duties, because he now has means to fulfill his desires. His duty is to fulfill his desires well. But Tracy finds that the notion of duty, like that of law, contains certain definite ideas: a pain that will follow infraction, a law that pronounces the penalty, and some agent that applies the law. Even in an isolated situation, however, there are certain penalties attached to a failure to minister efficiently to one's needs, e.g., a failure to achieve satisfaction of desire (which implies pain), or even self-destruction. Thus, we might be justified in extending some notion of duty to a nonsocial situation.

The third situation is not completely without concrete reference; it is illustrated by man's relationship with animals. Here the hypothetical man can sense, will, and act, and finds himself in relation to other sensate creatures; however, he can communicate with them only in a rudimentary way. Our subject still has the right to satisfy his desires and the duty to use all means at hand to do so. Because the beings surrounding him act according to their wills, he has the duty to captivate or subjugate these wills, to make them contribute to the satisfaction of his desires. Since it is supposed that he cannot truly communicate with them, he has no other way to proceed but to try to direct their wills by coercion.

Another element, however, has entered when we imagine the existence of more than one sensate creature: the newborn faculty of sympathy, which engenders the vicarious experience of another's pleasure and pain. Sympathy, then, is a newly activated need, which man has the duty to satisfy. This exposition of our relationship to animals indicates that a man has the duty to try to lessen the pain caused by the suffering of other creatures as much as is compatible with other duties. It also indicates that suffering is justified only by its utility.[57]

The fourth context considers the actual relationships among men. If men could communicate with others only imperfectly, as with animals, there would be no change in their rights and duties. Tracy notes that this was apparently Hobbes's view of a state of nature, although Hobbes was wrong to call such a situation a state of war. It would merely have been a state of "strangeness," the state we are in with animals who are not our natural predators.[58] In any event, this view ignores the crucial difference between the fourth situation and the preceding case: our subject can in fact communicate with other subjects, and thus can make agreements and conventions. Language obviates the use of force. Mutual understanding modifies judgments, desires, and rights, thereby transforming the manner of fulfilling duty. Only in this situation can the words *just* and *unjust* have any meaning. Tracy notes that, in the remaining part of his *Traité sur la volonté,* he will ignore the first three hypothetical situations, since men never in fact lived in isolation and never lived together without a system of signs.[59]

Unlike earlier expositors of sensationalist psychology, Tracy does not use his analysis of the social implications of man's sensitivity as a defense of the natural rights of man. Rights arc ultimately rooted in universal needs; however, since needs are always expressed as desires, and since desires are always formed in a social context through communication with others, it is meaningless to claim exclusive rights based on the individual capacity to feel, as if men were in fact isolated monads.

Furthermore, a precise and complete idea of *right* involves the notion of legal compulsion applied by the sovereign power. For this reason Tracy argues that it is nonsensical for a constitutional convention to begin by enumerating their alleged natural rights. The very fact that they are accepted as a constitutional convention indicates that they are in possession of the sovereign power and can define legal rights. Of course, declarations of rights may have been useful, even momentous in the past. "I know that this [practice] will forever mark an epoch in the history of human societies."[60] It was perhaps necessary for the oppressed to have a manifesto against oppression, in order to discourage its recurrence. In the future, however, the framers of representative governments should limit themselves to stating those general principles that underlie all sound government. Indeed, legislators can do no more than this, since it is impossible to tie the hands of future generations.

> One generation does not at all receive from a previous one, like a legacy, the right to live in society, and to live there under laws pleasing to [its forebears]. One generation has no right to say to another, if you wish to succeed us, this is how you must live and must manage your affairs; for from such a right it would follow that a law once made could never be changed.[61]

The impulse to clarify the implications of human sensitivity led theorists such as the Physiocrats, Volney, Condorcet, and Sieyès, to derive "natural" imperatives from the facts of human nature. They used individual psychology as a grounding mechanism to stress the inalienable and absolute character of rights. Destutt de Tracy, on the other hand, insists on the necessarily mutable and relative nature of rights. Individual psychology—always in some sense prior to, outside of, and separate from, society—continues to provide a logical, definitional structure for his social theory; Tracy uses his *idéologie*, however, to insist on the separation of logic from exhortation. Like that of Cabanis, his work calls into question the theoretical link between an abstract equal sensibility and equality in rights.

Tracy and the Question of Certainty

According to Destutt de Tracy, then, one can gain a true understanding of notions like *law* and *right* only by reflecting on the subsidiary ideas that are necessarily contained within them. His own analysis of these terms was put to a critical purpose; he argued that a neglect of essential elements in the meanings of *law* and *right*—elements related to their necessary social context—had encouraged irresponsible fanaticism under the false banner of "nature." But on what grounds can we be assured of the true significance of such terms? Tracy's entire intellectual project was in fact premised on the belief that analysis could yield certainty about the "real" meaning of ideas. In the pursuit of this goal, however, he continually encountered unsettling doubts that led him to a candid appraisal of his difficulties, and to an admission of inevitable uncertainty.

In attempting to establish the possibility of certitude in human reasoning, Tracy begins from Condillac's assumption that preliminary sense data are "true," i.e., that these data accurately reflect reality. Error must lie in the process by which the mind combines and distorts these perceptions. Rational thinking depends on accuracy in judging the relationships between ideas. Condillac, however, had explained this process in algebraic terms. He somewhat vaguely suggested, for example, that we can compare complex notions by reducing them to simple ideas, and then counting and comparing the number of ideas in each.[62] This analogy Tracy specifically rejects. Algebra is a peculiar and limited form of reasoning that considers ideas only under the principles of quantity and number. However, most reasoning is not a matter of equating identical propositions.[63] Ideas are composed of a mass of heterogeneous elements, considered under a multitude of different relations. The complex idea of "good," for example, is qualitatively different in relation to a man, a horse, or a tree.[64] Furthermore, Tracy insists that, even apart from the complexity of ideas and the imperfection of signs, it is impossible to develop methods of calculation that would be as successful in dealing with all kinds of ideas as is algebra in dealing with quantity. "If to calculate is to reason, to reason is not to calculate."[65] A judgment is not an equation; rather, an equation is a particular kind of judgment.

Judgment, in Tracy's theory, is an act of the mind by which we recognize that one idea contains another. Reasoning is but a series of consecutive judgments. In this view, error is to mistake one idea for another.

> Thus all our perceptions are originally accurate and true, and error finds its way in only when we admit an element which is contrary to them, that is, which distorts and changes them without our noticing it.[66]

The accuracy of our judgments depends on the correct classification of a present impression as being of the same kind as a previous one. This theory places the responsibility for certitude on memory.

Tracy most simply defines memory as perceiving sensations of recall. Insofar as these sensations are actually perceived by the mind, we can be as certain of their truth as of the truth of our primitive sensations. However, the exact relationship between such sensations of recall and original impressions remains obscure and probably inexplicable.[67] We do know that a memory is not a literal reproduction of a past sensation, although we must assume it to be some kind of representation or image. But, as to the faithfulness of this representation, it is impossible to judge. It may be that a simple sensation can be transmitted as a memory only with the admixture of some other element or sign. It is particularly clear to Tracy that, in the case of simple sensations of passion or desire, memories are essentially different from the sensations themselves, which "can in no way be the subject of really exact memories for us."[68]

According to Tracy, complex ideas are more susceptible to recall, since the intellectual operation of recall is similar to the process of perceiving a complex idea. However, in this case, a whole new set of difficulties arises. When ideas reappear as memories, they may have either gained or lost elements of meaning, without our knowledge. When we make new judgments about complex memories, the chance of error is compounded, for we are not in fact comparing the ideas themselves, but imperfect recollections of them. Finally, the intellectual act by which we remember a previous judgment is not at all the same as the original act of judgment, since one's general state of mind is necessarily different.[69]

The radically imperfect faculty of memory is thus the source of error in human reasoning. Time itself seems to render all associations and inferences unreliable. Tracy's desire to perfect human reason, to compensate in some way for the weaknesses he has recognized, leads him to an analysis of those influences on memory that seem to aid or inhibit accurate judgment. The most important of these are attention, habit, and language.

Condillac and Helvétius had both relied heavily on the concept of attention to explain the development of human intelligence. For Condillac, the pain associated with unmet needs focuses attention on certain objects and initiates the association of ideas.[70] In his final work, Condillac literally assimilated the notion of attention to a vivid sensation of pleasure or pain.[71] Helvétius's *De l'esprit* explains the function of attention in a similar way, and places it in an even more central position. Since Helvétius posited that all minds are equal at birth, he could explain differences in intellect only by the length of time impressions were heeded. Furthermore, his primary emphasis was on the manipulation of attention by the legislator through the use of pleasure and pain, reward and punishment.[72]

The response of the human organism to pleasure and pain also plays a central role in Tracy's analysis. Men have no control over the sensations with which they are bombarded; nor can they modify these sensations "to find agreeable or disagreeable that which is not such."[73] Thus free will, for Tracy as for Hobbes or Hume, is technically a nonsensical proposition. The will depends on a previous desire, which, in turn, is a consequence of an involuntary sensation of preference based on the pleasure or pain attending that sensation. One would expect, then, that Tracy would explain attention as the effect of preceding sensations of pleasure or pain. However, he is apparently unwilling to sacrifice the voluntaristic connotations of the term "attention" in this way. In attempting to affirm man's ability to become the master of his own thought processes, Tracy asserts that it is within all men's power to pay attention to certain perceptions, rather than others.

> It does not depend on us whether or not we perceive sensations . . . ; but it does depend on us, up to a certain point, to give our attention to one of these perceptions so that the others become meaningless to us.[74]

Tracy implies that attention can provide a corrective to faulty reasoning; he does not explain, however, how the desire to be attentive arises, or how attention is related to sensations and judgments. One must conclude that different capacities to pay attention are due in some ways to innate differences in energy or *force vitale*.

Tracy's discussion of habit similarly fails to establish the bases of accurate belief. *Habitude* is defined as "the disposition, the permanent attitude that arises from . . . frequent repetition."[75] Tracy agrees with the common observation that the repetition of the same movement leads to an ability to execute this movement with more facility and rapidity. Thus, many intellectual operations become easier with practice, and men may become habituated to correct judgment.[76] Tracy stresses, however, that movements become less vivid as they become easier:

> The easier and more rapid they are, the less perceptible; in other words, the perception they cause diminishes even to the point of extinction, even if the movement persists.[77]

Many kinds of movements, both physical and mental, become so familiar as to pass out of consciousness altogether. Tracy believes, in fact, that the functioning of bodily systems like circulation may be perceptible to infants; only with maturity do men become unaware of their operation.[78]

The phenomenon of habituation is crucial to the acquisition of knowledge; but it is also a powerful impediment to enlightenment. Habit makes some thought patterns easy and relatively automatic. A contrary idea, on the other hand, is unfamiliar, difficult, and attended with pain. Tracy assumes that a correct perception of objective reality exists, but he is unable to specify its connection to habitual behavior. The truth has no intrinsic power to persuade, and Tracy concedes the philosophic aptness of an old maxim: *"la raison éclaire et ne conduit pas."*[79]

The most powerful aid to the thinking process is language, or a system of signs that fix ideas in the memory. Without such an aid, men would be limited to the most rudimentary sorts of reasoning. Again following Condillac, Tracy seeks a solution to the problems inherent in his psychology of knowledge by studying the origin, nature, and function of language. "One is brought irresistibly to this study."[80]

In the eighteenth century, a number of treatises devoted to the genesis of language were published.[81] Members of the Institute continued to be fascinated by questions concerning the origin and functions of language. Indeed, they discussed many issues in the philosophy of language that were neglected in the subsequent development of a historical science of linguistics, but that have dominated twentieth-century linguistic studies.[82]

Most of the eighteenth-century theories of the genesis of human speech had assumed, as did Tracy, that gestures, cries, and touch made up the first kind of language, a language of action, rooted in original needs and sentiments. This primitive system of signs remains the "natural and necessary" basis of languages.[83] The original purpose of language was intimately related to the satisfaction of physical needs. Abstract thought, the comparing and analyzing of our ideas, is largely an unintended consequence of the invention of language.

In Tracy's view, primitive language is in some sense more pure than any developed system of signs, since a sign is perfectly meaningful only for the one who invents it. Those who inherit an existing system of signs can never be sure of understanding a word in precisely the same way as others do, and the original power of an idea must necessarily become attenuated. Furthermore, languages develop haphazardly, increasing the potential for misunderstanding and confusion.[84]

To use the analysis of language as a way to approach the verification of ideas, Tracy must assume that a "true" chain of ideas can be represented in a logical chain of speech. Since *actual* languages are incoherent and chaotic, Tracy has to suppose that there is an underlying "rational" language that corresponds to true ideas. This is in fact the unstated premise of the *Grammaire* (the second volume of his *Elémens d'idéologie*) which seeks to rectify, purify, and clarify language in order to achieve an accurate chain of ideas.[85] Tracy's entire analysis of language, however, points to the conclusion that all languages are irremediably imperfect representations of our ideas. Rather than establishing the possibility of certitude, language, with its inherent imperfections, vitiates this possiblity forever.

Tracy's own observations on the basic character of existing language undermine his effort. He notes that the same word includes many ideas and that words may change functions.[86] Furthermore, at times there is no verbal representation for an idea at all. An idea may be vaguely implied by the reasoning used, i.e., by unstated relations with the expressed idea (ellipses). The converse—signs without ideas—occurs in the case of the subjunctive, which Tracy believed to be a useless mode.[87] But the fatal flaw in language is that words do not represent ideas in a uniform, certain manner. The relationship between signs and words can never be constant, since it is established only by the radically imperfect faculty of memory.

> This sad truth is essentially what constitutes the radical defect in the mind of man; what condemns it always to fail of complete exactitude, except in extremely simple cases, and what causes almost all its reasoning to be founded, up to a certain point, on uncertain and variable data.[88]

Thus, Tracy denies the possibility of a universal language accurately reflective of objective reality. The attempts both to develop a new language and to perfect existing languages are doomed to failure. The creation of an artificial language would require the previous clarification and enumeration of all ideas, an impossible task.[89] And, even were such a language to be invented, it never would be adopted, since language is acquired slowly, without premeditated design, either by conquest, religion, or commerce.[90] Extant languages are no more susceptible of perfection in expression than are artificial ones, because of the inherent defects of the human mind. Finally, even if a language were to be created or perfected, and adopted by universal consent, it would immediately become corrupted and idiomatic.[91]

> I conclude that the project of a pasigraphy is a conception, vicious in its very origins, that will never produce a useful result, and that no one would tackle, if he had formed a really clear idea of it.[92]

According to Tracy, it is not only impossible, but undesirable, to create a learned universal language. Although such a language might facilitate communication between experts, it would inhibit the enlightenment of the masses. "Experts, in this position, communicate more easily with learned foreigners, but much less easily with the mass of their fellow citizens."[93] Tracy preferred to stress improvements in existing oral and written languages, improvements that would help the common man to correct his judgment and ideas.[94]

Tracy began his examination of the analysis of sensations and ideas with the hope of establishing more securely the grounds and limits of rational belief. Beyond those limits, he argued, one should maintain an attitude of agnosticism, of fruitful doubt. And although he often ex-

pressed considerable satisfaction that he had reached "incontestable conclusions,"[95] the result of his inability to give a satisfactory account of the
relationship of current to past impressions, of his recognition of the irremediable defects of memory, of his emphasis on the contrary effects of
habit, and of his pessimism about the accuracy of signs was to curtail
severely the areas in which one could speak with any certainty at all.[96]
The more Tracy sought to remain close to the indisputable evidence of
the senses, the more difficult it became to affirm general truths. He could
even remark to Stendhal that the immediate sensations conveyed through
the medium of the novel might be as close as men could come to experiencing "truth" directly.[97]

This radical retrenchment is obvious in his rejection of Condorcet's
vision of a social mathematics based on probability theory.[98] Condorcet
had hoped to subject the grounds for rational belief to precise and measured calculation through the science of probabilities. The mathematical
calculation of probabilities offered "the only solid reply that can be made
to the subtleties of pyrrhonism."[99] For Condorcet, the truths of the moral
sciences were less probable than those of the physical sciences, but, in
both cases, the expression of probabilities could be precisely measured
by mathematical calculation. Just as Tracy had rejected the connection
between human logic and algebra, so he denies that social knowledge is
subject to mathematical calculation.

The success of any kind of mathematical calculation, Tracy argues, rests
on the susceptibility of the materials in question to quantification and
mathematical manipulation.[100] However, there are many subjects (many
more than it was formerly believed) in which one cannot express the
relevant facts in terms of number, even were it possible to collect all the
"facts."

> Surely degrees of the capacity, of the integrity of men, those [degrees] of
> the energy and strength of their passions, of their prejudices, of their habits,
> are impossible to evaluate in numbers. It is the same with the degree of
> influence of certain fundamental legal structures or offices, with the degree
> of importance of certain institutions, with the degree of utility of certain
> inventions or certain methods.[101]

When one tries to apply the calculus of probabilities to subtle and complex data such as these, as Condorcet attempted to do in his work on the
decisions of assemblies, the results can only be called trifling.

The more they have followed out the consequences of the small number of data that they were able to grasp, the more [the consequences] became different from the consequences that these same data would have produced in combination with all those often more important [facts] which they were obliged to neglect, for want of the power to disentangle and appreciate them.[102]

Recognizing, choosing, evaluating, and ordering facts require ability and discernment, qualities to which it is difficult to apply precise rules. In the great majority of cases, according to Tracy, we have no other choice but to apply the ordinary instruments of reasoning to these tasks, i.e., to employ ordinary language. Only "ideology," intended as a clarification of language, can help us to reason well in complex matters. Research in the social sciences will always be difficult, and the results less than rigorous. At best, it may be possible to discern that the truth must lie within certain broad limits.[103]

One result of Tracy's encounter with epistemological uncertainty was his insistence on the positive social consequences of doubt. This reaction resembled that of the seventeenth-century English scientists of the Royal Society, who responded to the theological disputes of the Reformation with a theory of "constructive skepticism."[104] Indeed, the parallel between the ideological and fratricidal warfare of the Revolution and the wars of religion was much heeded at the time. In his *Lectures on History*, Volney rejected both the "ridiculous" opinion of doubting everything and the "more common and more dangerous disease" of doubting nothing.[105] The latter, he argued, led to convulsions of enthusiasm and frenzies of fanaticism. "Brutus and Casca seem destined to obtain the same influence in this age, that Ahod and the Maccabees possessed in the last."[106] Volney recommends, therefore, the middle road of constructive doubt:

that of forming an opinion after weighing and examining the reasons which ought to determine it—holding judgment in suspense while there is not a sufficient motive for fixing it, and proportioning our belief to the degree of proof and evidence with which each fact is accompanied.[107]

In an Institute lecture on the origin of printing, Daunou concludes with this typical observation.

It is that tendency to take too exalted a view of many of our attainments which gives rise to presumptuous claims, long quarrels, intolerance, or dissension . . . . [D]oubt is also a science, and it is the most peaceable one. It seems to me at least that skepticism . . . is the gentlest and sanest habit that the mind can contract.[108]

Ultimately, however, the Idéologues' desire to use constructive skepticism as a basis for creating a science of social happiness would remain a largely empty project. The underlying difficulty was that they never developed any real criteria for, in Volney's words, "weighing and examining the reasons which ought to determine opinion."

In the case of Tracy, this difficulty can be seen clearly in his attack on the syllogism. Tracy objects to the syllogistic form as a scholastic obfuscation because it suggests that particulars are deduced from universals. In fact, the major term of a syllogism (the universal) is *not* the evidence by which the conclusion is proved; "all that is false, and exactly the reverse of the way human reasoning proceeds."[109] A similar position led Hobbes and Condillac to reverse the logic of the Aristotelian syllogism, but to retain the ideas of an identity between the terms. In Hobbes' view, the terms of a syllogism are but different names for the same thing.[110] Tracy disputes this view as well because it continues to suggest that reasoning means comparing quantities of identical elements.

Tracy's solution is to suppress the major term altogether, and to begin with the minor term. The correctness of a conclusion arises from the fact that "the minor, the *first subject,* includes an initial predicate; that predicate a second, a third, a fourth if you will, and, finally, that of the conclusion."[111] Tracy employs the following example:

(1) Man is an animal.   (Major term)
(2) John is a man.   (Minor term)
(3) Therefore, John is an animal.   (Conclusion)

According to Tracy, the first statement is useless; the conclusion is in fact generated by following out the implications of our idea of *man.* "John is a man" is true because we recognize in John, independent of his particular attributes, all those ideas common to all men composing the idea of *man.* Similarly, "John is an animal" because we recognize in *man* all those ideas common to all animals. In this example, Tracy in fact suppresses the appeal to experiential evidence. He merely assumes that "real" experience exists, contained implicitly in our ideas as expressed in language.

However, his own examination of memory and language does not support the assumption of a universal set of perceptions.

We have seen an example of this difficulty already in his analysis of the term *right*. Tracy had argued that rights derive from needs, but only through the medium of socially conditioned desires. This account undercuts the revolutionary argument that universal needs beget universal rights. But it seems to rest the notion of "right" purely on social interaction and habit. Tracy is ultimately unsatisfied with this conclusion because it offers no way to distinguish rational experience from irrational custom. He notes that we may sometimes have true needs without desires, as well as desires without true needs. The obvious implication is that we "ought" to have some rights, whereas some existing rights are groundless. Tracy can only conclude that these cases are "exceptions" due to inherent defects in our intellect that prevent us from always judging correctly what is in our self-interest.[112]

Hume, whom Tracy does not seem to have read, had earlier faced the problem of distinguishing "natural" from "unnatural" beliefs in a much more self-conscious and systematic manner. If Hume's account of the distinction was still not entirely satisfactory, it did not pose a practical problem for him. He had little reforming zeal; custom, born of accumulating experience, provided the necessary structure of men's beliefs and Hume was more aware of the fragility of opinions than desirous of correcting them. But Tracy deliberately offered his *idéologie* as the basis of a theory of social and political action. His failure to specify any standard of correct judgment was, therefore, a formidable problem.

Throughout Tracy's discussion of society and politics, there is a tension between his desire to rationalize social and political life and his inability to offer any consistent basis for that rationalization. This tension is "resolved" in different ways in different places. At times Tracy falls back, as did Hume, on the customary beliefs that provide certainty in daily life. More often he oscillated between a projection into the future of a purified natural pattern of social interaction and troubled attempts to manage "unreason" in the present. But whenever he attempts to use *idéologie* to unravel complex perceptions like "property" or "liberty," his reasoning inevitably displays a somewhat arbitrary character. "Ideology" often stands apart—an isolated prolègomenon with uncertain application to Tracy's own assessment of social realities.

The major impulse of Cabanis and Tracy in developing "ideology" was to provide a serviceable method for the study of the social sciences, a metascience (*"la théorie des théories"*) [113] that would assure steady and certain progress in social analysis. The immediate result of their work, however, was to deflate the claims to certainty of earlier theorists, and to widen the perception of a breach between human aspirations and social reality, and between political ideas and the existing justifications for these ideas. In their work, the conception of the science of man as a set of first principles derived from sensationalist psychology was undergoing a subtle transformation. Cabanis's medical perspective on sensibility undermined the egalitarian logic implicit in the earlier conception, and indirectly fostered a more organic, functional approach to politics. Tracy, while maintaining a definition of social science based on the first principles of the human mind, was unable to show convincingly that this conception offered either a clear guide to action or a reasonable hope of certitude. In Tracy's own work, the radical uncertainty that lies at the heart of his method has particularly instructive consequences. It intrudes on his discussion of both economics and politics in such a way as to express the peculiar vulnerability of the utilitarian version of classic liberalism.

CHAPTER THREE

Political Economy and the Logic of the Will

DURING THE revolutionary period in France, the conceptual distinction between social and political was usually articulated as an antagonism between the natural needs of society and the unnatural demands of government. Sieyès focused dramatically on this theme in *Qu'est-ce que le Tiers Etat?* Throughout the *Rights of Man,* Thomas Paine made the same argument: government had theretofore been antagonistic to the substance of commercial society.[1] And Roederer took as the explicit theme of a set of lectures given in 1793 that "social science does not consist solely in the science of public law."[2]

Yet no consensus existed about the principles, or even about the subject matter, of social science. The phrase usually denoted a mixture of self-evident principles of right, moral axioms based on some variant of egoistic psychology, and generalizations borrowed from Montesquieu, Rousseau, and the Physiocrats. Furthermore, the immediate exigencies of revolution and war deflected attention from the detailed analysis of economic and social theory. After the demise of the Physiocratic school, interest in economics had lagged in France. In England, a systematic reconsideration of Adam Smith did not appear until the publication of Ricardo's *Principles of Political Economy* in 1817.

First discouraged by the failure of revolutionary efforts to create a virtuous society, then dismayed at Napoleonic Realpolitik, the Idéologues wished to establish an inviolable scientific substratum that would serve as a guide to social action. Hence they turned to those aspects of the contemporary notion of social science that appeared to be most "concrete."

This attraction explains the new concern with the physiological bases of psychology. It also accounts for the great appeal of the eighteenth-century economists who claimed to have discovered the invariable laws of human production. The problems of economic reconstruction and the first stirrings of the Industrial Revolution were to reinforce this new perspective, although they did not precipitate it.[3]

This chapter will examine the nature of "ideological" economics in the work of Destutt de Tracy, who combined the commitment to sensationalist psychology with the new interest in political economy in his notion of a "logic of the will and its effects." Because much of Tracy's theory was taken directly from J.B. Say, however, we must first turn to a brief consideration of Say's contribution to the emergence of classical political economy in France.

J.B. Say and the Definition of Political Economy

After his revolutionary career as a journalist and politician, Jean-Baptiste Say turned to the formal study of economics, and also became personally involved in manufacturing through his ownership of a cotton-spinning factory in Pas-de-Calais. He was deeply influenced by Adam Smith, whom he had read during an extended stay in England in the 1780s. But he also continued the traditions of French economic thinkers, in particular Turgot and Cantillon.[4] In 1803, the first edition of Say's *Traité d'économie politique* appeared. Several other theorists published general works on economics during the Napoleonic period, but the imperial regime was not particularly hospitable to speculative discussions, and these works stirred little comment. With the Restoration, the economists resumed their work. Say gave his first courses in political economy in 1815, and beginning in 1819 held a chair in *économie industrielle* at the *Conservatoire des arts et métiers*.

Say began with the assertion that political economy must be distinguished clearly from political theory.[5] Influenced by the Physiocratic notion of a rational theory of economics, his purpose was to elevate political economy to the status of a science. On Say's account, Adam Smith's work was much superior to that of the Physiocrats; nevertheless, Smith had been disorderly. He had confused economic facts with historical and philosophical speculations; he had not sufficiently treated the theory of value and commercial production; and he had not foreseen changes in circumstances and their effects on economic progress.[6]

Say's own method is in fact one example of applying "analysis," or the "rigorous method of philosophizing,"[7] to economics. He accepted Smith's view of the development of civil society, but was little concerned with the historical process itself. It was the principles governing the production of wealth in civilized society that interested Say.[8] An economist, like an experimental scientist, deduced general facts, or principles, from particular facts apparent to all neutral observers; a general fact disclosed the reciprocal action of substances on each other, i.e., the relations of cause and effect. Say argued that political economy should be careful to distinguish matters of fact from matters of right or opinion. He favored the expression *faits positifs* or *notions positives*. The objective of economics was to provide "a correct representation of the nature of things and the general laws necessarily resulting from it."[9]

Despite his emphasis on the autonomy of political economy, Say resisted the English tendency to construe this science within the narrowest possible limits. Thus, in many ways he continued to prefer Smithian economics to the rigorously logical system developed by Ricardo. Say believed that Ricardo had somehow falsified reality by straying too far from factual observation. "The reasoning proceeds in a straight line; but a vital force, often unperceived, and always unpredictable, makes the facts deviate very far from our calculations."[10] Say claimed that his theory was more closely tied to actual facts, i.e., to "objects that exist [and] events that take place"[11] in relation to wealth.

Moreover, Say explicitly retained the Idéologue conviction that all of the social sciences were theoretically unified. He reaffirmed that profound links existed between economics and other sciences, especially the sciences of morality and politics. But he was content to leave the establishment of these links, such matters as tracing the origin of property, to "speculative philosophy."[12]

It was in France, then, that Ricardo's image of economics as a deductive science first evolved; indeed, there may have been a direct link to Ricardo through James Mill, who was acquainted both with the Physiocrats and with the new French economists. As early as 1808 Mill was expounding Say's theory of markets (which was then adopted by Ricardo), and he later followed Say's general organization of economic subjects.[13] During the Restoration, the English and French economists also developed personal contacts. In 1814, just after the appearance of the second edition of his *Traité*, Say was sent to England by the French government to study the English economy. Received as something of a celebrity in reformist circles, he established relations with Bentham, James Mill, Malthus, and Ricardo.[14]

In France Say gained an immediate following, among both economists and liberal journalists. D'Hauterive and Storch, as well as Destutt de Tracy, relied heavily on Say's work.[15] His ideas were also adopted by the political journalists Charles Comte and Dunoyer, and by the historian, Augustin Thierry. Indeed, much of the defense of classic nineteenth-century economic liberalism on the continent can be traced to the influence of Say and his school.[16]

Tracy's Preface to Political Economy

Destutt de Tracy first turned to the study of economics in the course of commenting on those books of Montesquieu's *Esprit des lois* that deal with public revenue and taxation. But he works out his "logic of the will" most systematically in the final volume of the *Elémens d'idéologie*, the *Traité sur la volonté et de ses effets*. In this work, Tracy placed the underlying principles of economics at the heart of social science. In fact, he preferred the expression *économie sociale* to *économie politique*, in order to indicate that social science should be distinct from the traditional concerns of politics.[17] Only economics "leads us in a sure way to appreciate the value and utility of all our actions, to judge their merit by their consequences, and consequently [to judge] the merit of the feelings that incline us more to one action than to another."[18] Hence, economic science forms the largest part of social science, which Tracy defined as a system of principles indicating the way to promote the greatest amount of happiness in society.[19]

Tracy's indebtedness to Say, whom he termed "without contradiction the author of the best book on political economy ever written,"[20] was obvious throughout. Nevertheless, there were some points of doctrinal difference between them. Furthermore, Tracy's purpose in discussing economics differed from that of Say. Less interested in presenting economics as a self-contained set of relationships, Tracy wished to draw out underlying connections between philosophy, psychology, economics, and politics. Apologizing for the summary nature of much of his economic analysis, Tracy explained that his work was not really a treatise on political economy per se, but rather the first part of a study of the human will.[21]

This effort to justify classical liberal economics through "ideological" reasoning, an effort that has been called the "psychological preface of liberal political economy,"[22] was particularly irritating to Marx, who ridiculed Tracy as a "fish-blooded bourgeois doctrinaire."[23] But in fact, Tracy's effort both to demonstrate that political economy was inherently related to the nature of the human understanding and to draw out the social and political ramifications of economic laws provided less a doctrinaire defense of "bourgeois ideology" than a revelation of the contradictions and limitations of its utilitarian form.

The fundamental assumption underlying Tracy's analysis of political economy is that notions such as property, riches, labor, value, and exchange can be grasped in their entirety only by relating them to a universal model of human thought. Hence, economics must begin with "ideology."

From Xavier Bichat, Tracy borrows the distinction between two modes of existence: organic or interior life, and animal or exterior life.[24] He argues that the need to nourish oneself and to fight the forces of decomposition, i.e. organic life, is clearly the "most indispensable" mode of existence. It gives a definite direction to our exterior life by creating "a mass of interests that are particular and peculiar to ourselves."[25] These are the interests of *personnalité*.

According to Tracy, political economy concerns itself primarily with the necessary effects of personality, of which property is perhaps the most fundamental. His theory of property is prefigured in the Lockean notion that man has a property in his labor and in that which is mixed with labor; in the Physiocratic notion that a natural right in one's person is naturally extended into a natural right in physical goods; and in Sieyès's declaration that "everyman is the sole proprietor of his person."[26] Tracy, however, concentrates on defining the precise nature of this link between personality and property.

To understand the meaning of personality, we have to grasp the relationship between the faculty of willing and the concept of the self. The faculty of willing is based on our sensitivity to desires; it is an immediate and necessary response (attraction or repulsion) to the pleasure and pain occasioned by certain types of perception.

> . . . the will is truly and properly the general and universal faculty of finding anything whatever preferable to something else, [the faculty] of being affected in such a way as to prefer some impression, some feeling, some action, some possession, some object, to some other.[27]

Tracy argues that the self is coterminous with the general faculty of sensibility. "Thus . . . the existence of the *self* and the sensibility of *self* are two identical things."[28] Nevertheless, we often identify the self only with the faculty of willing (in fact but a part of sensibility), since to enjoy and to suffer constitute the whole of human existence, and since we enjoy or suffer only insofar as the will is satisfied or thwarted. Furthermore, Tracy assumes that a complete consciousness of self is possible only in a willing being, since one becomes aware of one's separate existence only by becoming aware of resistance to the will.[29] It is this awareness of other beings that develops in us the idea of our exclusivity and individuality, and of our peculiar relationship to our bodies and faculties.

The ideas of separateness and exclusivity are at the core of the idea of property. As soon as a person can recognize himself clearly as a separate entity, with a capacity to experience pleasure and pain and to act on these feelings,

> necessarily he also sees clearly that this *self* is the exclusive proprietor of the body to which it gives life [and] of the organs which it moves, of all their faculties, . . . powers, . . . effects, . . . passions, . . . and actions; for all these things begin and end with the *self*, exist through it alone, are set in motion only by its acts. No other moral person can employ the same instruments nor be affected in the same way by the results.[30]

The notion of property, then, is born in the awareness of our exclusive relationship to our faculties and activity; however, it is not limited to this awareness. Everywhere that he has been observed, man has tended to extend the psychological relationship of property to external things. When human activity, or labor, is expended on material objects, the feeling of proprietorship associated with the activity is extended to include those objects, e.g., tools, animals, or land.[31] A full conception of individuality necessarily includes the idea of owning exterior goods.

Tracy sought to prove that private property is a direct consequence of the concept of self.

> But *yours* and *mine* were never invented, they were recognized on the day that one could say *you* and *me*; . . . or rather, *me* and *other than me*. . . . There is property, if not precisely wherever there is a sensing individual, at least wherever there is an individual willing according to his sensations, and acting according to his will.[32]

He concludes from this analysis of possession that pure communism is impossible.[33] Tracy's defense of property, however, is not necessarily a defense of existing property relations. He notes that the advantages and disadvantages of various *kinds* of property will become clearer as his discussion proceeds. Rather than defending any property in particular he merely asserts that there is a fundamental sense in which property is anterior and superior to all institutions. And rather than concluding that man has an inalienable right to property, Tracy says merely that self-consciousness inevitably leads us to recognize ourselves as "possessors of our existence and its modes."[34]

According to Tracy, then, the notions of personality and property arise spontaneously as the individual interacts with his environment. So too does the concept of riches or wealth. Wealth consists of the capacity of the willing faculty to direct actions toward the satisfaction of desires. In its most general sense, wealth or riches includes anything that increases the power and effect of human volition, individually or collectively. Thus, ownership of property, knowledge of scientific laws, technical skills, the use of language, and social institutions securing peace or furthering cooperation can all be considered riches. They are all goods (*biens*) because they contribute to well-being (*bien-être*).[35]

Say had defined wealth in a similar fashion as the possession of anything that has the ability to satisfy needs.[36] Say called the "inherent fitness or capability of certain things to satisfy the various wants of mankind"[37] *utility* and he argued that utility was the basis of value. Utility was measured by price, i.e., by the amount of one good that a person was willing to give up for another good. Say was careful to note that price was a measure only of the value of social riches, i.e., the part of riches created by labor in the process of exploiting land and capital; nevertheless, he insisted that the exchange value of a commodity directly reflected its utility, rather than the labor expended to produce it.[38]

Despite Tracy's usual deference to Say, he rejects this contention that utility is the measure of value. Returning to Smith's theory of value, later elaborated by Ricardo and Marx, Tracy argues that there must be a natural and necessary basis of value, and that this basis can only be human labor.[39] Although the concepts of *richesse* and *valeur* refer to "anything that satisfies needs," they also necessarily imply for Tracy the more fundamental idea of the process of satisfying needs: movement, the exercise of faculties, labor. Tracy's theory of the development of self-awareness in infants had emphasized that the pleasurable sense of movement is one of the most primitive aspects of human consciousness.

> All pain, suffering, and even mere discomfort create in us the desire . . . to move, to bestir ourselves. This feeling of movement is a solace, a true comfort. We experience pleasure as long as it lasts.[40]

Thus the ability to use our powers—to labor—is the most primitive sense of wealth. We first develop the notion of value in relation to labor, which overcomes resistance to the will and transforms the things around us into a valuable state. Like the idea of property, the notion of value is then "communicated" to the things themselves.[41]

Tracy is quite certain that he is correct in attributing to labor the primitive basis of value because labor, unlike utility, can serve as an intelligible measure of value. The value of the labor performed by a worker in a certain period of time is measured in terms of the indispensable needs that arise in the worker during the same period. In saying this,

> we are really giving as a measure of this value the value of a certain quantity of labor, since the goods necessary for the satisfaction of these needs take their own natural and necessary value only from the work that their acquisition costs. Thus labor, our only original good, is given a value only by itself, and the unit [of measurement] is of the same kind as the quantities calculated.[42]

Like most classical economists who struggled to use the labor theory of value, Tracy encounters perplexing difficulties. He notes that all goods have two values: that of the sacrifices their production requires (natural or necessary value), and that of the advantage their possession procures (conventional value). The discussion of conventional value is really a reworking of Say's theory; Tracy's *valeur conventionnelle et vénale* is determined by supply and demand, is a measure of the utility of production, and is reflected in the market price.[43]

An adequate theory of value would have to show how the two conceptions of value are related; but Tracy does not offer such an explanation, and is apparently unconcerned about the failure to do so. He observes that if the natural value of a commodity is greater than the conventional value, a laborer engaged in its production must either change his occupation or perish; if the natural value is less, the laborer prospers; if the values are equal, the laborer merely subsists. Tracy does not suggest, however, that conventional value tends to approximate natural value in normal times. In fact, he merely juxtaposes his two definitions without specifying any relationship between them. He is even led to conclude that "this natural and necessary price has almost nothing in common with the venal or conventional price. . . . In themselves, these two things are foreign to one another."[44] The importance of Tracy's discussion of value, in his own view, is his demonstration that man creates nothing that does not already exist in nature; "since artificial and conventional values exist among us, there had to be a natural and necessary value somewhere."[45]

Having defined property, wealth, and value, Tracy then turns to economic interaction, which he understands as a continuous process of exchange. Tracy credits Adam Smith with the important discovery that man is the only animal to barter and trade, although he notes that Smith made no attempt to ascertain the causes of this phenomenon.[46] In Tracy's view, man's fundamental penchant to exchange can be traced to the peculiar intellectual abilities that cause men to develop language.

In his *Grammaire,* Tracy speculated that animals may be capable of a primitive communication by sounds or gestures expressing inchoate ideas. Men also originally communicated in this way, and the mode survives in the part of speech called interjections.[47] Men alone, however, are capable of breaking down these elliptical expressions into separate elements, of generalizing, of abstracting, and, finally, of forming propositions. As personality develops, man is led naturally to utilize this capacity in the satisfaction of his needs and desires. His ability to distinguish himself clearly from his attributes, to distinguish subject from predicate, makes it possible for him to form the general idea of value, an abstract quality that is distinct from its embodiment in specific goods or activities. He then can enter into a process of exchange with the object of increasing value.

The prototype of all exchange is a free and uncoerced transaction in which both parties perceive that they have gained. Thus the true utility of society is to render possible an uninterrupted series of advantageous trades among its members. The sum of these acts of exchange constitutes society, "for *commerce is the whole of society,* as labor is the whole of wealth."[48] The sum of the individual advantages gained constitutes the common good.

Tracy further explains his assertion that "commerce is the whole of society" by viewing all existing social relationships as some species of exchange, either: 1) rendering a service for a salary, 2) exchanging one product for another, or 3) executing some work in common. In the first two cases, the exchange process is clear. Tracy argues that it is no less real in the third. When men labor in common, they give up the advantages that would have been gained in working for their private benefit in order to gain a part of the common utility. Indeed, cooperative labor produces a synergistic increase in productivity.[49] Tracy also stresses the importance of economic cooperation to the growth of knowledge. Cooperation is the essence of learning because it fosters the invention and employment of language and signs, which "furnish our minds with many new means of combination and action."[50]

For Tracy, then, economic cooperation is paradigmatic of all social intercourse. In exploiting the dual senses of the words *commerce* and *exchange,* Tracy was drawing on a long tradition that recognized the softening, the *doux,* effects of commerce on manners. His emphasis on this economic model of society also results in a refinement and restatement of a defense of civil equality that was implicit in the works of many eighteenth-century thinkers, who took for granted a distinction between the independent and dependent poor. The latter usually figured as "victims" driven to seek aid from those with power and wealth.[51] Rousseau had brilliantly explored the social consequences of what he took to be the psychological and moral impoverishment characteristic of this dependent relationship. Tracy, on the contrary, stresses its economic disadvantages.

Tracy argues that inequalities in human abilities, intelligence, and faculties, apparent even among savages, increase as the human species develops and diversifies. These inequalities lead both to unequal power and influence, and to unequal property distribution. In primitive societies, inequality of power, manifested most clearly in the institution of slavery, is more important than inequality of wealth, since these societies are generally poor. Tracy assumes that it is precisely this inequality of power that impedes social and economic development. Primitive societies are inefficient. They satisfy human needs poorly because men are prevented from engaging in a free process of exchange, and thus from benefiting from the process of cooperation. Among savages, inequality of power "places the weakest at the mercy of the strongest. It is because of this that they have as little to do with each other as possible, for any relation would become insupportable."[52] Slowly, men perceive the drawbacks of this state of affairs; they diminish inequality of power through a gradual extension of equal legal protection, leading to a more general security. Secure from arbitrary violence and protected by the law, men can freely acquire property, keep what they acquire, and enter into contracts, i.e., they can freely increase individual and collective *richesse*.

Tracy's account of exchange, like his definitions of property, wealth, and value, follows a distinct pattern. He begins by drawing out a connection between each concept and his theory of mind, allegedly proceeding in a certain manner by examining the idea to ascertain which aspects of its meaning are fundamental, or consistently related internally. His implicit claim is that these definitions will clarify and point toward the beneficial reform of existing social and economic relationships. The connection between these preliminary "clarifications" and his subsequent economic discussion, however, will not be at all straightforward.

First, as in his discussion of the meaning of "natural right," Tracy will attempt to sever the connection between the psychological roots of an idea and its moral significance. Thus, while he affirms the primitive connection between personality and property, and between individual effort and value or wealth, he will continually insist that the legitimacy of actual human institutions is a matter of weighing "advantages and disadvantages." This juxtaposition of viewpoints, however, often suggests that "ideology" has no intelligible relationship to reality.

A related difficulty arises out of his discussion of society as *commerce*. This theory that individuals act so as to increase satisfaction through bargaining is a variation on a theme that was played over and over in the social philosophy of the Enlightenment. Public consensus was to be found in the peaceful interlocking of enlightened self-interests. At the same time, however, his work exposes the vulnerability of such a view. In explaining the development of *société*, Tracy relies explicitly on his analysis of the development of language. But his own methodical unmasking of the inherent deficiencies of language suggests that these optimistic assumptions about the results of social cooperation are unfounded. After sketching his model of increasingly beneficial social relations, Tracy records some obvious objections himself. People may be mistaken in what they desire, and thus enter into relations with others that are ultimately disadvantageous. They may subsequently change their perceptions and regret the exchange. They may, moreover, be forced by circumstances to enter unequal relations, sacrificing more than they gain. Yet he dismisses these strictures as particular cases "that are not related to the nature of the transaction."[53]

Tracy's discussion of the obvious utility of laws guaranteeing individual security and economic rights suggests one cause of this dismissal of doubts about the validity of his conception of society. For Tracy, the distorted perceptions that significantly mar the economic model of society are those of the powerful, who shortsightedly make *commerce* difficult by exercising personal tyranny. As long as he focuses on this source of conflict, which he hopes is remediable, he can ignore the more difficult questions that his critique of "universal reason" raises. And it is this conflict which figures most importantly in his discussion of production and distribution.

The Production of Value

While his theory of society as exchange assumes the increase in satisfaction that accrues to individuals, Tracy—in the spirit of keeping to "factual" observation—also asserts that proof of actual gain is the necessary condition for a favorable judgment on the evolution of social relations. "We shall also examine to what extent the progress of the species as a whole increases the happiness of individuals, which happiness is necessary before we can congratulate ourselves [on our progress]."[54] The actual progress of the species is first considered from the point of view of production.

Tracy's analysis of production was largely taken from the first edition of Say's *Traité sur l'économie politique*. His adoption of the theory of the *Traité* helped to popularize Say's conception of *industrie,* a view of the factors involved in production that had distinctive social implications.[55] Indeed, Tracy's exposition tended to accentuate the ideological tenor of Say's work.

Say's theory of production directly challenged the Physiocrats, who had attributed a unique productivity to agriculture. His definition of wealth as the "fitness of any object to satisfy wants" led to the assertion that the collection, fashioning, and transportation of these objects constitutes productive activity or *industrie.*[56] Thus the *industrieux* included all those involved in productive agriculture, manufacturing, and commerce. The important common element here was the application of human faculties, i.e., labor broadly conceived to include human skill and inventiveness. Say specifically notes that industry consisted of three distinct operations: *theory* (or the study of the laws and course of nature regarding the product) and *application* (the employment of this knowledge to produce a useful effect) as well as *execution* (manual labor).[57] In advanced societies these functions are separate, and are usually, though not always, performed by different people. Theory is the province of the scientist or scholar (*savant*), application that of the entrepreneur, and execution that of the worker.

Say's view of the different functions of *industrie* gives his notion of the laboring classes a different connotation from the English equivalent. It includes a defined role for intellectuals, as well as a special productive status for the *entrepreneur d'industrie.* Say argues that the return to the entrepreneur is partly a return on his capital, and partly the wages of his function of execution, although he never found a satisfactory way of expressing the relationship between these two kinds of revenue. He was certain, however, that *industrie* represented an independent source of net wealth.

The import of Say's theory, then, was to maintain the Physiocratic opposition between land and *industrie,* but to attribute productivity to the latter rather than to the former. But the terms had now somewhat shifted in meaning. *Industrie* included productive agriculture and excluded only those who squandered their resources in luxurious consumption. While those who did not take an active part in production need not be limited to landowners, in France this way of life was particularly associated with the ownership of landed estates.[58] Destutt de Tracy's treatment of production intensifies this denigration of landed wealth, and draws out even more sharply the distinction between the "industrious" and "idle" classes.

One of the points on which Tracy fundamentally disagreed with Say concerned the proper understanding of profits accruing to land. Say viewed land as a natural agent possessing productive properties; it contributed utility to the productive process, apart from any investment of human labor. Land rent was a function of the productive properties of land in conjunction with demand.[59] Tracy objected to the differentiation of land from other forms of capital, apparently seeing in this theory a vestige of the Physiocratic glorification of the landlord. For Tracy the rent of land reflected no more than the interest on the capital engaged in it.[60] He insists that agriculture is merely an unduly romanticized sort of manufacture. Indeed, agriculture is in most cases an arduous and largely unprofitable profession to which it is difficult to attract capital. However, so much are all men the "dupes of words"[61] that both landowners and their tenants often share this unwarranted reverence for agriculture.

> It is fruitless to say that agriculture is the very first of the arts, that it is as mother's milk to man, that it is man's natural destiny, that we are wrong not to honor it more, that the emperor of China plows a furrow every year, and a thousand more nice things in this vein; none of these things will serve any purpose or in any way alter the course of society.[62]

Even more vividly in Tracy's work than in Say's, the entrepreneur (from the richest manufacturer to the smallest independent farmer) emerges as the prototypically productive member of society. Tracy notes that the *savant* and *ouvrier* will always be in the pay of the entrepreneur, since there must first be an enterprise to which they can contribute. "Industrial entrepreneurs are really the heart of the body politic, and their capitals are its blood."[63]

Tracy also focuses more directly on the ways in which capitalists consume their income. Although any particular capitalist may spend his income in both productive and unproductive ways, Tracy distinguishes two distinct types for purposes of analysis: the idle capitalist and the active capitalist.

The idle capitalist has a fixed income, independent of any activity on his part, consisting of revenues from capital of some sort. He does not engage in productive labor and spends his entire income on personal pleasure. Although he may employ numerous workers, his expenditure is sterile. The active capitalist, on the other hand, does not live idly on his revenues, but works to increase his capital stock. He invests his own capital, and often capital borrowed from idle capitalists, in order to make a profit. The active capitalist thus lives on profit, rather than on rent or wages. What he consumes for his own or his family's benefit is unproductive, but those expenses going to the support of industry are productive. In advanced society, "those who live on wages, those who live on rent, and those who live on profits, form three essentially different classes of men." [64]

Tracy is most disturbed by the disproportionate social and political influence of those he calls idlers (*les oisifs*). The category of idle capitalist was introduced as an analytical tool to distinguish more clearly the effects of different outlays of capital. It is obvious, however, that Tracy, himself a count of the Old Regime, identifies these men primarily with the great landed proprietors of France and with those who aspire to join them. He disparages them in surprisingly harsh terms. They form the only truly sterile class, a class that does nothing but live "nobly, as it is called" [65] on the value produced by others. One ought not to treat them with a superstitious love and respect or to regard them as "pillars of the state" or as the "soul of society," [66] for they perform exactly the same function as avaricious moneylenders.

In condemning *les oisifs,* Tracy employs a mixture of economic and moral reasoning, rarely distinguishing clearly between them. His major argument is based on the economic notion of unproductive consumption. In one sense, any satisfaction of a desire is good; therefore, "even a frivolous pleasure, is useful." [67] An idle capitalist's consumption, then, is not evil in itself. However, it is a purely personal, evanescent consumption. In a strict sense, productive consumption includes only those expenses that increase the capital stock of society and generate profits. Tracy uses the phrase "utility that remains," referring to such things as the construction of bridges, roads, buildings and machinery, and the improvement of arable lands.[68] Taken to an extreme, this theory, which began by seeing all consumption as inherently good, regards personal consumption itself as a luxury; all personal satisfaction of needs is "lost" value.[69]

Tracy recognizes that this train of reasoning takes him too far. He then provides a more moderate definition of luxury as superfluous or exaggerated consumption, "unproductive expenses that are not necessary."[70] Although he never deals adequately with the definition of *necessary,* Tracy seems to suggest that there is a "conventional necessity" in civilized societies, having to do with those things necessary to do one's job adequately.

So far, Tracy has not really differentiated between the personal consumption of idle and active capitalists, who both live to some extent on the returns of capital. The real danger is that unproductive personal consumption will surpass the tenuous limits of the necessary, and will eventually decrease the total amount of goods in circulation by destroying society's capital base, thus destroying potential prosperity.[71] Yet, if it is simply the employment of revenue that distinguishes the idle from the active capitalist, an idle capitalist who lends money to an entrepreneur would seem to be acting in a productive manner.[72]

At this point the original ambivalence in Tracy's discussion of conventional and natural value reappears. The real objection that Tracy makes to idle capitalists, to the way of life of the old nobility, and to all state *rentiers* is that they are content to live on unearned increment. The labor theory of value underlies a moral indictment of *les oisifs.* If it is labor that is our sole original wealth, to be idle is by definition to live at someone else's expense. The active capitalist includes both industrial entrepreneurs and those engaged in active farming, both rich and poor. But all these are part of the *classe laborieuse* because they add personal activity and talent to capital in order to direct labor in profitable directions. From this point of view the contribution of capital disappears; "the whole laboring class of society equally merits the name of productive."[73] The villain is idleness:

> In short, it [idleness] enervates the spirit while diminishing the mind, and it produces these sad effects not only in those who enjoy it, but also in all those who serve it, or who admire it, or who imitate it, or who envy it.[74]

Those who do not work are drones supplying neither theory, opportunity, nor execution to the labor process.

The only apparent "idleness" Tracy condones is that of those devoted to study, especially to the study of man. In a clearly self-justificatory note, Tracy adds ironically that these are the only *oisifs* that are persecuted. "There is a reason for that. They show how useless the others are, and they are not the strongest."[75] According to Tracy, one of the primary aims of "ideology" is to undermine the pretensions of landed wealth, which belong socially and politically to the dead past.

> How can these great rural landowners, who are praised so much, be persuaded that they are but moneylenders, burdensome to agriculture and alien to all its interests? How can these idle rich, who are so revered, be made to admit that they are absolutely good for nothing, and that their existence is an evil in that it diminishes the number of useful laborers?[76]

Tracy deplores the existence of the *oisifs* because their existence is a direct burden on producers, but even more because they endanger the very bases of the economic model of society by exacerbating the effects of inequality. Economic inequality, though inevitable and irreversible, is also dangerous to the extent that it creates serious imbalances in education, capacity, and influence. This process is greatly aggravated by the political predominance of the *oisifs*, who attempt to use their position to create legal privileges. Those favored by economic development even short-sightedly attempt to overturn the conditions of their own prosperity by suppressing equality of opportunity and the equality of civil rights.

> Some declaimers have maintained that *inequality* in general is useful, and that it is a benefit for which we should thank Providence. . . . [However] inequality is an evil, not because it is an injustice in itself, but because it is a powerful support for injustice whenever justice favors the weak.[77]

Since the sole aim of social policy is to increase wealth as much as possible, the tendency to establish legal class privileges and legal monopolies, a tendency that undermines the conditions of prosperity, ought to be combatted continually.

Tracy does recognize other antagonisms that arise within the class of producers. Each individual is apt to view others as obstacles to his own satisfaction. There results a kind of universal war, in which men seek to buttress their particular claims by pressuring the government to act in their favor.[78] And the short-range interests of the various contributors do differ. Employers wish to minimize the number of competitors, while maximizing the supply of workers and consumers. The employed would prefer many entrepreneurs and few laborers in order to keep the price of labor high. But Tracy believes that these apparent conflicts are often fleeting: "often under one aspect we have an interest that is opposed to one that we have under another, so that we find ourselves linked with those to whom we were opposed the moment before."[79] Moreover, as consumers, everyone shares a common long-range interest in increased production. Conflicts among producers in fact tend to cancel one another out.

Thus Tracy's analysis of production largely confirms his underlying conviction that everyone gains by social interaction. Only those who hold themselves aloof from this process are problematical. Even the critical division between idler and worker, however, is overshadowed by the triumphs of the productive process. After a five-page tribute to the benefits of cooperative labor, Tracy concludes:

> What an immense accumulation of the means of well-being! What prodigious results from the portion of our predecessors' work that was not immediately necessary to support their existence, and that was not utterly destroyed with them! Even the imagination is astounded at it.[80]

When viewed from the perspective of distribution, however, the economic picture looks strikingly different.

> This tableau is very satisfying; but it changes color greatly, when we pass from the examination of the formation of our wealth to that of its distribution among various individuals. Here we recognize everywhere the superiority of needs over means, the weakness of the individual, and his inevitable suffering.[81]

The Distribution of Value

Destutt de Tracy signals the importance of the problem of distribution in a way that was new in political economy. Say had tended to blunt the pessimism of Malthus, but Tracy was more cognizant of the significance of the "population problem," and this recognition imbues his theory with a pessimistic undercurrent. There is a greater willingness to stress the tragedy in the species point of view, an insistence on the necessary parameters of progress, and an awareness of the plight of the working class.[82]

The sobering fact about distribution is the inherent scarcity of the social product. Malthus's book on population "ought to be regarded as the latest scientific advance on this important subject."[83] Beyond merely noting the relationship between the means of existence and production, Malthus has shown that in civilized nations population tends everywhere to outstrip resources; "it is too great for the happiness of men."[84] Tracy reiterates Say's admonition that we should not confuse means of subsistence (which concern purely alimentary matters) with the means of existence (which concern the sum of profits we can make by our labor and include all the resources furnished by the arts and sciences), agreeing that Malthus used these terms ambiguously. Nevertheless, Tracy's assumption of a relatively fixed number of jobs led him to conclude that population growth would eventually depress wages, resulting in progressive immiseration.[85] Like Malthus, Tracy believed that the only hope for men was to "diminish the effects of their own fecundity."[86]

If Malthusian arithmetic assures that the numbers of the human species will always be greater than its productive capacity, the problem of distribution is further compounded by the environment of inevitable inequality in which the social product is divided. Tracy now directly confronts the inevitable sufferings of the majority of the population, which earns its living by wages alone.

Tracy's psychological explanation of property had stressed its intimate "natural" connection to the evolution of human reason, but this defense expressly set aside the question of the utility of existing property relations. His economic model of society further suggested that individual property would have to be protected by law in order to induce men to join in social *commerce,* but he there implied that inequalities in property would reflect inequalities in labor. However, in his substantive discussion of production and distribution, Tracy generally accepted the utility of established property relations as self-evident, despite the presence of great inequalities. This acceptance is obvious in his account of capital accumulation.

If some security in civil rights was a necessary precondition of prosperity, this security, nevertheless, did not prevent the growth of inequality in material resources. As society developed, inequality of wealth increased to a degree that could hardly be accounted for by differences in individual abilities. This increased inequality was due to the introduction of new ways to acquire property. Just as human conventions had everywhere recognized the special relationship between man and his goods, so it was "naturally" decreed that after death property should descend to the nearest relations of the deceased. Thus inheritance became a new means of acquisition, and what is more, or, in Tracy's view, "rather what is worse," a way of acquiring property without labor.[87] Under conditions of scarcity, inheritance laws resulted in a very skewed distribution of resources.

Although Tracy termed inheritance a "worse" way of acquiring property than labor, his ideological explanation of property is in fact largely irrelevant to the evaluation of existing property relations. He briefly suggests a "natural" connection that would explain inheritance, but his major argument is that expectations formed by the system are too strong to be changed by legislation. Any extensive attempt to reverse the expectations produced by existing property relations would result in decreasing the sum of capitals invested, and, ultimately, in stifling industrial activity to the detriment of the entire community. Tracy's final position in fact differs little from that of Say, who argued that justifications of property "make no difference whatever in the business of the production and distribution of its product or revenue."[88]

Inheritance laws, then, produce two identifiable classes: wage earners and employers of labor. Tracy argues that it is incorrect to call these propertied and nonpropertied, since everyone retains a property in his own faculties. But since workers receive remuneration according to the rarity of the skill they offer, the wage worker will always receive a lower wage than either entrepreneurs or *savants*. Population pressure tends to keep this wage at the subsistence level among the unskilled.

Thus, the distributive process seems to contradict the promise of progress held forth by man's production. "The human species, taken as a whole, is rich and powerful, and every day sees its resources and means of existence increase; but it is not the same for individuals."[89] All men suffer and die; and some more and sooner than others. It is even unclear if the majority of men are better off in civilized society.[90]

Since the *raison d'être* of human society is to increase individual pleasures, Tracy argues that the object of social organization, from the point of view of the distribution of the social product, can only be to limit inevitable suffering as much as possible. To a great extent, this involves an attempt to combat the unfortunate effects of inequality, which Tracy deplores as "the source of all our misfortunes."[91]

We have seen that pronounced inequality imperils the productive process itself, since great wealth tempts one to parasitic consumption and even to misguided attempts to undermine the legal bases of prosperity. Tracy further argues directly that discrepancies in distribution seem to doom the majority of society to a life of more pain than pleasure. However, "justice" regards every individual's pleasure as equally valuable, and always obliges us to take the number of interested beings into account.[92] Since the wage-earning class is always the largest, its interests should be preferred to those of other classes by virtue of numbers alone.

> Humanity, justice, and statecraft alike require that of all interests, those of the poor should be always the most constantly considered and respected; and by the poor I mean simple wage-earners, and above all those whose work is the worst paid.[93]

The word *interest,* then, has a totally different degree of energy when used in relation to the poor; it often means not just more or less enjoyment, but the possibility of life or death. Interests of this kind can hardly be weighed against simple conveniences. Finally, Tracy restates the familiar argument that a sovereign's power and wealth is increased by the power and wealth of his subjects in terms of the need of the rich and powerful to succor the poor and weak.

> I believe the whole world will agree that when a considerable portion of society suffers too much, and consequently is too brutalized, neither repose, security, nor liberty is possible, even for the rich and powerful, and that on the contrary, these preeminent citizens of a state are more truly great and happy when they are at the head of a people enjoying a decent comfort that develops in it all the faculties, moral and intellectual.[94]

Although Tracy seems determined not to shrink from the unfortunate "facts" about distribution, his solutions do not go beyond those proposed by earlier economic thinkers. He struggles to show that the real interests of the poor do not contradict the general interests of society, repeating his assertions of a general interest in production and consumption, and adding a plea for wage incentives and stable prices. Furthermore, he rejects any violent or "forced" remedy for the effects of inequality. Instead, he recommends education of the classes in their true interests, complete liberty of trade, and freedom to emigrate.[95] The only governmental measures he specifically endorses are prohibitions on wage- or price-fixing, some restrictions on inheritance, and taxes on luxury items. Again, the main task is one of persuasion.

> How can all those who pay for labor be made to admit that the high price of manpower is a desirable thing, and that in general all the true interests of the poor are exactly the same as the true interests of the whole society?[96]

Even Tracy's advocacy of a free market lacks complete assurance, however. He notes that the employer often has the opportunity to fix wages and prices and is in fact likely to abuse this power. And though it is absolutely necessary to leave the worker freedom to emigrate, emigration is never an adequate solution. For it to occur in numbers considerable enough to relieve population pressure, the domestic situation would have to be intolerable. In that case, we should be concerned more with the frightful suffering of the poor than with the decrease in their numbers. Men are not abstract and insensitive beings who can be transported like cargo.[97] In his discussion of distribution, then, Tracy seems determined to "bring us back from romance to history."[98]

Government and the Economy

Although Tracy concludes from his analysis of distribution that social policy must always favor the interests of the poor as much as possible, his belief that the market is the best adjustor and conciliator of interests greatly reduces the "possible." His scrutiny of the effects of governmental revenues and expenses confirms and deepens this disparagement of governmental intervention. Government performs essential functions, but political economy considers only its effects on public wealth and national prosperity. Tracy follows Smith and Say in arguing that the major portion of governmental consumption is sterile and unproductive.[99]

Throughout his discussion of government in the *Traité sur la volonté*, Tracy looks at government from this restricted point of view, ignoring his own earlier equation of productivity with usefulness. The merchant is judged to be productive because he facilitates exchange. The intellectual is productive because he increases knowledge and thus makes it easier to exploit the laws of nature. But the costs of defense and administration are said to be "doubtless very useful, and even necessary on the whole, if one means by that that the whole economy is desirable; but none of all that is productive."[100] Tracy consequently advises the utmost frugality in government spending and in fiscal matters generally. He joins Say in decrying the public debt and in deploring governmental issue of paper currency, which he assumes to be the cause of ruinous inflation.[101] The *rentiers* created by state borrowing are particularly dangerous, in Tracy's view, because they are indifferent to the fortunes of the industrious classes and have a strong vested interest in the continuance of the borrowing government, whatever its policies; at the same time, they desire to see the state in continuous financial difficulties. Thus, the very position of the state *rentier* is likely to render him a bad citizen.[102]

The only substantive policy issue that Tracy treats in any detail is taxation.[103] His position here is consistent with his general view of the restricted role of government. Taxation is a *prima facie* evil, a sacrifice of individual pleasure and well-being to be weighed against the good resulting from the government's disposition of tax revenues. What is interesting in this discussion, however, is Tracy's position on the problem of linking theory to practice.

The best system of taxation, he argues, imposes moderate sacrifices in an equitable manner, through a variety of taxes that disturb existing expectations (which have entered into the calculation of current prices) as little as possible. The only guiding principle Tracy offers is that government should try not to distrub "productive consumption." The least harmful taxes are those that bear principally on the idle capitalist. If taxes reach the industrial capital of the entrepreneur, society as a whole eventually suffers. When taxes fall primarily on the workers, immediate suffering ensues; thus, these taxes cause the most evil. Unfortunately, regressive sales taxes on necessities are very popular with governments, because they bring in great amounts of revenue, are simple to administer, and can generally be imposed without provoking complaint. Consequently, such taxes will always be judged necessary to supplement other methods of taxation.[104]

Tracy's discussion of taxation is characteristic of his unwillingness to use the conclusions of rational analysis as an unequivocal basis for social action. He shrinks from cutting a bold theoretical swath through the complex field of men's interests, because of the impossibility of calculating all the relevant data.

> I know that these separate, differentiated and modified results will appear less satisfying than a clear-cut conclusion, which, by treating the series of men's interests like a run of billiard balls, would assert that no matter which of them was hit, only the last would be put into play. But I have felt compelled to represent things as I see them rather than as they might be imagined.[105]

He makes a similar argument about monetary reform. Although it would be simpler and more rational to indicate the worth of metal coin by weight, rather than by arbitrary names like *livre* and *sou*, "once these arbitrary denominations have been admitted, and used in all the obligations contracted, one must guard against changing anything."[106] And even while he tries to divide foreign trade into rational categories, he insists on the drawbacks and deficiencies attending such a classification: "real beings yield only with difficulty to these general and abstract ways of considering them."[107]

The problem of taxation finds him at his most practical and least abstract. Reluctant to recommend sweeping reforms, he recognizes the inherent utility of custom.

> In matters that are a little complicated, practice is provisionally tolerably reasonable long before theory becomes so, and when the subject has been truly examined thoroughly, it will be recognized that the good sense of the public, I might almost say the general instinct, has strayed less from the correct path than have the earliest scientific speculations.[108]

Practice or custom is at least close to the raw data of human experience. In speculative combinations of these data, according to Tracy, there is always the danger that an initial false assumption or definition will lead to grave errors. Thus, even blind attachment to customary practice and extreme resistance to novelty, though often exaggerated, are not intrinsically unreasonable.

"Ideological" Economics

The work of J.B. Say and Destutt de Tracy significantly shifted the focus of social science in France away from the "Machiavellian" world of power or the subtleties of moral philosophy toward the solid realm of scientific economic laws. Or so they would have described their own intentions. Aghast at the results of the exercise of will in revolutionary politics, they were strongly attracted to the certitude promised by natural economic laws, to that view of social relations that found social benefit in individual freedoms.

Such a view had informed the program of eighteenth-century economic thinkers like Turgot, who sought improvement to the state and working orders at the expense of aristocratic privilege and certain monopolists. The theory of Say and Tracy reflected a marriage of this earlier program with their reactions to the French Revolution. New in their work was a thoroughly functional view of the state, and a sharper articulation of the bases of and threats to social peace. The role of force in social life was the most compelling issue of their time; they wished to tame and rationalize state power, to insist on its place in supporting and structuring a certain conception of social relations. The *nobilité* was now largely excluded from this conception—a nation of producers united by their *industrie*. Thus their work helped to solidify that belief in civil equality that was the most lasting passion of the Revolution.

In this distinct alignment of social forces, capitalists were certainly cast in a favored role. Indeed, the work of Say and Tracy has been intimately linked with the defense of manufacturing interests and strict laissez-faire economics in both Europe and America. But what is at least as significant is the extent to which their work depends on the past rather than heralds the future. They relied heavily on an earlier notion of implicit social harmony, and continued to address those disruptive issues that had vexed earlier *philosophes:* the relationship between *pauvreté* and *luxe,* and the crucial distinction between respectable poverty and miserable dependence. Like many eighteenth-century economic thinkers, they rejected the utility of poverty as well as of luxury and insisted that the dependent status of the poor inhibited both *sociabilité* and economic growth. Moreover, they sought to end slow growth and excessive misery through the traditional remedies of better administration, price stability, and the legal protection of the poor from victimization.[109]

This vision of economic life was already becoming somewhat difficult to maintain, as can be seen from Tracy's troubled attempts to deal with distribution. At times he portrayed nature not as a *mère,* but as a *marâtre* (harsh step-mother) who condemned mankind to suffer.[110] But, paradoxically, the conviction of a solidarity of interests in society became more necessary to French moderates like Say and Tracy in the wake of their revolutionary past. Thus they turn decisively toward that current of thinking about society that celebrated the utility of *commerce* in its largest sense.

In concentrating on the conditions necessary for the production of the greatest amount of pleasure in society, Say and Tracy apparently neglected the perspective of the individual's right to happiness, i.e., that perspective which had been expressed so powerfully in the theory of the inalienable rights of man. Yet Tracy's "ideological" preface to political economy shows that the individual perspective was neglected precisely because it was assumed that individual gains in satisfaction would take place "naturally" in a rational society purged of corporate interests. Tracy's definitions of property, riches, and value presupposed the possibility of such a society, and contained an implicit statement of the moral claims of individuals, claims now clothed in the peremptory language not of "right" but of "science." Individual happiness required the (intrinsically pleasurable) development of all human faculties, and required the possession of material goods.

Tracy could seemingly tolerate the discrepancies between his "ideological" definitions and reality as long as he viewed society as temporarily perverted by the *oisifs.* The labor theory of value, which he could not reconcile with his theory of conventional value or with his defense of existing property, was, nevertheless, "vindicated" by its apparent support of his attack on idle capitalists. Moreover, this attack on a class of idlers who *deliberately* kept people in ignorance allowed him to avoid facing the contradiction between an ideal model of social *commerce* in which everyone would gain, and his own perception that radical defects in the human mind precluded the ideal. His arguments that these defects necessarily caused individual interests to conflict, and that they complicated the task of administration so much that one hesitated to challenge existing practices for fear of causing more harm than good, remain minor discordant notes in his celebration of the benefits of social cooperation. When a challenge was made to the view that the only significant division in society was between the *oisifs* and the *industrieux,* however, the inconsistencies in Tracy's position would be impossible for successors to tolerate.[111]

CHAPTER FOUR
"Ideological" Politics

T RACY'S economic "logic of the will" represented a synthesis of earlier assumptions about the nature of man as an exchanging animal with his reactions to the social and political tensions of the revolutionary years. The first set of assumptions disposed him to argue, on the basis of the fundamental principles of human nature, for the possibility of a rationalized society of self-interested individuals; the second set of reactions suggested a defense of laissez-faire on the grounds that it was the best arrangement given men's circumstances. These points of view are separable, and there was indeed some tension between them. Nevertheless, they were fused in Tracy's mind, especially insofar as the nobility was perceived as an irritant from both perspectives.

An analogous pattern of argument emerges in his political theory as well. This chapter will consider the arguments advanced by Destutt de Tracy and by Pierre Daunou in favor of liberal representative government. Tracy's *Commentaire sur l'Esprit des lois de Montesquieu*, along with Daunou's *Essai sur les garanties individuelles que réclame l'état actuel de la société*, which offered a similar analysis of the modern state, at once kept alive the Revolution's hopes for a qualitatively new polity, and offered a defense of representative institutions as the best possible form of government given men's circumstances and the limitations on their knowledge. In the works of Tracy and Daunou, the belief in a future level of civilization that would correspond to "right reason" is evident, but their attempts to demonstrate the correctness of this belief on the basis of a psychological science of man recede steadily into the background. Daunou concedes the relevance of human nature to social science, but deliberately neglects the task of analyzing man's organization and needs, preferring to illustrate man's nature through historical example.[1] And Tracy's use of "ideology" to clarify political concepts is problematical and inconclusive. The main arguments that Tracy and Daunou in fact advance in favor of civil and political liberties assert that liberties are both historically inevitable and functionally necessary in modern societies, and that these liberties are desirable because of their consequences.

In making these largely consequentialist arguments for liberalism, Tracy and Daunou joined other postrevolutionary liberals who attempted to find in the machinery of the constitutional state a framework of coexistence for a nation still deeply divided on social and political ends. Indeed, constitutional principles took on a new significance in their thought. Although they shared with Condorcet the overwhelming desire to make politics the handmaiden of science, the experience of continual revolutionary dictatorships left them more suspicious of power. And both their epistemological doubts and their perceptions of a lamentable indifference to "enlightenment" made them more uncertain about the persuasive power of reason. The result was not an abandonment of politics but rather an increased attachment to the notion of inviolable constitutional procedure, i.e. to a "middle ground" between will and reason.

The Sociology of Power

Legitimacy

Hume's essay "Of the Original Contract" had clearly set forth the historical arguments against the idea of the contract origin of society and government. Few of the *philosophes* or theorists of the French Revolution had any quarrel with this refutation or with the insistence that man was naturally a social animal. Hume, however, was at the same time disputing the utility of insisting that legitimate governments have no other basis than popular consent. To insist on the contract analogy, on the "philosophical origin,"[2] of government, was both wrong and dangerous. Condorcet, Sieyès, and the English apologists for the French Revolution had made precisely the opposite ideological judgment. They universally described the bases of society and government as contractual in an effort to legitimize the new order. Tracy and Daunou, however, were no longer concerned with defending a living revolution. On the contrary, they were trying to salvage liberal principles under conditions they considered to be socially and politically regressive, without calling for renewed violence. Thus, they were led to develop Humean arguments against radical political rhetoric. But they combined these arguments with a social messianism that was utterly foreign to Hume.

In his pamphlet in support of Brumaire (an event that could hardly be seen as a resumption by the people of their constituent power) Cabanis had succinctly repeated the case against arguing from the premise of a "state of nature." He argued that this pretended state was not even a particularly useful fiction: the farther one traveled from human nature as it currently existed, the less light one shed on ways of perfecting nature and increasing happiness. The only truth contained in this "confused" mode of argument was that one must first study the passions and interests of individuals before understanding the relations born of those passions and interests.[3]

Tracy and Daunou continue this theme that only the function, not the origin, of society and authority should be at issue in political discussion. Tracy, for example, cites anthropological evidence that human beings have been found only in groups or tribes, in order to conclude that "it is the social which is our natural state, and the only one with which we should be concerned."[4] To explain the growth of society in terms of a sacrifice of natural liberty gives a wholly false idea of the process, since there was never a real perception of liberty outside of society. The very idea of liberty is social, since it develops with language itself.[5] And social conventions have always included some form of political authority, which protects the society against outside aggression and settles internal disputes: "some kind of government is unquestionably necessary to every political society because its members must be judged, administered, protected, defended, guaranteed from all violence."[6]

Daunou's *Essai sur les garanties* also abruptly dismisses questions about the origins of authority. Abandoning the arguments of his revolutionary pamphlets, Daunou self-consciously shuns "abstract questions" such as the origin of sovereignty, the hypothesis of a social compact, or the anterior or natural rights that these concepts presuppose.[7] He now states that every political system projects certain "myths" about the basis of its power. With increasingly rapid communication among countries, however, these political rationales begin to lose their mysterious hold over men. The disregard of those in power for political articles of faith further undermines the credibility of these myths. Finally, Daunou argues, people obey a government not because of its alleged origins, but because of its present actions.[8]

In their discussions of the history of civil society, Tracy and Daunou deliberately slight the significance of origins. Daunou explicitly adopts Adam Smith's theory of an historical progression from hunting to manufacturing. On Daunou's account, each stage would have established leaders and laws, probably in that order, since the initial impulse would have been to accept one man's will as law. But since the historical record tells us very little about the early development of society, all such generalizations are risky and largely irrelevant.[9] Tracy's view of the growth of society from tribal organization to sophisticated commercial economy is also in the tradition of Smith, Turgot, and Condorcet. Like Condorcet, he considers social progress to be inherent in the application of men's faculties to the physical and social environments. Tracy's categorization of historical periods, however, is more provocative, and his discussion of politics more deliberately contextualist.

He recognizes three important stages in history, defined by the type of government, system of culture, and theory of punishment.[10] The first "degree of civilization" can still be seen in contemporary "savage societies." Depending on the character of the people, the governments of these societies are either direct democracies or simple monarchies. Tracy thinks the character of a primitive people is probably very much affected by climate and geography.[11] Primitive societies are formless; their culture is based on ignorance, animistic religion, and frequent violence. The principle behind their codes of law is satisfaction of the urge for vengeance.

The second degree of civilization emerges gradually, as distinctions of strength, riches, talent, and power develop. Those who possess such advantages use them to acquire more goods and to establish social and political dominance. They form into groups and are attracted to religious and civil ideas that support their power. The emerging elite puts pressure on the political system, and finally succeeds either in subverting primitive democracy, or in forcing a despotic chief to share his power. Thus the government changes to a form of aristocracy, under one or many leaders.

Tracy's account of the change from the first to the second stage of civilization is perhaps purposely vague. Both during the Old Regime and during the Bourbon Restoration, the nobility supported its political claims with historical arguments. A consistent opponent of the *thèse nobiliaire*, Tracy wished to deny prestige to the origin of aristocracy. By arguing that the past can never be truly known, he again suggests that it should not be evoked to justify the present.[12]

The culture of the aristocratic period is predominantly religious. Eventually the clerical class dominates the formation of all social opinion and attempts to make theology into a systematic science. In Tracy's view, however, this theology is the inverse of science, i.e., it is *metaphysics*. Religious ideas, which are temporary and illusory hypotheses about the functioning of the world, are transformed into real objects. In Christian societies, "absurd" religious doctrines are especially deep-rooted because of the fusion of theology with Greek logic.[13] Whereas primitive peoples have a system of punishment based on human vengeance, the second level of civilization develops the more sophisticated notion of divine retribution. However, the "barbaric" idea of vengeance is retained; it is merely transposed in part onto an angry God.

Tracy thought that most peoples had achieved only this second degree of civilization; some were in a transitional state leading to a higher level, but nowhere had the third degree of civilization been completely realized. This higher degree of civilization would be manifested in representative government, a positive philosophy based on reason, and a utilitarian theory of punishment.

Insofar as Tracy ascribes any necessity to the direction of history, he sees it in the gradual development of the potentialities of the human mind.[14] Yet, he suggests that intellectual, economic, moral, and political progress are interrelated in complex ways. Although intellectual progress accelerates the change in morals and politics, economic or geographic causes have precipitated certain advances in knowledge. Indeed, commerce is an especially powerful spur to the acquisition of knowledge, and becomes more influential as society becomes more complex.

> Commerce, exchange, being society itself, is the unique link among men, the source of all their moral sentiments, and the first and most powerful cause

of the development of their mutual sensibility and reciprocal benevolence.
. . . it begins by reconciling all the men of the same tribe, then it links
societies together, and it ends up by uniting the whole world.[15]

Commercial society breeds the qualities of industriousness, prudence, and
moderation, which, in turn, dispose men to become more aware of their
true interests as producers and citizens.[16]

Destutt de Tracy's tripartite view of the evolution of society undoubtedly influenced the conceptions of Saint-Simon and Auguste Comte.[17]
Although Tracy was relatively unconcerned with the historical process as
such, he emphasized the "necessity" of the first two degrees of civilization
in a way that tempered his own pervasive hostility to the past. There is
in his work more than an echo of Condorcet, for whom religion was
primarily a manifestation of human error and superstition compounded by clerical duplicity and cunning. More distinctly than his predecessors, however, Tracy suggests that theological thinking is a necessary step in the development of human reason.

> In reality, the tendency to make suppositions and to formulate hypotheses
> must have been born before the spirit of observation and the aptitude for
> experimentation; the spirit of credulity and of enthusiasm necessarily pre-
> ceded that of doubt and restraint and the knowledge necessary for well-
> grounded opinions.[18]

Tracy does not examine the relation of "truth" to error, except to speculate that true statements can be developed and clarified only in relation
to false; but he plainly anticipates what was to become the positivist view
of the historical function of both political and religious ideology.[19]

It is clear, then, that both Tracy and Daunou wished to separate questions of legitimacy from questions of origin. But they go further; they
also attempt to argue, at least initially, that legitimacy is distinct from
consent. One ought to judge the worth of a political system only in
terms of how well it promotes the happiness of its members.

> But, all things considered, this organization is made only to lead to good
> results; it is preferable to anarchy only . . . because of the evil it avoids and
> the goods it procures; its degree of perfection should be judged only by the
> effects it produces.[20]

Tracy insists that social science cannot establish the precise degree to
which one social organization is preferable to another; nevertheless,

analysis can indicate the parameters of absolute perfection and total fail-ure.[21]

He observes that men have lived under an "almost infinite host of social organizations," among which hardly one resembles another in all respects."[22] He rejects Montesquieu's division of these organizations into republican, monarchical, and despotic on the grounds that these distinc-tions are vague and do not permit a definitive classification of any con-temporary government.[23] Furthermore, these categories are not even ad-equate to Montesquieu's own discussion, which seems to Tracy to be based on a different and more logical formulation: 1) direct democracy; 2) aristocracy with many leaders; 3) aristocracy with one leader; and 4) pure monarchy.[24] Tracy also argues that Montesquieu's "moving princi-ples"—virtue, honor, and fear—are really not principles of action, but rather conservative sentiments. In keeping with his definition of law, Tracy argues that the active principle in a state is always found in the body of governing officials, those who can command the use of force.[25]

Although Tracy rejects Montesquieu's classification, neither does he accept the "peremptory" decision of Helvétius, i.e., that there are only two kinds of government—good and bad.[26] Any government has both good and bad effects. If one ignores practical operation and looks only at the theory of a government, it is necessary to discuss first principles, and to decide which are true and which false. But this evaluation of principles is exactly what Tracy claims he wishes to avoid in his prelimi-nary factual classification.

> I would like, as did Montesquieu, only to say what is, to show the various
> consequences of the different social organizations, and to let the reader draw
> his own conclusions in favor of one or another.[27]

Just as he sought the essential descriptive elements of "law" and of "right," so Tracy tries to fathom the "essence of the [political] organiza-tion."[28] To this end, he divides all governments into two basic catego-ries: "national" and "special" (or "public" and "private"). National gov-ernments, no matter what their particular form, openly profess that their power and their rights emanate from, and exist for, the entire people. All public functionaries are considered to be servants of the nation. Insofar as the national principle of these governments remains intact ("is not called into question"), they can always be modified, or even abrogated, by the nation, i.e., by the general will as expressed through accepted procedures.[29]

Special governments, on the other hand, recognize legitimate sources of rights and powers other than the general will: divine authority, conquest, birth, or express or tacit social pacts in which each party stipulates conditions. Special governments also may appear in various forms: as democracies, aristocracies, or monarchies. These differ from national governments, however, in that "there are, so to speak, different powers in the same society."[30] The organization of special governments actually depends on a series of conventions among groups recognized to have independent rights; it can be changed only by the free consent of the contracting parties. Thus Tracy uses the language of contract—now associated with instability—to describe special, rather than national, governments.

His classificatory device, of course, is far from neutral. The admitted purpose is to discover the kind of social organization most likely to lead to general happiness. But the answer is implicit in Tracy's categories. Special governments are plainly less "satisfactory" than national ones. The more interesting aspect of his distinction is his effort to deal with the problematical notion of the *volonté générale*. He does not want to argue that the general will (the will of the majority expressed through democratic institutions) is the only legitimate source of power.

> I repeat that I do not claim to decide, or even to be discussing . . . whether one can legitimately oppose them [particular sources of rights] to the clearly pronounced general will. These questions are always resolved by force, and besides, they have nothing to do with my present concern.[31]

Indeed, in describing actual governments, he sometimes uses *volonté générale* to mean tacit consent to whatever authority is in power. "The existing legislative organ (whatever it is) . . . is always to be deemed the organ of the existing general will."[32]

Nevertheless, Tracy does not completely abandon the participatory connotations of the *volonté générale* by dissolving it into the factual question of obedience or disobedience. He was convinced that the people as a whole—even if they could not be expected to act completely rationally at present—were a safer *point d'appui* for the general interest than any conglomeration of partial interests, or any royal house. Tracy, then, attempts to reintroduce some conception of political participation into his distinction between national and special governments: national governments 1) acknowledge no other mandate than the general will, and 2) contain some mechanism of representation.

First, Tracy describes national governments as those that both openly admit the general interest to be the sole purpose of their rule and openly claim that they rule by virtue of the general will rather than by private right. This is not to claim that national governments exist only at the pleasure of the majority. Rather, in national governments the governors *assent* to the proposition that they rule by virtue of the general will; they *"profess to think* that all rights and all powers belong to the body of the nation," and *"declare* that they derive their rights only from the general will."[33] Thus Tracy suggests that those governments that do not claim any basis other than the popular will are in fact more likely to serve the general interest.

This use of *volonté générale* as a justification for the power of national governments, however, would not exclude the phenomenon of modern caesarism. A government might clothe itself in the mantle of the general will, while pursuing a narrowly partisan policy, stifling public opinion, and arrogating effective power into its own hands. Tracy considered this to be the case under the ultimately "special" and "private" regime of Napoleon. Therefore, he includes in his notion of national government a second element: some mechanism (as yet vaguely defined) of popular participation. Not only do national governments admit the *volonté générale* to be the source of their rule, but they can be modified or even nullified without violence by the "nation."

In discussing the degree to which actual governments fulfill their utilitarian function, Tracy uses both his distinction between national and special, and the categories he found to be implicit in Montesquieu's *Esprit des lois* (direct democracy, aristocracy under many leaders, aristocracy under one leader, and pure monarchy). It becomes obvious in the course of his analysis that governments in these categories—whether national or special—are historically bound phenomena, destined to disappear as the third stage of civilization establishes itself more securely, making possible an appropriately modern form of national government.

Tracy argues that pure (direct) democracy and pure monarchy are functionally suited only to primitive tribes. These forms in fact belong to the "childhood of society."[34] The remaining historical forms of rule—characteristic of the "second degree of civilization"—have all been aristocracies of one sort or another. Although these have included national governments, Tracy rejects Montesquieu's argument that tempered monarchy (or aristocracy under one leader) is an essentially modern regime of moderation and balance. The pride and honor of nobility have usually engendered scorn for the people and an open rejection of the national principle. Tracy agrees with Montesquieu that "honor" is a passion particularly associated with European aristocratic monarchies; however, he views it either as a hypocritical mask for corporate interests, or as but another name for the corrupt vanity of *les oisifs:* "a false honor that seeks all that glitters, and plumes itself on the vicious, and even on the ridiculous, when they are fashionable."[35] Tracy obviously viewed the *Esprit des lois* as a dangerous source of political arguments for a renascent nobility.

According to Tracy, then, even national aristocracies are likely to exploit and oppress. Special aristocracies—historically the more frequent variety—are even less likely to promote the public good. Special governments are based on conventions among groups recognized to have independent rights. Since it is unrealistic to assume that these groups were originally equal, special governments legitimize inequalities in power, providing but a fragile basis for unity. Warring private interests constantly threaten to erupt and disturb the peace, and the public interest is even more easily sacrificed to class "honor."

Tracy's criticisms of hereditary monarchy are especially pointed. He argued that hereditary power was by its very nature illimitable and expansionist. Such power coexisted uneasily with that of aristocratic chiefs and other corporate bodies; it was to some degree checked by rival centers of power, but it also exploited these social divisions to expand its claims. The victim, in Tracy's view, was the nation. In a representative system, hereditary power must eventually come into conflict with the general will. Tracy goes so far as to say that the monarchical principle and the principle of national government may be mutually exclusive.[36]

Tracy concludes that the only national government intrinsically favorable to the interests of modern men is "pure representative government." This governmental type can be considered a new invention, unknown in Montesquieu's time. Tracy argues that the modern concept of representation requires a grasp of the full implications of the art of printing, which facilitates communication between citizens and their delegates and minimizes sudden disorders excited by demagogues in assemblies.[37] Moreover, unlike direct democracy, a representative democracy need not be limited by territorial considerations. Since it lacks the expensive affectations of a court, it is less costly for small states; since a representative legislature will enhance the moral and persuasive power of the executive, it is also more suitable for large states.[38]

Thus Tracy's canvassing of governmental types leads to the conclusion that an "enlightened republic" is the logical consequence of a utilitarian standard. Beneath this judgment lay an obvious commitment to his own version of the republican ideal, an ideal that was the indelible mark of the Revolution.

From the rising of August 10, 1792, to the triumph of Napoleon, *la république* had symbolized revolutionary hopes. This powerful new vision—evoking shifting images of democracy, social justice, patriotism, national independence, heroic self-sacrifice, and the end of historical irrationality and violence—was to become the leitmotiv of political protest in the nineteenth century. French moderates had rejected Robespierre's version of republicanism, but most had not lost faith in a "true" republic, purified of Jacobin excrescences. Indeed, during the Directory years, the republican/royalist dilemma had a significance far surpassing the question of governmental form. The Republic was associated with a whole series of vague and imprecise hopes for social salvation through the stabilization of the Revolution.[39]

The difficulty was to separate the Republic from its association with the Terror. As early as Thermidor, moderates began to counter charges that the Revolution was all of a piece, i.e., that its excesses were implicit in its beginnings. Most often this campaign took the form of an attack on the cult of antiquity, an attempted debunking of the models of Sparta and Rome.[40] A minority of French liberal opinion had in fact always insisted that the moderns had triumphed over the ancients on all fronts, including politics. Condorcet, for example, denied the Greeks and Romans any true knowledge of liberty, equality, or rights.[41] And some conservatives had argued that republicanism would bring on the ancient evils of disorder and despotism, because the French were a large corrupt nation.[42] After the experience of the Terror, a common ground was found in these critiques of the ancient city. The ideal of ancient republicanism was portrayed as both inherently flawed and particularly menacing.

Tracy's analysis of direct democracy as anachronistic was part of this general effort to divorce republicanism from the notions of direct assembly rule and heroic virtue. On the basis of his theory of motivation, he denies the possibility of any virtue involving renunciation of the self. The alleged rectitude of republics has generally amounted to little more than the primitive sense of tribal independence.[43] And although savage people show extraordinary devotion and courage, these qualities are inextricably linked to brutality. In modern societies, he argues, social relations are much more polished, complicated, and delicate.[44] Any attempt to revive simple forms of rule in such a context is doomed to provoke social instability and chaos; reimposition of order will then require naked force. Moreover, this repression may take on a new savagery. The revival of atavistic forms stimulates primitive passions and customs. Hence, the Committee of Public Safety's "law," according to Tracy, was based on the lust for vengeance. Because the French were no longer uncivilized, however, such an experiment was necessarily transient.[45]

This notion of the danger in forcing outmoded forms of rule on modern societies also serves Tracy as an explanation of Bonapartism. Moderates had always believed that the Jacobin regime and the rule of Bonaparte were somehow linked; they were usually classed together as "despotisms." Tracy's pairing of pure democracy and pure monarchy enables him to offer a different explanation. According to Tracy, despotism is not a separate category of government, but rather describes any situation where power is abused.[46] Both the Jacobins and Bonaparte were despotic because both abused power, but this abuse was not caused only by the universal tendency of power to corrupt. Rather, the reliance on violence was *intrinsic* to the operation of these regimes because they attempted to impose simple forms of rule on complex societies.

Tracy's depiction of Bonapartism as "pure monarchy" is a further indictment of monarchical government. Insofar as a monarch is not responsible to the nation—and Tracy believed irresponsibility to be the irresistible tendency of kingly prerogative—he would be seduced by a conception of absolute power that was antithetical to the needs of modern society. This situation would be highly unstable and would lead to continual coups and senseless oscillation between inappropriate regimes: transient popular tyrannies and attempted revivals of aristocracy.[47]

The concept of a "republic," then, was not inherently subversive of order as many counterrevolutionaries claimed. On the contrary, it was the only form of government capable of providing peace. Tracy asserts that the term has often been used imprecisely and carelessly;

> *republic* is a very vague term that is used to refer to a multitude of governments prodigiously different from one another, from the turbulent democracy of Athens, to the repressive aristocracy of Berne and the dismal oligarchy of Venice.[48]

Moreover, the word was sullied by the actions of the First French Republic. Nevertheless, Tracy did not wish to surrender the association between national governments and republics. Indeed, his retention of the term *republic* was a significant action that would place the *Commentaire* outside the mainstream of political argument under the Restoration and would help to keep alive the association of republicanism with wholesale political regeneration.

In his historical lectures, Daunou adopts and helps to popularize Tracy's distinction between national and special governments and also encourages the notion that the term *republic,* because it refers to the "public thing," is especially suited to national governments.[49] Daunou prefers Tracy's classification because it does not depend on ideas of "primitive sovereignty," but rather on the important distinction between the social body and the political system.[50] Only on the basis of this distinction, he argues, can one divide governments into two general classes: 1) those that have for their end the best possible condition of persons and things, and 2) those that act only in the interests of the governing bodies composing the political system. Daunou notes that special governments have been historically more frequent, and earlier in time, than national governments, and he stresses the element that also underlies Tracy's theory: national governments require some popular participation. He concludes that, in practice, only some form of representative government "announces, develops, and guarantees the progress of large societies."[51] Whatever its specific form (which depends on historical conditions), the representative system encourages prudence, morality, and civilized sentiments; renders the common people honest and hard-working; and preserves and directs those with great energies. Abandoning Tracy's feigned neutrality, Daunou sometimes calls special governments with no representative element usurped and illegitimate.[52]

Revolution

Because they were repelled by revolutionary violence and repression, Tracy and Daunou attempted to disown the language of its legitimation. Yet in light of their desire to vindicate certain revolutionary achievements, this new caution posed a certain theoretical problem about the proper justification of resistance. They had favored the utilitarian aspects of revolutionary ideology partly in order to deny that a violation of supposed "natural" rights was an adequate reason for continued revolutionary upheaval. But could not a people rebel to replace an inefficient government with a more useful one, to hasten the transition from the second to the third "degree of civilization"?

In confronting the question of resistance, Tracy and Daunou employed two themes developed more fully by other Restoration liberals faced with an implacable conservative coalition that repudiated the Revolution completely. They adopt a pragmatic approach to present and future resistance, while formulating a rudimentary historical explanation of the French Revolution that views it as inevitable.

The most simple explanation offered for the phenomenon of revolution is that a people that finds its lot intolerable will rebel. The success or failure of the rebellion depends on the balance of forces involved and the support for the revolutionaries within the nation. Tracy offers no specific advice on the point at which one is justified in rebelling against authority. The issue is always one of weighing the consequences of resistance versus obedience in specific circumstances.[53] His instincts, however, are deeply cautious. "Let time do its work, let us not rush to realize these dreams, and let us rush even less to fight and destroy the hopes of men of means."[54] Daunou argues that under a despotic regime it is usually best to avoid useless resistance that will intensify oppression.[55] Patience is even more reasonable under an imperfect regime offering peaceful opportunities for improvement. A just lament for the failings of a regime does not excuse disobedience of its laws. Daunou publicly counsels steadfast opposition (but not active resistance) to a government's violations of its own constitution.[56]

For Tracy and Daunou neither the situation under Napoleon, nor that under the restored Bourbons, justified a violent revolution, since the opportunities for success would be quite small. In the original American version of the *Commentaire,* Tracy had made very strong statements about the evils of hereditary monarchy; in later French editions, however, he added the following note:

> Despite its imperfections, constitutional monarchy, or representative government with a single hereditary leader, is and will remain for an extremely long time the best possible government for all the peoples of Europe, and especially for France. . . . I firmly believe that I do nothing but establish the very important difference, unfailingly recognized by all wise men, between the abstractions of theory and the realities of practice.[57]

Tracy's clarification was undoubtedly intended partly to ensure that his work would be published in France. It is significant that he failed to change the text, or to omit a sentence such as "To hope for liberty and monarchy is to hope for two mutually exclusive things."[58] In a letter to Jefferson in 1821, however, Tracy observed that the opinion expressed in the new footnote was a sincere, if sad, commentary on the real conditions in Europe.[59]

While attempting to establish a certain distance from questions of present resistance, Tracy and Daunou constantly introduce the theme of the historical inevitability of the 1789 Revolution.[60] We have seen that they had little real appreciation of the historicist point of view. Daunou was a medieval historian who could never disguise his distaste for the Middle Ages, and who saw no inherited liberty in traditional customs and privileges. But the model of historical development upon which they insist in order to justify the inevitability of representative government throws into relief the idea of a necessary correlation between society and politics. Their heightened interest in economic laws as the major organizing force in modern society also suggested that the political system had to undergo a significant alteration.[61]

Tracy argues that economic development is the measure of a society's greatness. Despite commercial and political reverses, for example, the Dutch always remained formidable because of their economic base.[62] The Canadians were making less progress than the Americans because a much greater portion of the Canadian population were gentlemen attempting to "live nobly."[63] In the case of the French, the Revolution assured France's emergence as a world power precisely because it favored the productive sectors of society.

Before the Revolution, according to Tracy, the French were not as wretched as they portrayed themselves. Nor was the *Ancien Régime* a despotism, but rather a tempered monarchy. However, the French—a potentially rich and powerful people—found themselves not only stagnating, but incapable of supporting the expenses of their own government, and in a weak position with regard to other European powers.

The Revolution brought civil and foreign war, loss of colonial possessions, devastation of the countryside and great loss of life. Yet during that period the French also supported enormous taxes and a huge army. On Tracy's account, the reason for this release of energy—and the lasting significance of the Revolution—was the liberation of the productive part of society from its legal subservience to a class of largely unproductive idlers. During the Old Regime, the greatest part of useful work went towards supporting the Court and upper classes. With the Revolution and the abolition of feudalism, almost all these revenues were divided between the new government and the industrious class (*classe laborieuse*). A much greater percentage of the population was engaged in useful labor. Tracy also attributes the profound changes in French society to a multitude of "moral" causes; these moral factors, however, were merely the immediate causes of the Revolution. It was the better employment of labor that ensured their success.

> I concede that the passion for domestic liberty and national independence, and the indignation against unjust oppression and an even more unjust aggression, were sufficient in themselves to produce great upheavals in France, but I insist that only because these great upheavals produced a better utilization of all resources were they able to furnish these passions with so many means of success, this despite the errors and the horrors to which their violence led.[64]

> I know that moral causes have more power than economic calculations; but I say that these moral causes so prodigiously increase all resources only because they direct all efforts towards concrete objectives.[65]

Daunou explains the French Revolution in part as a specific example of the general trend of increasing tension between the "people" and their

rulers, and he attributes this interior struggle to the fact that governments become solidly entrenched in a society and change more slowly
and with more difficulty than the social and economic systems. This helps
to explain the necessity of revolution, or "internal war."[66]

In modern societies, according to Daunou, the economic aspect has
become all-absorbing. He describes society as an "immense workshop"
in which men labor to satisfy their needs.[67] Because of the advances in
the science of political economy, we understand the organizational laws
of this society better than those of earlier systems.[68] Therefore, the proper
correlation between economic and political systems becomes manifest. A
civilized society requires a national government that will interfere as little
as possible with private lives.

> National constitutions become established only when the majority of citizens
> live much more in their families, in their private affairs, in the particulars of
> their industry or trade, in short, in what we have called the social body, than
> in the commotion of the political system.[69]

Any attempt to reimpose a special government was doomed to eventual
failure, and would provoke continuing resistance.

Daunou and Tracy thus suggest that social and economic development
necessitates a redistribution of power and the emergence of "national"
representative governments. If a government persists in inhibiting progress, it will be overthrown. One is justified in contributing to this overthrow if the good expected from the policies of a new government out-
weighs the evil associated with a violent disruption of society. In general
peaceful reform is vastly preferable to abrupt forceful change, but the
Revolution of 1789 was inevitable and justifiable, if sometimes misguided.

What we have been examining in the works of Tracy and Daunou is
the historically new conjunction of a soberly "realistic" politics, which
exploited the historical and sociological strands of Enlightenment thought,
with an implicitly visionary politics, which revealed an intensified belief
in the immanence and imminence of a new age. Tracy and Daunou drew
on existing histories of civil society as a basis for a theory of "types" of
social organization with corresponding functional requirements. And,
much more than thinkers like Smith or Turgot, they used this analysis to

explore the significance of contemporary political crises. But, at the same time, they insisted on an ideal conception of social relations yet to be realized. Destutt de Tracy in particular seemed to gain solace by indicating the emerging outlines of a new order that would put an end to the contrarieties and uncertainties of the present.

> The moment when men finally bring together a great stock of acquired knowledge, an excellent method, and complete liberty is, then, the beginning of an absolutely new era in their history. This era is truly the FRENCH ERA; we must look forward to a development of reason and an increase of happiness that can hardly even be judged by the examples of the past centuries, for none resembles the one that is beginning.[70]

This hope was strangely akin to the theocratic dreaming of De Maistre or Bonald in its expression of a generalized yearning for a world reborn, and it was as much a legacy of the Revolution as was the attempt to demythologize the actual events of 1789 to 1815.

When Tracy and Daunou turn to an explicit consideration of constitutional design, these two strands of thinking are also apparent. In the future, the benefits of representative government would be obvious and its defense easy. Then government would be "founded only on right reason and [would profess] to be forever ready to submit to it, in the same way as to the general will, as soon as they make themselves known."[71] But contemporary "transitional" states, they found, were marred by willful stupidity, the clash of interests, and uncontrollable irrationality. In this context, the benefits of liberal democracy were not as obvious. Their arguments for the necessity of representative democracy in the intractably contentious present largely took the form of heralding the usefulness of liberty in promoting stability, enlightenment, and good government, although this defense was not entirely unproblematical. One also finds a renewed commitment to the notion of fundamental constitutional law.

The Theory of Representative Government

Tracy's Model Republic

Like the economic defense of civil equality discussed in chapter 3, Tracy's more general discussion of civil liberties considers primarily the beneficial consequences of such freedoms. For Tracy, the view of society as a collection of individuals engaging in a series of free and mutually productive exchanges is a model for that increased efficacy of the human will that is assumed to be a part of all cooperative ventures. Social cooperation leads not only to increased material productivity, but also to greater collective intellectual power, and greater moral satisfaction (through the increased satisfaction of the need for love and esteem permitted by closer social ties). Tracy's underlying supposition is that each person, if left "free," will so act as to join in the cooperative social venture. Thus, he can at times overstate his own position by asserting that the ideal government fosters human happiness by permitting individual passions and wills to operate completely freely: "it has only to let [nature] act."[72] However, Tracy also recognizes that defects in the human intellect always preclude wholly rational development; hence, the coercive arm of the law must preserve as much of this development as possible. Governments can best "let nature act," then, by guaranteeing that each person retains enough liberty of action to join in the *commerce* of society. The law ought to protect a sphere of individual action through legal sanctions. Tracy usually uses the broad term *individual liberty,* which includes economic freedoms and those guarantees of liberty of action he believed to be most important: proscription of arbitrary arrest, detention, and exile; freedom of speech, press, assembly, and religion; provisions for jury trials; and divorce. Equality refers to the extension of these rights to all.[73]

To the extent that Tracy gives specific arguments for these liberties, he emphasizes their social usefulness in contributing to enlightenment, or their contribution to the maintenance of utilitarian government. Freedom of expression, for example, was particularly important, because it was necessary in order for the truths of social science to emerge and to pass into the ranks of those unquestioned assumptions upon which people act. Democratic government requires these freedoms to ensure that the *volonté générale* will be informed.[74] Furthermore, freedom of the press is necessary in order to keep a watchful eye on government.[75]

Tracy argues that a state religion always endangers this atmosphere of free debate. The dogmatic teachings of organized religon ought not to be granted a favored status in the marketplace of ideas, because these opinions tend to confer dangerous powers on those who preach them. Thus, while tolerating individual beliefs, the government ought not to ally itself with any particular religion.

> The spirit of the laws in this regard ought to be neither to offend nor to restrain the religious opinions of any citizen, to adopt none [of these opinions], and to prevent any of them from having the slightest influence on civil affairs.[76]

For the same reason, governments should never use writers and teachers for propaganda, or require textbooks in schools, or draw up catechisms of acceptable dogma.

In Tracy's view, the use of juries is most important for its social and political consequences. Indeed, he doubts whether a jury "is always a very efficient way to render judgments more just."[77] A jury, however, is a powerful obstacle to the tyranny of judges and of those who appoint judges. It also educates people in the political process, and accustoms them to pay more attention to their fellow citizens.

Just as economic freedom leads to prosperity, then, liberty of opinion and action in general leads to social happiness. These freedoms maximize the sum of private pleasures and make possible the essential activities of citizenship. Tracy admitted no inherent conflict between his consequentialist justification of economic freedom and his "ideological" clarification, which traced the origin of economic rights to the necessary effects of human *personnalité*. Yet he had certain difficulties in reconciling the two perspectives. In his more general discussion of liberty, the same ambivalence is evident. Intermittently Tracy cast his opinions about civil equality in the form of deductions from *idéologie*, but apparently never to his complete satisfaction. He wrote to Fauriel, for example, that the manuscript of the *Commentaire sur l'Esprit des lois* was "too intertwined with ideological reminiscences."[78] But the very difficulty that Tracy had in communicating the coherence of his position gives his work its importance for the contemporary reader.

Tracy prefaces his analysis of *liberty* in the *Elémens d'idéologie* with a characteristic warning against political rhetoric, which "electrifies" the soul, and consequently makes agreement difficult.

> Nothing would be easier than to inspire interest in all generous souls by beginning this chapter with a kind of hymn to the first of all the goods of sensitive nature, *liberty*. But these explosions of sentiment are meant only to electrify oneself, or to arouse those whom one addresses. . . . thus let us not seek to excite but to satisfy, and let us speak of liberty as coldly as if this word alone did not set in motion all the power of the soul.[79]

In Tracy's view, the quality common to all types of liberty is that they all apparently procure for the one who enjoys the particular liberty a greater development of the exercise of will. He understands liberty, "with Locke, [as] the power to execute one's will, to act according to one's desire."[80] Liberty and happiness are merely two ways of explaining the same idea, since man is happy only insofar as his desires are fulfilled, and since liberty is the power to fulfill desires. Constraint, on the other hand, is the cause of powerlessness, suffering, and unhappiness. Tracy suggests a measure of happiness in terms of active power to produce pleasure; "it is always the possession of a sum of power, the annihilation of a portion of constraint, that constitutes a certain quantity of happiness."[81] When confronted with mutually exclusive objects of desire, men calculate the competing pleasures and pains and choose accordingly. Although it may be man's fate to lead a limited and constrained life, the idea of *"all-powerfulness,* or what is the same thing, *total liberty,* is inseparable from *perfect happiness."*[82]

Tracy equates happiness with power in a formula that appears very Hobbesian. However, unlike Hobbes, Tracy's equation of happiness with power has liberty as the decisive middle term. It is liberty—the sense of movement involved in overcoming constraint—that is most closely identified with pleasure for Tracy. He does not share Hobbes' preoccupation with securing individual power in ruthless competition with others because he assumes that the joint quest for power and satisfaction is not inherently a zero sum game. Not a geometrical increase in anxiety, but a joint liberation of power against the environment characterizes the "natural" pattern of human interaction.

Thus Tracy's "ideological" explanation of liberty focuses not on its positive social consequences, but on the individual increase in pleasure that comes from the active development of one's personal faculties. Yet this explanation was neglected in his substantive discussion of social guarantees, apparently because it would have challenged "ideology's" claim to be both noninflammatory and "scientific." If Tracy used his analysis of liberty as the basis of an individual "right" to happiness, the theory could easily be taken as a subversive indictment of the existing social and political order. But if used as a factual analysis of that order, Tracy's theory embroiled him in obvious contradiction.

The subversive possibilities of Tracy's "ideological" equation of liberty and happiness emerge in "De l'amour," the first chapter of the incompleted fifth part of the *Elémens d'idéologie*. This chapter, which was not published in France in Tracy's lifetime, contains some of his most utopian ideas about social organization.[83]

Tracy's main purpose in "De l'amour" was to discover how sexual love could best be regulated by human institutions; therefore, he necessarily turns to a discussion of the status of women. Tracy certainly does not challenge women's traditional roles, but rather sees marriage and the family as the fundamental units of social order. And he elsewhere explicitly denies that women ought to be granted political rights. What is significant in his analysis here, however, is the degree to which he calls for social reform based on the notion that personal freedom—for both sexes—is necessary to individual happiness.

Unlike most of his contemporaries, Tracy does not attribute to women a distinctly female sensibility. They share the general human sensibility and capacity for pleasure and "do not have a different nature."[84] Physical differences may prevent women from entering certain occupations, but do not justify denying them the opportunity to develop their personalities through experience.

Tracy contends that women have never been allowed to develop their natures fully. In the early stages of civilization the general rule was domination by the strong, and women suffered in the general oppression of the weak. Forms of oppression were perpetuated through custom and traditional law. In the Middle Ages, relations between the sexes became an unstable mixture of glory, religion, and desire. The true nature of love—a combination of sexual attraction and friendship between the sexes—was never adequately recognized by human institutions, and this failure led to unnecessary unhappiness among both sexes.

Tracy indicts the social relationships in contemporary France, as well as those of past societies. While the foundation of human relationships should be reciprocal liberty and equality, in order to maximize power and pleasure, society is in fact based on anachronisms, of which the corruptive notion of sexual conquest is but one example.[85] Tracy seeks nothing less than the total regeneration of social relations, so that personal character would be valued more than artifice, vanity, birth, or wealth, and eventually "an entirely new national character" would emerge.[86] To achieve this end, he recommends fundamental changes in the regulation of the institutions of courtship and marriage. The core of marriage, a combination of sexual attraction, friendship, and fidelity, cannot be created by legislation. Indeed, love and fidelity often exist outside the institution of marriage. We can see from an analysis of extramarital relationships, according to Tracy, that it is the "delicacy and constancy" of love that makes us approve a relationship, not mere legality.[87]

The guiding spirit of legislation, then, should be to grant both sexes the greatest possible liberty, and to remove all considerations other than personal choice from marriage. This analysis leads to a bitter critique of marriages of interest; an endorsement of education for women and much freer social interaction between the sexes; and a strong advocacy of liberalized divorce laws. The arguments given for divorce are particularly revealing. Besides discouraging marriages of interest, a liberal divorce law would encourage more spontaneous sentiments and increase individual chances of happiness, and it would end the agony of people "chained" against their will, especially that of the woman, whose very person is alienated in an unhappy marriage.[88]

Tracy's discussion of the painful constraints of traditional sexual mores exploits his equation of liberty, pleasure, and happiness, and indicts society's failure to recognize the proper claims of individuals for personal freedom and fulfillment. But this discussion remained an unpublished fragment, too "radical" for French public opinion.[89] If "De l'amour" reveals Tracy's assumption that every individual's pleasure ought to be increased by social interaction, his discussion of the relationship of freedom and pleasure in a repressive society illustrates his difficulty in maintaining that "ideology" could clarify existing reality.

Tracy was writing the *Commentaire* in 1806. Napoleon was then at the height of his power and was successfully consolidating his personal rule, with the evident approval of most of the French public. When Tracy attempts to illustrate his definition of liberty in reference to this situation, he is forced to recognize that on his principles, a nation may be regarded as free whenever its government is pleasing to it, i.e., "where the greatest number is the most happy."[90] For example, the Constitution of 1795 seemingly granted the French a considerable amount of liberty. In reality, however, they must have been in subjection, since they did not actually desire the liberties granted by that constitution. Formal civil liberties and liberty of the press were suppressed by Napoleon "without a murmur, and even with pleasure."[91] Tracy even concedes that were an omnipotent despot to administer perfectly, "under his rule one would reach the height of happiness, which is one and the same thing as liberty."[92] The anomalous surfacing of primitive forms of government, and the unexpected but undeniable symbiosis between these regimes and popular opinion, were phenomena that Tracy could never quite apprehend.

Tracy's inability to reconcile political "ideology" and political reality is reflected in his regretful admission that to advocate a regime because it corresponds to the true principles of reason is a rather feeble recommendation, for "when all is said and done, worldly affairs are not a matter of speculation and theory, but of practice and results."[93] Despite his discouragement with the state of public opinion in France, however, and his recognition that his own definitions could be used in support of repression, he continually struggles to incorporate "liberty" into the criterion by which governments should be judged.

> Thus the only thing that makes one social organization preferable to another is that it is more likely to make the members of society happy, and, *if you wish, in general,* that it leaves them many ways in which to manifest their will, for only then is it likely that they will be governed to their liking.[94]

So far we have considered only Tracy's arguments for civil liberties. But beyond the protection of a sphere of personal freedom of thought and action, he maintains that national governments require popular political rights. Tracy's argument for the necessity of public liberty has two important dimensions: first, he defends popular sovereignty on the grounds of utility rather than right, and second, he worries obsessively about the exercise of that power. The first dimension emerges most clearly in his discussion of the suffrage, the second in his speculation about an "ideal constitution."

The underlying rationale for popular control of the government can be simply stated. Although those in positions of authority do not have different long-range interests than those of the general population, the temptations inherent in their positions make a proper calculation of interests difficult. Tracy notes that it is exceedingly rare "to find a man capable of governing, who, in the long run, does not become unworthy of it."[95] In fact, a good constitution is but a collection of measures combined in such a way that those charged with repressing offenses do not have the occasion to commit crimes themselves.[96] To prevent the abuse of power, citizens should elect most public officials, hold them responsible for their actions, and limit them to very short terms in office.[97] Public happiness, then, is largely dependent on public (or political) liberty.

In order to illustrate how a nation might reform its political institutions, Tracy conjectures a situation in which a nation appeals to a special assembly to set up a new political constitution, as did the Americans (in 1776 and 1787) and the French (in 1789 and 1792). Tracy favors such a convention not because its determinations will necessarily be just, or because the people retain a constituent power (which is in some sense a truism), but because this method of regenerating a nation unites the most advantages with the least disadvantages.[98]

In his discussion of the election of this hypothetical constituent assembly, and of voting rights in general, Tracy demonstrates the extent to which his political theory depends on the analysis of divisions in society that he shared with Say. In a society with aristocratic traditions, the problem of procuring a disinterested assembly which will represent the universal interests of the *industrieux* is particularly acute. Tracy proposes regional assemblies to choose delegates, with universal male suffrage and universal male eligibility for office: "all citizens equally should be summoned to vote, in an equal manner, in the assemblies deliberating on the proper way to give a new organization to society."[99]

The argument for universal suffrage begins from his description of society as a collection of individuals. Since every man's very existence will be affected by the new rules of organization, each has an equal interest in the collective decisions to be made.

> It matters little that the existence of some is more substantial, or more valuable, or more agreeable than that of others. The existence of each person is everything to him; and the idea of everything does not admit of more or less.[100]

But Tracy does not conclude from this equality in interest that every individual in principle has a right to the vote. The *principle* involved is the prevention of the emergence of "special" government. An equal interest in political decisions merely signifies that no one can be excluded from the suffrage a priori.

Before any person is shut out of the political process, it ought to be proved that such an exclusion will lead to a better result than will inclusion. Tracy examines and rejects as spurious, however, the traditional arguments used in defense of a limited suffrage: birth, prestige, and wealth. His examination of the process of social *commerce* had indicated that the most serious potential division in society was between idlers and the industrious classes. But he argues that only the former would benefit from a restricted suffrage. To give men with a superior position in society a political advantage would endanger the bases of *industrie*. In Tracy's view, any attempt to fix suffrage on property qualifications is particularly useless. Since everyone recognizes the gradations and nuances that exist between rich and poor, it is unwise to erect additional arbitrary barriers. Property qualifications for the vote in fact encourage class warfare by making certain divisions more explicit than they already are: "these are awkward classifications, which cause internal warfare that would not arise without them." [101]

Tracy concedes that a property qualification on the suffrage is usually justified not in terms of the claims of wealth alone, but because of a presumption of a correlation between wealth and political capacity. On its face, this justification has merit, but he finds no evidence that knowledge is constantly linked to a certain degree of wealth, or to any other factor. Given an opportunity, the talented individuals in every class will emerge and attain recognition on their merits. To presume that enlightenment is a monopoly of a certain part of society, he argues, would be to degrade the very concept of reason.

Tracy also here considers the question of women's suffrage. While conceding that some "very respectable" men have held the opinion that women should vote, he disagrees. As sensitive and reasonable creatures, women are nearly the equals of men, but they are not called on to perform the same functions. They have an interest that everything in society should go well, but that interest does not require taking a direct part in public affairs. Because Tracy is not really concerned with establishing the link between individual reason and an inherent *right* to self-rule, but rather with the practical difficulty of preventing private government, he can conclude that the question of votes for women "is more curious than useful." [102]

In the primary assemblies, citizens may either vote directly for deputies to the constitutional convention, or limit themselves to voting for electors. Tracy favors the latter approach, although, in contrast to the Constitution of 1795, he rejects any property qualification for electors or deputies.[103] These offices ought to be open to all, for the same reasons that the suffrage should be universal.

Deputies to a constitutional convention are responsible for devising a national constitution that will suit the concrete circumstances of the country, but that will also encompass the discoveries of social science. These laws of social happiness, Tracy again insists, are not in themselves positive laws; they take on the character of positive law only when ordered by a coercive tribunal. He distinguishes three such guiding principles.

1) Governments are made for the good of the governed, not for the good of the governors. Consequently, they ought to exist only by virtue of the will of the majority of the governed and ought to change when the majority changes. It follows from this principle that no class should be legally favored or oppressed at the expense of another class.

2) There should be no power in society that cannot be changed without violence, or whose replacement will cause the whole fabric of society to change. Accordingly, all authority in the nation should not be given to a single person, the same body should not enact and administer a constitution, and a careful separation between governmental powers should be maintained.

3) A reasonable government should always have as its end the conservation of national independence, the liberty of its citizens, foreign peace and domestic tranquility. It follows from this that the government should seek indisputable and defensible boundaries, but should not seek to encompass highly diverse populations and should favor the establishment of a regular international federation. It also follows that government ought not to abridge the security of citizens, or their freedom to express opinions on all kinds of subjects, or their freedom to follow their own inclination in matters of religion.[104]

These principles are illustrated in a sketch of an ideal political constitution, a sketch that clearly reveals Tracy's preoccupation not only with the problem of private interests, but also with the threats posed by concentrated political power.

As in his discussion of the election of a constituent assembly, Tracy is obviously most disturbed by the possibility of aristocratic influence.

Therefore, he argues that the legislative power is best given to a representative assembly, indirectly elected by universal suffrage. Only in this way is it probable that the laws will reflect public rather than minority interests, will obtain general confidence, and will be obeyed readily.[105] He is hostile to bicameralism, except in the sense that a single assembly may be divided into sections with different functions but without different eligibility requirements and without the right of absolute veto over one another. "The legislative body must be essentially a unity."[106] The single assembly should be elected for a limited time and renewed in part each year. Tracy does not discuss the matter of responsibility to electors in the context of his ideal legislature, implying that elected deputies should have a certain liberty to act on their own judgment. But he also indicates that a deputy's major duty is to represent the state of opinion in his province.[107]

Although Tracy gives ultimate power to the majority, he worries about the exercise of such power on a number of levels. It is not so much that he fears the interests of the masses. Rather, he questions the capacity of the majority's representatives to enact "reasonable" laws, and worries about the possibilities for the subversion of constitutional government.

One concern, then, is that the public authorities will not have the knowledge to enact necessary reforms. The primary task of a representative legislature in Tracy's view was to encourage the development and maintenance of a law-abiding population aware of its true interests. It must above all create an effective system of public education, and a comprehensive civil and criminal code with a rational system of punishment.

In the *Commentaire,* Tracy repeats the themes of the earlier *Observations sur l'état de l'instruction publique* on the importance of habituating men to a correct calculation of their interests. There is now a greater emphasis, however, on the necessity to reduce that "cruel" inequality that supports the claims of privilege. The spread of popular knowledge will help to assimilate all classes to a middling (*mitoyenne*) class.[108] The most direct tool for accustoming men to a certain manner of judgment, however, is not education but the power of legal retribution.

> Education continues throughout life, and laws are the education of mature men. There is no law, of whatever kind, that does not instill certain opinions and discourage others, that does not lead to certain actions and away from their opposites.[109]

The direct hand of the law has definite limits; for instance, it would be fruitless to legislate against fundamental human instincts. Such instincts form the parameters of social experimentation, "against [which] one can never successfully battle for long, either in the physical or in the moral order."[110] Nevertheless, law remains important because it can mete out physical suffering, and man is a creature ruled by pleasure and pain.

The problem with existing laws is that they inflict pain irrationally and inefficiently. In contrast, civilized man should inflict suffering only to avert a greater evil.

> We must never forget that the only reasonable grounds of punishments, the only motive that makes them just, is not to make amends for the evil act, which is impossible; it is not to appease the hatred inspired by vice, which would be to yield to blind passion; it is solely to prevent future evil, which is the only thing both useful and possible.[111]

Modern legal codes, Tracy argues, are burdened with archaic and contradictory laws that create new opportunities for injuries and even encourage transgressions by forbidding things harmless in themselves. Negligence and corruption in administration further undermine public authority and encourage intrigue and fraud. Modern societies require a simple, clear, internally consistent code of law, specifying punishments that are not so much the severe as the inevitable consequences of crime.

Tracy's passion for clarity and order disposes him to favor a simplification and rationalization of the legal system. However, the antinomy between the simplicities of theory and the complexities of reality that bedeviled his efforts to demonstrate a certain basis for knowledge, to illustrate the economic unity of interest in society, and to classify political systems, emerges again in his discussion of law. Legal clarity and simplicity are indispensable goals, but "as social relations become more various and delicate, the laws that regulate them necessarily become more complicated."[112] As a result of the intricacy of modern social relationships, laws supplement and support each other in subtle ways. The problem of reform is exacerbated by the phenomenon of unintended consequences; laws often have unanticipated effects contrary to the aims of the legislator.[113] Because of the inherent difficulty of imposing order on the clutter of modern law, Tracy questions the ability of any assembly to accomplish such reform. Therefore, he is curiously attracted to the position, which "may seem paradoxical,"[114] that the legislative power should be invested in the hands of one man.

This attraction to the notion of a rational legislator illustrates Tracy's continuing search for a conduit through which "correct judgment" could enter the political arena, but he quickly abandons the idea as too dangerous. Indeed the possible seizure and abuse of power by one man or a small group—and the consequent undermining of the idea of legality—is the other preoccupation apparent in his constitutional theory.

Tracy's fear of the subversion of legally constituted authority causes him to give a sympathetic hearing to the proponents of federalism, but he notes that this issue must be referred to a consideration of national defense. For a state with powerful enemies on its borders, federalism is impossible.[115] He also takes up Montesquieu's theory of the separation of powers in a very qualified manner. Although most alleged systems of checks and balances are pointless tricks (*singeries*),[116] and although there should be no other justification for governing authority than the will of the majority, it is important that executive and legislative power should be institutionally separate. Again implicitly drawing a parallel between Bonaparte and the Jacobins, Tracy argues that the confusion of executive and legislative authority is similar to that which occurs when a constituent assembly assumes ordinary governmental power. Both blurrings of what should be distinct functions facilitate the seizure of despotic power.

The issue of constitutional stability is also evident in Tracy's discussion of the organization of the legislative and executive branches. An additional reason for giving the legislative power to a broadly representative assembly is that such a body can be renewed in sections, thereby promoting peaceful political continuity.[117] The organization of the executive is even more problematical because the executive's necessary command over the armed forces renders this position inherently dangerous. If one man is given executive power for a short time, he will tend to extend it; if given power for life, he will strive to make it hereditary—and hereditary power is by nature unlimited and illimitable. Despite his disclaimer of 1819, Tracy did not really believe that a hereditary monarch could fill the role of executive in a constitutional state.[118] He recommends, therefore, a plural executive of eight to ten members, elected for short terms and renewed at staggered intervals.

Tracy argues that it is singleness of conception and will (i.e., the legislative power) that is vital to government, not singleness in execution. Even in a monarchical or presidential regime, power is carried out by a group of ministers. In England, the king is important only in terms of the influence he retains over the legislative process. "The king is but a parasite, a cog unnecessary to the running of the machine; he only increases the friction and the expense." [119] Since the ministers execute policy, they might as well be given the constitutional authority. Jefferson's one major criticism of the *Commentaire* concerned this proposal of a plural executive. Citing the positive experience of the United States, and the disastrous experience of the French Directory, Jefferson suggested that a collegial executive is always inefficient and likely to lead to usurpation. [120] One might certainly object that Tracy here recreates a system that had already proven dismally inadequate in the face of disagreement between the legislature and the executive. He believed, however, that his system could avoid intragovernmental paralysis in several ways.

First, unlike the directors chosen under the provisions of the Constitution of 1795, Tracy's executive ministers could be chosen from the ranks of the deputies. Hence there is at least the possibility that the executive body would consist of the leadership of the legislature, although there would be no formal ministerial responsibility. But more important, Tracy proposes that the executive body be elected by a third *corps conservateur,* whose general function would be to mediate and to adjudicate differences between the legislative and executive powers.

Tracy's notion of a conservative force was probably inspired by Sieyès's 1795 proposal of a constitutional jury. His *corps conservateur* would be made up of distinguished former public servants ineligible for any subsequent office and "past the age of passion and great endeavors." [121] The members would be elected for life, at first by the constitutional convention, thereafter by the popularly elected regional assemblies, according to lists of eligibles drawn up by the executive and legislative branches. Besides participating in the choice of the executive council, the conservative body would nominate members of the high courts, judge the constitutionality of acts of the other branches of government, verify elections, act as grand jury in court cases involving deputies, dismiss the executive council on the demand of the legislature (if cause were found), and play a central role in any amendment of the constitution.

For Tracy, the *corps conservateur* is the cornerstone of the constitution, that part which facilitates and regulates the actions of the other branches. If he has what appears to be unreasoning confidence in this institutional innovation, it is because it speaks to his most fundamental fears about the exercise of political power. He takes pains to argue that such a body could guide the majority without representing "antipublic" interests, i.e., without halting *la marche de la société*. But neither would it become a useless "phantom" subservient to a powerful executive like the Napoleonic Senate. He notes that the manner of election he is proposing is very different from that of 1799 or subsequent Napoleonic constitutions.[122]

Perhaps most revealing is Tracy's comment that the *corps conservateur* could preserve public life from *le hasard et la violence*. His scheme has been compared both to the "neutral power" that liberal constitutionalists like Constant granted to the king, and to the American Supreme Court.[123] It is difficult to compare such different conceptions on an institutional level, but Tracy's proposal is very like these in that it expresses the psychological need among liberals for an external judge to arbitrate and regulate the political process, even when their epistemology has discredited the idea of any such standard. Tracy refers the most difficult cases of public *jugement* and *verification* to this constitutional jury. He does not explain why this group of men would possess a clear standard with which to decide on public interests. Indeed, the lesson revealed particularly sharply in his "idéologie" was that men had to act under conditions of irremediable doubt in politics. But to absorb this lesson fully would be to acknowledge the centrality of the "chance and violence" which Tracy still hoped to banish from social and political life.

Daunou and an Idéologue Interpretation of the Charte

Pierre Daunou's *Essai sur les garanties* was first published in 1818. Like his earlier pamphlets, this work is above all a contribution to current political controversies. His specific purpose was to force a liberal interpretation on the *Charte*, the ambiguous document granted by Louis XVIII on his accession. Like other Restoration liberals, Daunou claimed to demand only what the Charter promised.[124] The spirit of his work, however, is different from that of many who attempted to push the Restoration monarchy in a liberal direction. Daunou, like Destutt de Tracy, avoids a defense of historical French *liberties,* in favor of a utilitarian defense of *liberty.*[125] The point was to insist on the appropriateness and even necessity of civil rights in a "cultivated and industrious" state, to give convincing arguments for their usefulness, and to threaten the government—cautiously and obliquely—with the dangerous consequences of denying such rights.

The first part of the *Essai* discusses those spheres of action that ought to be protected as spheres of right; the second examines the political institutions necessary for such legal protections to be real. Daunou takes the word *garantie* to mean "the obligation to let someone enjoy a specific thing: it implies a recognized right and a contracted promise."[126] Without going into a discussion of the ultimate basis of rights, he takes it as given that individuals have the desire to be preserved from governmental, as well as from individual, aggression. In all languages words like *despotic* and *oppressive* have connotations of disapproval, indicating that in order to be happy all peoples desire some limitations on the activity of governors.[127]

Personal security is the most important of all guarantees. By this phrase, Daunou means something very like due process. Breaches would include retroactive laws or punishments, internment without trial, and unreasonable length of imprisonment.[128] Intimately linked to the need for personal security is the need for secure property rights. Positive law, the ultimate regulator of property, ought to recognize the fundamental link between assured property rights and public prosperity. He advocates efficient government with a minimum of economic regulation and taxation. Among his many criticisms of the restored Bourbons is the charge that Louis XVIII's government was unnecessarily extravagant.[129] In economic matters, the government can best assure prosperity by noninterference.

> Thus, in the last analysis, public prosperity is not more in our eyes than the most active private industry, which will introduce and distribute comfort in the greatest possible number of residences.[130]

Finally, a government ought to recognize complete liberty of opinion and liberty of conscience. Daunou devotes most of the first part of the

Essai to these issues, which were debated intensely during the Restoration.[131]

Daunou's primary defense of freedom of speech is that such freedom is necessary for intellectual progress. To judge whether an opinion is permissible on the basis of certain standards is to enclose conventional notions in a protective circle.[132] No one is free enough from error to make these judgments. Progress results only from the freedom to examine any opinion. Daunou further argues that speech is not seditious or libelous unless it "expressly" provokes disobedience, or is "immediately" revolutionary.[133] The law ought to restrict freedom of speech or press only by narrowly and specifically defining criminal or seditious provocation, calumny, and injury in the criminal code. Finally, it is the worst of all possible policies to promise freedom of the press while officially declaring certain doctrines false and pernicious. Forcing the elites of society to profess things that they do not believe corrupts society and creates an intellectual exchange based on lies.

Like Tracy and other liberals in the French anticlerical tradition, Daunou does not treat religious liberty as desirable in itself. Rather, he states that all accommodations between law and religion, except for complete separation with toleration for all religious opinions, are dangerous because of religious pretensions to intellectual superiority. Such ascendance, he argued, would eventually destroy guarantees.[134]

Daunou concludes that the prosperity and happiness of modern societies depend on granting a large area of personal liberty in which individuals are free to judge their own interests. *Liberty* is the general expression for these concrete personal guarantees. *Equality* means according these rights to all men. Any enlightened, industrious people to whom one refuses guarantees exists in a critical state during which storms "are born, grow, and burst into fury."[135] Thus it is prudent to grant people these rights. It is even impossible to avoid doing so.

In his post-Revolutionary writings, Daunou keeps constantly in view the restricted scope of a truly "national" government: the enforcement of a criminal and civil code that includes social guarantees, with only the minimum contribution of military service and taxation from the citizen.[136] The difficulty is always to get such a government, i.e., to produce "the conditions under which the guarantor will have the will and the power to keep [the guarantees]."[137]

This general problem of getting a government in the interest of the governed was particularly acute in post-Revolutionary France, and Daunou addresses it directly in the final chapter of the *Essai,* entitled "How individual guarantees can become inviolable in a country where they have never been so." [138] Like Tracy, Daunou was a consistent critic of the Old Regime. But also like Tracy and other liberals of the period, he feared not so much the practices of a traditional monarchy as those of the "new" systems of rule thrown up by the Revolution.

Daunou's portrait of the Napoleonic era is particularly striking. [139] Not only was such a regime a double expense to the taxpayer, who had to support both the cosmetic trappings of constitutionalism and real absolute power, but it was a psychological trial unlike either a natural disaster or an "age-old" despotism. The atmosphere was one of perpetual anticipation breeding inner anxiety and even "torment." Beneath masks of outward calm men jockeyed for favor, pursued various interests, and harbored nebulous plans of action. But without publicity and freedom of action, these interests and plans never became clear, even to their authors. Thus the regime distracted men from their private pursuits to a debilitating and sterile preoccupation with the uncertain future. "More than any other plague the arbitrary regime battles against the vigor of the body politic." [140]

It is the possibility of the reincarnation of aspects of such a system that most distressed Daunou. He feared the evolution of a monarchy that was constitutional in form but arbitrary in substance and hence unable to provide real stability. A veteran of the revolutionary assemblies, Daunou was permanently impressed with the hidden levels of meaning that lurked—dangerously he thought—in public discourse. Though people ostensibly argued about the provisions of the *Charte,* he observed, in reality they saw it as a "bridge to who knows what other regime." [141] In particular, Daunou warned of a tactical alliance between Bonapartists and ultraroyalists that would destabilize the government and permit the emergence of a repressive regime that would wipe out the fragile consensus in favor of the social guarantees established by the Revolution.

According to Daunou, the "solution" to the problem of good government does not lie in political institutions alone; nevertheless he recommends the following as essential: an independent judiciary, the use of juries, representation of national interests in a national assembly, and a precise written constitution. Daunou's devotion to the concept of an impartial judiciary was long-standing; and like many French liberals before and after him he admired and even romanticized the English jury system.[142] His constitutional theory, however, is almost wholly tied to French experience.

For Daunou *droits politiques* or *droits de cité* are essential to the guarantee of civil rights. The most important participatory activity of the citizen, besides local functions such as jury duty, is the election of the national assembly. Daunou avoids a direct discussion of the suffrage, saying only that its extent should be determined with reference to the particular characteristics of each population. The aim of the electoral system, however, ought to be to produce a body of representatives whose interests are not opposed to those of the entire body of citizens.[143] The most serious threat to this outcome comes from "privileged castes" who are especially opposed to guarantees if they themselves have been the victims of arbitrariness.[144] Thus Daunou is extremely tepid in support of an upper chamber, noting that such a chamber is tolerable only if it does not interfere with the lower house or try to deprive the industrious classes of the vote.[145] He states explicitly that a new form of dangerous rhetoric has replaced the vague propositions and denunciations of the revolutionary years. Now the term *grande propriété* is used to mask ominous projects and to dictate "fatal" laws.[146] Daunou, therefore, is against distinguishing various classes of electors, and clearly opposes the highly restrictive and complex electoral system of Restoration France.[147] One of his most impassioned speeches concerns the Electoral law of 1820, which was aimed at curbing the liberal strength shown in the 1819 elections. Daunou focuses his remarks on the constitutional issue of whether electoral rights should be considered under the supposed "regulative" rather than the "fundamental" articles of the Charter. He will not acquiesce in this change because it would give an aura of legitimacy to the government's tampering with fundamental constitutional law.[148]

Daunou's concern about the perils of constitutional tinkering is more than just a reflection of the liberals' belief that they could use the Charter to further their interests, although he certainly thought that to be the case. His belief in the necessity of an "inviolable" written constitution was analogous to Tracy's faith in a *corps conservateur;* it was the tangible symbol of his hopes for a reasonable mediating force in French politics.

Daunou's insistence on the importance of a detailed ordering of power grew with his experience of continued constitutional instability. This belief was already evident in his opposition to the trial of Louis XVI on the ground that the Convention could not constitutionally assume judicial functions, and in his resistance to all attempts to involve him in the Eighteenth Brumaire.[149]

An obsession with written constitutions was characteristic of a certain type of liberal reformer in the early nineteenth century; in view of the succession of French constitutions from 1789 to 1848, it has appeared to most observers a particularly naive and unrealistic concern. What is particularly puzzling in the case of Daunou is that he saw clearly the limits of written constitutions. Like Tracy he criticized the idea of attempting to institutionalize a balance of power. Moreover, he rejected Tracy's scheme for a constitutional jury on the grounds that such a body would probably become a vehicle for manipulating the constitution, rather than the "guardian" of its provisions. Finally, he states repeatedly that political passions are naturally so active and capricious that only ingrained habit, a conviction that *cela ne se peut pas,* can restrain them. A consensus on rights would be possible, he thought, only with the growth of enlightenment and industry.[150] Presumably, with "enlightenment," men would be gradually convinced of the relative truths of social science.

Daunou, like other Idéologues, claimed to prefer the political consequences of doubting and suspending judgment to the consequences of self-confident zeal. Ultimately, however, he is unable to trust fully that the kind of psychological certainty associated with the relative truths of social science will be enough to sustain "progressive" political action. He needs to enshrine what he called civilized principles in a constitution, which he almost always describes as both *inviolable* and *précise.*

What Daunou hoped that the constitution would provide was a rational touchstone for public debate. Without such a document, he argued, public discourse will more easily stray into senseless argument over illusory interests. Thus Daunou accused the royalists of opposing a constitution so that they could mask their play for absolute power by arguing at will from this or that "tradition." He hoped, then, that even if a liberal constitution did not correspond to any social consensus, it would generate its own constituency.

This hope can be seen in his distinction between *opinions populaires* (a type of easily manipulated ignorance which prevailed, Daunou argued, in different ways under the Old Regime, the Jacobins, and Napoleon) and *opinion publique* (beliefs that are founded on observing, experiencing, comparing, and analyzing facts).[151] A written constitution, for Daunou, is a method for rationalizing politics by forcing men to justify their opinions against a "clear standard." Those who oppose such a document inhibit the emergence of real public opinion. Daunou's perception of the composition of this opposition is telling. He charged the ultras with desiring: 1) ignorant masses, 2) a tiny middle class, and 3) a stifling of all intellectual activity.[152] The elements in his positive vision are, correspondingly, a large and learned middle class united by their enlightened opinions, who take a leading role in politics. In Daunou's constitutional theory, a precise written constitution has become a symbol for the infusion of "enlightened reason" into political discourse.

Daunou thus shared with Tracy a preference for moderate political authority, responsive to the general interest and will, but demarcated and limited by constitutional rules. Rather than attempt to sum up the significant aspects of this view as I have developed it in this chapter, I will try to make its outlines clearer by addressing explicitly what has been implicit throughout this essay: the argument that the reinterpretation of the revolutionary heritage exemplified in the work of Destutt de Tracy and Pierre Daunou was a form of utilitarianism indigenous to France, but plainly analogous to the development of Benthamite radicalism in England.

CHAPTER FIVE

French and English Utilitarians

I N THE FACE of growing attacks on sensationalism and the *philosophes'* method of analysis, both English Utilitarians and French Idéologues defiantly insisted on a method based on the association of sense impressions. They championed the economic reforms urged by the classical political economists; they traced all morality to enlightened self-interest; they developed a remarkably similar political position; and finally, they neglected the traditional natural rights basis for this position in favor of arguments based on "social science."[1]

The significant issue here is not the possibility of mutual influence. There certainly were contacts between the two groups, but the theoretical affinities are probably due to common intellectual roots, and, more importantly, to similar reactions to the particular kind of political radicalism unleashed in England as well as in Europe by the French Revolution.[2] An explicit comparison between English and French utilitarianism is illuminating for other reasons. It clarifies some aspects of classic English utilitarianism that have been continually disputed by commentators: the character of its claim to be scientific, the basis of civil and political rights in the theory, and the relationship between utilitarian political ideology and middle-class interests. Moreover, such a comparison helps to explain the relatively rapid demise of utilitarian reform movements in the nineteenth century. The claim here, then, is that the logic of the utilitarian position, and also its political vulnerability, come into focus more clearly through a comparison with the French case.

Utilitarianism, Benthamism, and *philosophical radicalism* are terms which have their own—sometimes very different—associations. The first has come to connote a broad movement in ethical and legal theory that is only loosely connected to the first utilitarians. The second was used by Tories and Whigs purely as a term of abuse in the political struggles of the 1820s. The third was closely linked to a short-lived group of parliamentary reformers, not all of whom were "utilitarians" strictly speaking.[3] I will use "English utilitarianism" or "philosophical radicalism" in this chapter to mean certain leading ideas of Bentham and James Mill that became important components of a new radical program in England. This is not to deny that there were differences between Bentham and Mill, or between them and their followers. But I wish to deemphasize these differences in order to stress important aspects of what undeniably became a shared doctrine. Those parts of Bentham's and Mill's writings that are most significant for the following analysis are the critique of natural rights, the defense of civil liberties, and the theoretical and practical justifications of political democracy.

Rights and Utility

Bentham's writings on natural rights are still considered to be the *locus classicus* for the logical demolition of the theory; in the celebrated phrase he labeled such rights "nonsense on stilts." The most perceptive readers of Bentham, however, have always seen that his main concern with the language of natural rights and contract was political and contemporary, rather than historical or logical.[4] Much of his attack on natural rights is but a précis of Hume's argument against a historical contract.[5] Beyond his rejection of contract, the major contentions of his argument are two: 1) rights are not anterior to political society, but are created by law, and 2) to claim "pre" or "ultra" legal rights is to speak in an ambiguous and dangerous manner that inflames antisocial passions and encourages rebellion. These points, especially the second, form the constant theme of Bentham's attack on the French declarations of rights. The basic fallacy of the French was to use the "cutthroat" words *can* and *cannot* where *ought* and *ought not* should have been used. To speak of what sovereign authority cannot do is either nonsense or treason, for such a manner of speech undermines the authority that is essential to happiness.[6]

This sort of criticism, as we have seen, was also common among the

Idéologues, who wanted to deprive *liberty* of its status as a political fetish. The reaction of liberals like Daunou and Tracy to the use of words as weapons during the Revolution was to insist on the limits of politics, and to celebrate the concrete advantages of society conceived as a *compagnie* organized around human satisfaction and pleasure. Accordingly they decisively resolved the ambivalence in the philosophical party's understanding of the principles of 1789 in favor of a utilitarian defense of the rights necessary to modern society, and largely banished the concepts of contract, inalienable rights, and republican virtue from their political vocabulary.

Idéologues like Tracy, however, rarely attacked the *motives* of natural rights theorists, whereas Bentham depicted such men as "turned crazy by self-conceit."[7] When Bentham took up the cause of democratic reform and began to attack the fallacies of the right, he indeed was embarrassed by these earlier vituperative attacks. When the question of an English edition of his general work on political fallacies arose, Bentham wondered whether to

> print [the critique of natural rights] as it stands, conveying as it does the
> sentiments entertained A°1811; and then subjoin the change produced
> A°1819 by regarding the same subject in a different point of view.[8]

He ultimately decided to omit the earlier critique entirely. Bentham certainly had not changed his mind about the obscurity of natural rights language, but he may have changed his mind about the extent of the danger involved in its use. Natural rights thinkers were now political allies, to be gently corrected rather than brusquely alienated.[9]

Both Tracy and Bentham, then, distrusted the too hasty employment of complex linguistic "fictions" like natural rights because of what they saw as the potential abuse of such terms. To argue against rhetoric in this way is certainly not to deny all relevance to a natural or higher law standard. Bentham, for example, concedes that terms like natural law and rights have meaning if they refer to interests and claims that are common to human nature, i.e., to interests and claims that can be defined without reference to social conditions created by, or arising with, social and political institutions. His description of natural law, in fact, is almost identical to Tracy's.

> The *law of nature* is a figurative expression in which nature is represented as
> a being; and such a disposition is attributed to her, which is figuratively

called a law. In this sense, all the general inclinations of men, all those which appear to exist independently of human societies, and from which must proceed the establishment of civil law are called *laws of nature*.[10]

The attacks on rhetoric do, however, reveal a heightened awareness of the autonomy of the public realm of coercion and power. In both cases, the impulse is to find a different referee for the inevitable conflict that occurs in politics. Yet this new referee—utility—continues to rely on the observer's (presumably careful and impartial) generalizations of social experience according to some common conception of "the natural and social man."

Utility and Social Science

Tracy's social and political theory is explicitly based on the premise that we can retrace the necessary association of sense impressions in the succession from needs to desires to actions; we can penetrate the true "logic of the will." When the meanings of contentious words are clarified, men will be able to organize their common life in such a way as to produce maximum general happiness. Yet logic and experience always confront one another uneasily in his work. Although his view of society and politics ultimately depends on the universal psychology of abstract sentient individuals and on the notion of the "natural" development of the will, he is often unable to use this model as an unequivocal guide to present political action. His reconsideration of Hobbes and Condillac had led him to the judgment that the basic constituents of the ideas involving the will, if traceable to pleasure and pain, are nevertheless incommensurable and thus unquantifiable. He is skeptical about placing any faith in the science of statistics, and argues that the mathematical temper itself is misplaced in most social analysis. One's only hope, then, is to use ordinary reasoning to clarify language. But Tracy's examination of logic and grammar indicated that absolute linguistic clarity is a chimera as well. Thus he concludes that the theorist can offer only gross guidelines to the legislator; his own theoretical discussions reveal continual difficulties in dealing with contradictory evidence. Tracy's utilitarianism, then, is much different in tone from the practical hard-edged theory of Bentham, which becomes even more dogmatic in James Mill's version.

Many of the assumptions underlying Bentham's view of society, and especially of political society, reflect an unquestioning acceptance of the possibility of a rational social development. No less than Tracy, Bentham believed that the fundamental facts of social science could be unearthed by creating a *"logic* of the *will* as well as of the understanding."[11] However, Bentham's "bastard mixture of theory and practice that was the logic of the will"[12] has a very different and implicitly more activist bias than Tracy's. Once Bentham had found the facts of human experience in units of pleasure and pain, he constantly returned to these concrete ideas as an infallible guide through the maze of linguistic fictions. His attitude toward the foundations of his system was fundamentally practical and manipulative.

The illusion of scientific certainty in Bentham's work depends on the illusion of quantification, to which he returns again and again—in the felicific calculus, in the axioms of mental pathology, in the table of the springs of action. This use of the language of mathematics gives a clinical tone to his work, although he rarely engaged in anything more than irrepressible reclassification and ever more extensive application of the same insights to new areas. Indeed, Bentham thought of his axioms not really as empirical generalizations, but as guidelines essentially incapable of demonstration, "since, referring to universal experience as their immediate basis . . . [they] require only to be developed and illustrated in order to be recognized as incontestable."[13] The creator of countless neologisms, Bentham never despaired of a new scientific language based on his axioms. "Postulate: That all words and phrases necessary to the substitution of truth to error—of clearness to obscurity or ambiguity—conciseness to verbosity—be coined, uttered, and received."[14] James Mill's *Analysis of the Phenomena of the Human Mind* (first published in 1829) was equally remarkable for its banishment of the legacy of doubt in associationist psychology.[15] This analysis can be seen as an attempt to fulfill his earlier expressed wish "to make the mind as plain as the road from Charing Cross to St. Pauls."[16]

Bentham's and Mill's use of sensationalist psychology exploited only its image of certainty, while Tracy exposed its weaknesses *malgré lui*. The different implications for action are suggested in Tracy's "ideological" parsing of the sentence, *the man is happy*.[17] According to the notion that the ideas in the predicate are implied by the ideas in the subject, Tracy postulates several definitions of *happy*. He then attempts to decide whether these definitions in fact are consonant with *man*. First, *happy* might be supposed to mean a state in which a being experiences only agreeable sensations. Tracy finds that a relationship between *man* and *happy* based on this definition does not exist, because this conception of happiness does not correspond to the ideas associated with *man*. Second, *happy* might be supposed to mean a state in which a being experiences a greater sum of pleasures than pains. Initially, this seems a much more reasonable assumption. However, since we cannot measure the intensity of agreeable and disagreeable sensations on any common scale, we must suspend judgment, or give only a provisional acquiescence to this possibility. Third, *happy* might be supposed to mean a state in which a being prefers existence to destruction. Tracy assumes this idea to be clearly contained in the idea of all men who do not kill themselves. Thus we are justified in adopting this relationship of *man* to *happy,* even if it expresses only a minimum level of meaning. This is not a conclusion that encourages self-confident reform.

In "ideological" utilitarianism, then, the underlying premise of an ideally rational society, which Tracy, Bentham, and Mill shared with earlier Enlightenment thinkers, is more clearly exposed because this vision is continually juxtaposed to a contrary "experience." Bentham and Mill generally admitted no such painful contradictions to complicate their claims for social science.

Society as *Commerce:* Tracy and Bentham on Civil Equality

It has often been argued that "classical maximizing utilitarianism" provides an inadequate basis for political liberalism because it does not offer a solid foundation for individual liberty and equality; i.e., its first concern is with the greatest net balance of pleasure or happiness, regardless of the distribution of advantages.[18] However, it is undeniable that early utilitarians failed to recognize any divergence between equally protected civil rights and maximum utility. They made no such distinction because they viewed society as a process of exchange that yields a series of gains for the species and for the individual. Despite their greater attention to the role of force and law in guaranteeing and organizing this process, they did not abandon the notion of a series of identities existing among all men.

Destutt de Tracy's defense of the necessity of equality before the law gives a concise statement of the logic of this argument. Tracy assumes that the greater the number of individuals cooperating in the production of *richesse* — material, social, or intellectual — the greater the total amount of satisfaction. The increase is due not to the mere addition of individual pleasures, but to the process of cooperation, which assures that each person gains by every act of exchange, and that the total increases not arithmetically but synergistically. Since he assumes that absolute legal guarantees of equality in rights are necessary to induce entrance into the social process, these rights are in one sense the logical counterpart of maximum happiness.

Like Tracy, Bentham came to view the ends of civil law as substantially similar to, if broader than, the ends of political economy. He defined the principles of legislation in matters of civil law as "more distinctively termed *private distributive, or distributive* law."[19] The objectives of this law are subsistence, abundance, security, and equality.

Bentham assumed that specific laws designed to create subsistence and abundance would be unnecessary. His account of the economic growth of society could easily have been written by a Physiocrat or an Idéologue.

> Before the idea of laws existed, *needs* and *enjoyments* had done in that respect all that the best concerted laws could do. Need, armed with pains of all kinds, even death itself, commanded labour, excited courage, inspired foresight, developed all the faculties of man. Enjoyment, the inseparable companion of every need satisfied, formed an inexhaustible fund of rewards for those who surmounted obstacles and fulfilled the end of nature. . . . Desires extend with means. The horizon elevates itself as we advance; and each new want, attended on the one hand by pain, on the other by pleasure, becomes a new principle of action. . . . The greater our means, the greater the scale on which we labour; the greater is the recompense, and consequently, the greater also the force of motive which animates the labour. Now what is the wealth of society, if not the sum of all individual wealth? And what more is necessary than the force of these natural motives, to carry wealth, by successive movements, to the highest possible point?[20]

Bentham, then, argues that in the economic sphere, laws directly promoting subsistence and abundance are superfluous and even positively harmful. However, the law has a crucial function in guaranteeing security, and Bentham anchors his defense of civil liberties on this notion.

For Bentham, subsistence, abundance, and security tend to "coincide and run into one another"[21] because laws that establish general security are a generic part of the process of production. They impose on us the duty of refraining from meddling with the person or property of others by specifically defining the behavior that will be considered meddlesome.[22] "For the subsistence [as also for the abundance] of all . . . provision will to a certain degree have been made by the provision for security in all its shapes."[23] Security is necessary to prosperity in order to induce individual effort. Slavery, the extreme case of insecurity of person, is the most inefficient method of social organization:

> Fear rather leads [the slave laborer] to conceal his power than to show it. . . . The sad feeling of insecurity, inseparable from [his] condition nourishes all the faults destructive of industry, and all the habits most fatal to society, and that too without compensation and without remedy. This is not an empty theory. It is an actual result, at all times, in all places.[24]

Bentham sometimes states the matter in terms of the value of human capital. Since liberty augments the value of human labor, the productive capital of a country will be stronger as the servitude of personal obligations is reduced.[25]

Liberty, in fact, is a necessary branch of security, even "the cornerstone"[26] of Bentham's system. Liberty in this sense is not solely defined by the equal application of law, although the *generality* of law is an important part of its ability to produce a sense of security. But Bentham also refers here to the content of law. It should assure liberty of person (i.e., guarantees against arbitrary violence from private persons or governors), security of property, and economic freedoms. The presumption of the manifest utility of personal freedom, an assumption never "proved" by the felicific calculus, underlies Bentham's defense of freedom of contract in the *Defense of Usury*: "you who fetter contracts; you who lay restraints on the liberty of man, it is for you . . . to assign a reason for your doing so."[27] Security generally requires a suppression of legal monopoly and of economic privilege. Thus, for Bentham, as for Tracy, an equality in civil liberties is the implicit counterpart of the greatest happiness principle. Or, as stated by James Mill, "That men are susceptible of happiness only in proportion as rights are protected is a proposition which, taken generally, it is unnecessary to prove."[28]

An eighteenth-century view of the harmony of individual and social purposes (and thus of the presumed utility of individual liberty) continues, then, to inform Bentham's and Tracy's conception of social science. Bentham, however, is more consistently hostile to evoking the traditional associations of what he called "sentimental liberalism" and more insistent on the novelty of his strictly utilitarian method: first, because of his strong impulse to organize the social universe in terms of absolute sovereignty and an imperative theory of law; second, because of his intuitive judgments about the most important psychological components of happiness.

Bentham consistently defines liberty as the absence of coercion. Law, on the other hand, is by definition coercive and operates only at the expense of liberty. The logical background of Bentham's thought, like that of Hobbes, is a boundless theoretical realm of individual freedom. To make law is to add something new to the world. What is added cannot be liberty, for that was there already. What is added are restrictions that take away liberty.[29] Thus, for Bentham, the law technically does not create liberty; it indirectly permits a degree of liberty by granting to an individual a sphere of *right*, i.e., by restricting others. In his resistance to viewing the hypothetical ground of liberty, which he sometimes calls the "universal law of liberty," as in any way outside a system of positive law, Bentham argues that the substratum of freedom on which positive laws are superimposed should itself be seen as general permissive law ordered by the theoretically absolute sovereign.[30]

In any strictly theoretical context, then, Bentham's *liberty* functions as an evaluatively neutral term. We have seen, however, that when he views civil society from the economic aspect, Bentham assumes that the general law of liberty is (or should be presumed to be) favorable to individual and social happiness, since individual motivation is presumed to be adequate to produce this result. This process does not occur entirely "naturally"; it involves harnessing motives by laws guaranteeing security. The same assumption ultimately underlies Bentham's social and political thought as well, although his preoccupation with the behavior-changing properties of legal sanctions tends to obscure it. When harnessed by a rational code of law and a system of education, human motives can be trusted to produce maximum happiness because they are in harmony with the "rational will" of each individual. Halévy has argued, in an interpretation of Bentham that has become standard, that Bentham adopted a theory of the spontaneous identification of interests in the economy, but that his theory of politics and legislation is based on the principle of the artificial identification of interests through the application of punishment. However, the implication of a theoretical duality in Bentham's system is misleading. In both areas, he was concerned to alter motives in such a way that the implicitly rational course of conduct, which would benefit both the individual and society, would be chosen.[31] Nevertheless, because Bentham was mostly concerned with the problems of rationalizing the legal and penal structure, the "omnicompetence" of the sovereign looms large, and he often appears as the quintessential manipulator of sanctions.

Tracy initially described liberty in a similar Hobbesian fashion as a boundless "field" of human potentiality upon which social and legal constraints are superimposed. Tracy, however, has a less rigorously legalistic view of this field. His "ideological" method tends to stress the apparently spontaneous aspects of judgment as it recognizes and wills the path of greatest satisfaction, the "natural" standards for conventions. For Tracy, the optimistic model of *économie sociale,* with its assumptions about the utility of liberty, serves as the acknowledged model for social rationality in a wider context. He certainly insists on the role of coercive law in this process; law, however, appears less as the positive structure necessary for the emergence of rationally self-interested individuals, than as the eternally necessary corrective to the wayward human will.

Bentham's bias toward the positive functions of law, rather than the inherent pleasures of freedom, also stems in part from his intuitions about the kinds of pleasures and pains that are important in social life. The pleasures to be fostered by the civil law are mostly those derived from the possession of material satisfaction; the principal pains to be prevented are those derived from disappointment of the expectation of satisfaction. Thus, the "moral thermometer to make perceptible all the degrees of happiness and misery,"[32] registers primarily portions of wealth and degrees of anticipation and dread. Bentham never considers the pleasures that may be directly involved in exercising freedom of assembly or expression. These rights are justified only on the basis of their presumed contribution to enlightened self-interest and thus to the effective will of the legislator.

Tracy clearly also relies on this consequentialist argument for liberties. However, his explicit expansion of society as *commerce* to serve as a theoretical paradigm for all social and intellectual intercourse also directs attention to the individual motives for social action: the desire for the pleasurable exercise of the will, which satisfies the individual need for power while creating the opportunities for other men to satisfy their needs. If Tracy does not adequately define the relationship between pleasure and freedom, even in terms of his own "analytical" method, his assertion of this link nevertheless helps to illustrate why *liberty,* defined as the absence of specific legal constraints on the will, was generally presumed to be beneficial.

Utilitarian Theories of Democracy

A comparative examination of Bentham's and Tracy's views on civil society has underlined the continuing importance of the perceived coincidence of individual freedom and social needs in their thought. Indeed, in some ways this theme becomes even more prominent, since the "laws" of political economy loom so large in their conceptions of social science. What was new was the effort to comprehend, and to rationalize, the role of coercive institutions in achieving the identity of interests. This presumed identity, I shall argue, was the single most important aspect of early utilitarian political theory.

The utilitarian theory of liberal democracy—especially as put forth in James Mill's *Essay on Government*—is still often treated as primarily a defense of middle-class interests, and, indeed, of middle-class suffrage.[33] A somewhat related reading of the *Essay on Government* sees Mill as the first to have espoused a theory of market democracy akin to the later theories of Joseph Schumpeter and Anthony Downs.[34] On this interpretation, Mill saw the middle class as "rational bargainers" who would efficiently represent the interests of the lower classes. He is said to have offered a defense of deference voting and functional apathy as potentially rational democratic behavior. There is an analogous view of Idéologue political theory which suggests that the political difficulties of the Revolutionary period not only discredited the language of 1789, but initiated a rejection of the existing democratic ideal, a division of society into those capable of acting on reason and those capable only of acting on emotion, and a deep distrust of political participation. This view notes the Idéologues' growing willingness to entrust the direction of society to those capable of calculating public interests correctly.[35]

Both of these views seem to me mistaken. They take little account of the view of society that underlies the utilitarian vision of the political process, and that provided both "philosophical radicalism" and "ideology" with their appeal to nineteenth-century radicals. For the early utilitarians, the major emphasis is always on the *equality and extension* of political rights. A consideration of the similarities between the theory of politics developed by French and English utilitarians helps to clarify the alleged class nature of this theory, the status of universal suffrage, and the inherent limitations of utilitarianism as an ideology of political reform.

The early utilitarians' defense of democracy begins from their revised view of government as legitimated only by its function of promoting the general interest. The argument is of course quite simple. To further the public interest is in actuality no different than to further the rational long-term interests of all individuals in society, including those of governors. The circumstances surrounding the exercise of power, however, provide governors with great opportunities to indulge a myopic view of their interests; consequently, the calculation of their rational utility breaks down. Governors tend to amass money and privilege, monopolies and sinecures.[36] Thus, governors need to be checked, i.e., made responsible to the people through democratic institutions. By definition the people can have no corporate interest, or in Bentham's preferred terminology, no "sinister" interest. There is never a sympathetic discussion of political parties among Idéologues or Benthamites, because parties are by definition partial associations held together by ties of place and patronage, i.e., they seek purely private interests.[37] Since pure democracy is impossible, the nonruling "people," or their major part, must control the rulers.

The question of political rights, then, is related primarily to the problem of choosing and controlling representatives in order to increase the chances of their consulting only the long-range interests that they share with the people. Because there is absolutely no way to distinguish the theoretical interest that one person has in the business of government from another's, the capacity to act on rational self-interest constitutes presumptive evidence of capacity to exercise political rights. Hence, Bentham argues:

> If, in the instance of any one individual it be *right* that he should possess a *share,* of a certain degree of *magnitude,* in the choice of a [representative]—how can it be right that in the instance of any other individual the share should be either less or greater?[38]

Tracy expressed the same fundamental position:

> [All citizens] are equally interested by virtue of everything they possess, all their interests, and their entire existence. . . . The existence of each man is everything for him; and the idea of everything does not contain that of more or less.[39]

It was fully compatible with this perspective, however, to require any element of the population to support its claim to the vote with arguments showing that its voting rights would in fact further the aim of keeping the government from falling prey to sinister interests (or, in Tracy's terms, from becoming "special"). The essential problem was to look at the population in terms of who was most likely to indulge short-term interests. Let us first reconsider Tracy's theory of political rights.

According to Tracy, the only invidious social antagonism was that between idlers and the industrious classes. The idle classes were dangerous because their great wealth led to a complacency which dried up the urge for activity that encouraged people to take part in *commerce.* Living "nobly" was inimical to the public interest. But it was this group that was most likely to be in a position to influence public policy. The aim was to ensure the political predominance of *les industrieux,* an aim that could only be enhanced, Tracy argued, by universal suffrage. This perspective on the question of political rights explains why Tracy could treat women's suffrage, which he perceived as unrelated to the significant split in society, as a useless curiosity. In this view of politics, as in Daunou's, the middle classes were crucial not so much for their interests as for their presumed susceptibility to "sane reason."

A reading of James Mill's notoriously ambiguous discussion of the suffrage in his *Essay on Government,* in the light of Tracy's position, may prove instructive. The interpretation of Mill's *Essay* as a thinly veiled defense of middle-class suffrage ignores the more fundamental vision of the political situation that underlies Mill's argument.[40]

Mill began the *Essay on Government* with a significant statement of the proper "end" of all governments. As a more exact statement of the greatest happiness principle in relation to politics, he asserted that the purpose of government was to provide secure civil guarantees so that the "allurement of advantage" would induce all men to produce: "To obtain all the objects of desire in the greatest possible quantity, and to obtain labour in the greatest possible quantity, we must raise to the greatest possible height the advantage attached to labour."[41]

From the beginning this perspective directed attention to the most relevant distinction to be discussed by Mill in relation to possible restriction of the suffrage: that between the "productive" and the "privileged." In this area, Mill was most concerned to extend the suffrage as widely as possible. Far from defending middle-class suffrage, he saw no relevant divergence between the interest of the middle ranks and that of those with less property. Mill's explicit concessions from the principle of universal suffrage were in reality limited to two groups: women, and men under forty. His reasoning in the case of women is similar to Tracy's. Because the interests of women were assumed to be comprehended in those of their husbands or fathers, the issue was unimportant. The discussion of an age limitation, which directly precedes that of a pecuniary qualification, seems to be in part a rhetorical device to make a property qualification appear even less defensible. In agreeing to a hypothetical restriction of the suffrage to men over forty, Mill was suggesting that *if* it could be proved that a restriction was not dangerous, then there would be no objection to restriction in principle. He then goes on to discuss the obvious dangers of a property qualification. Unless such a qualification was "very low," it was manifestly dangerous because it would tend inexorably to contradict the very end of government by creating "Aristocratic Government, . . . That organ of misrule."[42] And once the benefits of a wide extension of the suffrage had been granted, according to Mill, there was little reason not to extend the suffrage further to include those comparatively few who would be excluded by a small pecuniary qualification. Hence, the balance of utility always lay with the absence of a property qualification.

The classic utilitarian rationale for democracy can be explained only by the tendency to see the power of existing "partial" interests, i.e., the aristocracy, the crown, and the church, as the only structural obstacle to the creation of a utilitarian polity. There were differences in the perceptions of the collusion between these interests. Tracy and Daunou saw great evil in a hereditary monarchy, which must either surround itself with a permanent aristocracy in an attempt to make its power stable or drift toward despotic personal rule. They were republicans because of the historical association in France between monarchy and privilege. In England the preference for a republic remained rather academic. Bentham, and especially James Mill and the Philosophic Radicals, were more worried about the predominance of aristocratic influence *tout court* as manifested in both the Whig and Tory parties. In their eyes, the king might be the Corrupter-General, but he was a less poisonous influence in England than the entrenched aristocracy. In both cases, however, the collusion of interests was thought to be dangerous because it reinforced the power of the very elements in society most likely to act on immediate self-interests and least likely to become enlightened. An established church merely intensified the problem by perverting the educational process.

Thus the combined political influence of corporate interests was fundamentally opposed to the general interest because such influence threatened the bases of the model of society as *commerce*. Unchecked, these private interests endangered the very structure of prosperity: civil equality. Both Tracy and Daunou feared that a revived French aristocracy meant a return to the civil inequality of the Old Regime. At best, they thought, aristocratic influence would inhibit sociability, hamper production, and bleed the populace through extravagance and corruption. Bentham and Mill, less fearful of political threats to individual liberty, tended to concentrate on the dangers of corruption. But even Mill gave dire warnings of the heights to which aristocratic power might climb.[43]

I have tried to show that a conception of society as a free exchange underlay utilitarian political thought; nevertheless, this economic analogy ought not be pushed too far. Although politics exists to guarantee the functioning of a "market" of self-interested producers who labor in exchange for satisfaction, politics is not precisely itself a market in which citizens shop for representatives who offer policies as goods. It is true that the exercise of political "virtue" has become a derivative activity, secondary to other pleasures, but there is little reason to suggest that the exercise of political rights has fallen into the category of potentially avoidable pain or has become a fit occupation only for a rational elite.[44]

On the contrary, widespread intelligent use of political rights was viewed as the condition and fruit of a society organized around utility.

French and English utilitarians, then, assumed that in a democracy characterized by widespread education, guaranteed civil liberties, a frequently renewed national assembly, and universal suffrage,[45] the underlying identity of interests among the people would become manifest. There were hints of other benefits intrinsic to the democratic process. Tracy, for example, approved the effects of local political participation on character, and saw the representative legislature both as a way to achieve policies acceptable to all parts of the nation, and as a way to foster a law-abiding population. Bentham too discussed a principle of "universal interest comprehension" that suggested that the democratic majority might be viewed as a complex collection of partial interests.[46] But these themes remained distinctly secondary.

Before turning to some brief remarks on the fate of philosophical radicalism as a reform movement, it is necessary to make a final point about the early utilitarians' attitudes toward political power. If the French and English shared a simple conception of representative government, their characterizations of the power of this government nevertheless differed profoundly. According to Bentham, for example, the only dangerous dimension of power was duration:

> When it is to the dimension of its [i.e., political power's] *duration* that the defalcating-knife is applied, no power so ample in its other two dimensions [extent and intensity] but may be conferred with comparative safety.[47]

He then turned to the problem of maximizing the efficiency of power.

The French, on the other hand, were preoccupied with the dangers inherent in the extent and intensity of political power. Thus Tracy warned that any authority, even a popularly elected one, that had the arbitrary power to order imprisonments, exile, or reparations, would become powerful enough to ignore all constitutional limits and to bypass the voters with impunity.[48] Despite his view that government must be one and indivisible, and that checks on government had been in the past mere bulwarks of privilege, Tracy insisted that governmental powers should be functionally separate and independent. Despite his opinion that legislators could not and ought not tie the hands of future generations, he urged that constitutional tampering be made difficult. And his *corps con-*

servateur was designed precisely to adjudicate disputes between organs of government seeking to expand their power. Finally, Daunou's *Essai sur les garanties* is a veritable *credo* in the power of precisely formulated constitutional limits.

The differences between the English and French views of power emerge clearly in the rationales given for the rejection of the traditional constitutional theory of checks and balances. Bentham scorned its inefficiency: "Know ye not, that in a machine of any kind, when forces *balance* each other the machine is at a stand?"[49] Tracy feared that an improper division of power would destabilize the government and encourage arbitrary power: checks and balances were either meaningless gimmickry, "or a real civil war."[50] One anticipated stasis, the other political revolution.

Tracy and Daunou quite agreed with Bentham and Mill that government was an evil in the sense that it was a necessary "cost" to society. But their vision was considerably more complex. The succession of failures in French political experiments left them with a permanent awareness of government as a potentially uncontrollable institution with a monopoly on violence. Thus they wrestled constantly with the problem of bridling power through constitutionalism and neutral procedures. Moreover, their epistemological skepticism intensified this tendency in their thought. If the link between knowledge and power was forever uncertain, they would—paradoxically—attempt to instantiate reason in institutions and in precise fundamental law.

Philosophic Radicalism and Reform

These qualms about the ability to control political power were quite foreign to Bentham and Mill, who saw their task as the reformation of a corrupt, but functioning, representative system. By the end of the eighteenth century there was a general consensus in England about Parliament's role in representing the national interest, although there was no corresponding agreement about how "interests" were to be translated into the "public interest." To the rising generation of the 1820s the utilitarian version of this process of translation had a growing appeal.

The decade of the 1820s in Britain has seemed a period of relative calm between the violent radical agitation of the postwar period and the turbulent years of Chartism. But this sense of calm is deceiving. Throughout the period, as the British attempted to find a new social equilibrium after twenty years of war, there was a growing sense of the urgent need for reform to accommodate manufacturing interests and to address the needs of the industrial towns. The generally unpopular government, sporadically resorting to harsh repression in the face of discontent, clung to power with the support of a spiritless opposition. Yet at first the proponents of reform seemed to be locked in a sterile debate that did not correspond to the needs of the postrevolutionary period.

The ideology of High Whig reformism, with its claims for the Whigs' historic role as the defenders of the people against the court, had a strange air of unreality. At the same time, what has been called the "generalized libertarian rhetoric" of the Tom Paine tradition also appeared increasingly strident and equally irrelevant.[51] Moreover, English radicalism had still to struggle continually against the hostility generated by its association with the French Revolution. Hence the appeal of a newer sort of Whiggism exemplified in the *Edinburgh Review,* a Whiggism less tied to the past and freer of doctrinaire politics. And hence also the appeal of utilitarianism, which offered an allegedly neutral and scientific standard with which to revitalize public life.

The self-styled Philosophic Radicals, largely under the tutelage of James Mill, launched a political movement to begin this radical revitalization.[52] The intellectual foundation for the attack was Mill's distinction between the sinister interests of the British aristocratic political elite and the general interests of the numerous classes (or the "people"). They sought annual parliaments, near universal suffrage, and the secret ballot, and their goal was to establish a new political party that would replace the Whigs (whose interests they believed to be indistinguishable from those of the Tories) as the primary opposition in Parliament.

Although the Philosophic Radicals enjoyed some successes (for example, their innovative campaign of press mobilization and pressure politics helped to ensure passage of the Reform Bill of 1832), their political program as a whole failed quite completely. They never forced the Whigs to rally to the Tories on the basis of shared aristocratic interests, and they never became a powerful force in the British Parliament. Furthermore, other middle-class reformers continued to prefer moderate measures, under Whig leadership, to radical or "organic" constitutional reform. The most serious blow to their program, however, undoubtedly came from the explicitly working-class-based activism of the Chartist and Anti-Corn Law Movements. The Chartists' fundamental antagonism to the middle classes threatened to shatter the faith in a theory of society that stressed the universal interests of all producers, a faith that was the *raison d'être* of the Philosophic Radicals' version of a Radical party.

It is easy to make an argument that the utilitarian concept of a unified "people" endured only so long as the working classes were subordinate to middle-class leadership.[53] It is certainly true that the theory was used in defense of reforms particularly desired by the middle ranks of society, and that the Philosophic Radicals opposed the rise of autonomous working-class organizations and came to fear and distrust them. But my examination of the utilitarian theory of democracy suggests that the theory was particularly vulnerable to the emergence of any new political cleavages in society. The perception of any division that challenged the centrality of the distinction between aristocracy and people would tend to make classic utilitarianism untenable as an ideology of democratic reform. In England, this ideology foundered largely on the deepening split between working and middle classes, although the Philosophic Radicals' bitter denunciations of their middle-class allies should not be totally ignored.[54] Indeed, in France it was largely the perception of critical distinctions within the middle classes that would doom "ideology" as an ideology of political reform.

The Philosophic Radicals' illusion of methodological certainty, their sweeping attack on the legal system, and their unswerving conviction that the key to reform lay in the redistribution of political power made their program temporarily attractive as a bludgeon in the fight for parliamentary reform. The precariously balanced vision of "ideology"—with its equivocal claims for social science, its exposure of the conflicting realms of reason and experience, and its ambivalence about political solutions—was more vulnerable. And it was to face the most severe of tests in the largely hostile atmosphere of Restoration France.

CHAPTER SIX
Diaspora and Dissolution

UNDER THE REGIME of the restored Bourbons, France embarked on her first extended trial of constitutional government. The Charter, though it affirmed that Louis XVIII ruled "by the grace of God," nevertheless represented a real compromise with the new France. It affirmed the civil rights of Frenchmen, guaranteed a certain amount of freedom of speech and press, and provided for an elected chamber of deputies. There was a great outpouring of political discussion in France during the Restoration, but the language and imperatives of politics had changed considerably since the revolutionary period.

It was soon apparent that any direct assault on the alliance of Church, aristocracy, and crown in the name of the principles of 1789 was unthinkable. Hence many liberals turned to history, heretofore the monopoly of Burkean conservatives, in order to defend the Revolution without undermining the basis of the present regime. Their central theme was sounded in Madame de Staël's *Considérations sur la Révolution française,* which argued that "liberty is ancient."[1] At the same time, liberals seized on the Charter as the definitive settlement of the Revolution. By supporting their own interpretations of the Charter, they could claim to be both the true royalists and the true conservatives, thus neatly turning the tables on their opponents.

There was also an unstated agreement among all but the ultraroyalists (who insisted with growing shrillness on the absolute and divine sovereignty of the Bourbon kings) to remove the issue of "rightful sovereignty" from political discourse. Many moderate royalists still believed that the king held his power from God, although they equivocated on his right to absolute use of this power. The preeminent Doctrinaires declared that "reason" was sovereign, to be exercised through a balance of powers under the directive force of the king. Benjamin Constant, who wished to avoid slippery metaphysical ground, tended to the view that there was no real sovereign power, but only "nature."[2] Daunou captured this mood very well in his observation that wherever one placed the power of "reconstituting" society, in France it was a scourge.[3]

The distinctions among Restoration liberals are not always clear because of the absence of organized parties, and because of the common perception that they needed to join together to preserve their interests against the emigré reaction. But two major groups are often distinguished: 1) the Doctrinaires, among whom the most important were Guizot, Royer-Collard, and Cousin, and 2) the parliamentary left, or Independents. The Independent left, as its name implies, included a particularly disparate collection of individuals. Benjamin Constant was an important force here, but the term also referred to the vaguely "republican" left associated with the names of Lafayette, Destutt de Tracy, Daunou, and Voyer d'Argenson and the various coteries of disciples that formed around them. It is the neglected intellectual milieu of this last group that I wish to chronicle in this chapter. I will argue that the perspective on society and politics developed by Say, Tracy, and Daunou during the Napoleonic period was crucial to the articulation of radical political dissent during the Restoration.

The depth of the continental aversion to any philosophic position associated with the chaos and disorder of the Revolution placed "ideology"—no matter how purged of its revolutionary taint—in an increasingly isolated position.[4] Nevertheless, precisely because the Idéologues were associated with both revolutionary liberalism and a "scientific" theory of society, they were eagerly taken up by the more dissatisfied members of the new generation that gained its first political awareness under the Restoration. In the works of younger economists and historians, in the reading circles and conspiratorial groups of the slowly reawakening republican movement, and finally, in the sects of new-born socialists, "ideology" helped to shape the passionately negative response to the new political and social orthodoxies of the Restoration.

During the early years of the Restoration, liberal pressure was focused most sharply on the issue of freedom of the press; therefore, when the Decazes ministry lifted the censorship in 1819, the hopes of the liberal party soared. Tracy's *Commentaire* and Daunou's *Essai sur les garanties* appeared in France in 1819, and were reprinted in 1822. Both of these works, but especially Tracy's *Commentaire,* which appeared in sixth and seventh editions in 1827 and 1828, gained a certain notoriety as handbooks of "advanced" liberal ideas. The wave of revolution that broke out in Europe in the early 1820s carried with it a flood of Italian, Spanish, and German translations of Tracy's works. Tracy's *Commentaire* also became the political handbook of the Russian Decembrist leader Pestel.[5]

The texts of "ideology" also passed into the new world. Keenly interested in the Latin American independence movements, Tracy had befriended Bernadino Rivadavia, an Argentinian diplomat who spent the years 1814–1818 in Europe attempting to raise support for the cause of Latin American revolutionaries. On his return to Argentina, Rivadavia (first as minister, then as president) attempted to realize many liberal reforms espoused by the Idéologues. With Bentham and Holbach, Tracy became extremely popular in Brazil and Argentina, while "ideology" became the official philosophy of the state schools in Bolivia in the 1820s and '30s.[6]

In France, many disciples of "ideology" remained prominent in the schools. J.B. Say lectured in political economy at the Athenée, a free academy founded in 1792. Andrieux taught grammar at the Ecole Polytechnique. Daunou lectured in history at the Collège de France. Laromiguière, a disciple of Tracy, who, like Maine de Biran, had revised "ideology" in a more spiritualist direction, held a chair in philosophy at the Sorbonne. His *Leçons de philosophie* went through five editions from 1815 to 1833.[7] Until 1824 Tracy's friend François Thurot also lectured in philosophy and history at the Sorbonne; he was then named to the Collège de France.[8] At the Sorbonne the lectures of Laromiguière and Thurot were perceived as the "classical" alternative to Cousin's new Eclecticism, which was rapidly winning converts among French youth.[9]

Tracy's salon was another important gathering place for sympathetic politicians, as well as writers and scientists. There revolutionary veterans like Lafayette (whose son had married one of Tracy's daughters in 1802), were joined by much younger men—Charles Dunoyer, Charles Comte, Ary Scheffer, Augustin Thierry, François de Corcelles, Victor Jacquemont, and Stendhal.[10]

The *Economistes*

In the *Censeur européen* (published from 1817 to 1819) and in separate works published in the 1820s, Dunoyer and Comte directly continued the ideas of the Idéologues.[11] Tracy followed the *Censeur européen* closely, and had protested the imprisonment of Dunoyer and Comte in August of 1817, offering bail for their release. Stendhal speaks of Dunoyer's "goggling admiration" for the liberal patriarchs in the Tracy salon, and of the "ultra-Liberal" Thierry brothers who had the privilege of conversing with Tracy for hours on end.[12]

The liberal writers of the *Censeur,* also called the *Economistes,* became the propagandists of a new society based on *industrialisme.* They energetically developed the idea that the practical sphere of production provided the conditions for the development of freedom. This attitude was clearly dominant in the Tracy salon.

> M. de Tracy said that the Church, war, and feudalism would find themselves eclipsed by modern administration; that industry would have its day and would become, if the general peace lasted long enough, the passion of the world. It would change the spirit of French society.[13]

What the works of Say, Tracy, and Daunou appeared to offer was a radical critique of the new Restoration coalition of throne and altar, without directly attacking either the government's origin or its legitimacy.[14] In an enthusiastic review of Tracy's *Commentaire* in 1818, Thierry argued that Tracy had provided a defense of "liberty without violence, as the specious doctrines of the last century led us to violence without liberty."[15] The works of the Idéologues were received as "luminous and entirely positive"[16] because they apparently successfully separated liberalism from its suspect revolutionary past.

In the *Censeur européen,* the notion of a spontaneously self-regulating society increasingly displaced politics as the proper subject matter of social science. Dunoyer wrote, "We shall repeat it a thousand times. Man's concern is not with government [which is] no more than a very secondary affair—we might say almost a minor thing. His goal is industry, labor, and the production of everything needed for his happiness. . . .

The height of perfection would be attained if all the world worked and no one governed." [17] Until the end of 1816, Augustin Thierry was Saint-Simon's secretary, and the two were engaged in publishing the journal, *l'Industrie,* whose point of view was virtually indistinguishable from that of Comte and Dunoyer. After breaking with Saint-Simon, Thierry joined the staff of the *Censeur.* Thus the editors of the two journals were friends, almost collaborators, and it is impossible to tell which deserves the credit for developing the notion of a nation of *industrieux* or *industriels.* [18]

The Economists never completely separated the idea of industrial society from representative government. Indeed, after Thierry, the most important collaborator on the *Censeur* was Daunou, whose *Essai sur les garanties* first appeared as a long article. [19] But they systematically neglected both philosophical and political questions. All existing disharmonies were attributed to feudal excrescences. Dunoyer and Comte saw themselves as embattled partisans of the new system; in their works the categories of *oisifs* and *industrieux* were transformed into a dichotomy representing the basic ideological conflict of the age: the parasitic remains of feudalism versus the productive classes.

Furthermore, through the school of the *Censeur,* the theories of the Idéologues began to be fused with some of the new strands of historical thinking. Charles Comte looked at European history from the beginnings of the city of Rome to the nineteenth century as a gradual unfolding of the true principles of industry. Augustin Thierry also approached history with the preconceptions of an Idéologue, desiring to follow Daunou's advice on the scientific study of history through "facts." Above all, he wanted to explore the struggle between idlers and workers—oppressors and oppressed—in its historical dimension. [20]

The theories of the Idéologues, then, helped to inform the militant economic liberalism that emerged in France in the 1820s. In the clandestine circles of student radicals, "ideology" encouraged a more direct sort of militancy.

"Idéologue" Conspirators

At the end of the Empire, the republican ideal appeared to be moribund in France. But soon a younger generation of students, often the sons or protegés of old republicans, took up the banner of *la république*. Indeed, throughout the Restoration the alliance between the very old and the very young was to symbolize the republican temper in French politics. The new radicals at first distinguished but little between republicanism and liberalism. For them, the republic represented a hazy ideal of a just government: virtuous, strong, and founded on the consent of the people.[21] But soon a more explicitly republican ideology was reborn in France.

Political radicalism first erupted in the many secret societies that flourished during the reign of Louis XVIII in that twilight era between criticism and conspiracy.[22] The *Mémoires* of Joseph Rey, a young Grenoblois who was involved for many years in the life of these societies, serve as one of the best primary sources on this early period. Rey had arrived in Paris in 1802 and sought the intellectual guidance of Destutt de Tracy, who became his patron.

> [Tracy] welcomed me with extreme generosity, with no other recommendation than my strong desire for instruction. From that moment he became a second father to me, not only in the intellectual sense, but also as regards everything that afterwards might constitute any sort of interest in my life.[23]

Through Tracy's intercession, Rey obtained an official position with the Ministry of Justice, and spent the last seven years of the Empire serving as magistrate in various annexed lands.

Unemployed after Waterloo, Rey began a new "career" as a conspirator. He founded the secret society, the *Union,* in Grenoble and then established related groups in Germany, Savoy, Switzerland, and Lyons. In Paris, he joined with Lafayette in founding the *Union parisienne.* The *Union* was to be a secret organization, but its goal (the spread of liberal ideas) was pacific, its methods legal, and its membership (for example, Victor Cousin) eminently respectable. However, in 1818 a portion of the membership adopted a more militantly republican position, partly in response to the Chamber's refusal to seat the "regicide" Gregoire, whose candidacy had been supported by the *Union.*

These *Union* members joined with other young radicals to form the *Amis de la verité,* an organization loosely tied to the Freemasons.[24] Led by the future Saint-Simonians Bazard and Buchez, the new group established a certain intellectual and organizational ascendancy over the student left. Bazard and his friends also called themselves the *Société diable-*

ment philosophique, a reference to their attempts to clarify the theoretical basis of their criticisms of the Bourbon regime.

In 1820 the *Amis de la verité* and the *Union* joined forces to combat the reaction that followed the assassination of the Duc de Berri. An uprising of students and certain elements of the army was planned for August 1820. The government discovered the plot, however, and began a wholesale prosecution of those involved. Many of the conspirators took refuge in Italy, where they were converted to Carbonarism. Joseph Rey was condemned to death, but escaped to exile in England.

In the 1820s both the *Union* and the *Amis de la verité* largely yielded to French Carbonarism, but lack of military support and internal dissension continually plagued the conspirators.[25] In 1822 there were several ill-planned and ill-timed military uprisings that occasioned bloody retaliations. By 1824 revolutionary Carbonarism too had succumbed to vigorous governmental repression.

A great many of those involved in the political activities of societies like the *Amis de la verité* and the Carbonari later emerged as leaders of socialist or republican dissent under the July Monarchy. Hence, some have claimed that this first wave of post-Revolutionary radicalism was largely inspired by Jacobin, or even by Babouviste ideals.[26] These claims appear to be unfounded and to distort the picture of emerging republican opinion in a fundamental way. The philosophical speculation that immediately preceded and followed the intense political activity of the Carbonari was, on the contrary, closely tied to the ideas of the Idéologues. The book most often cited as the conduit for the radicals' vaguely republican sentiments is Tracy's *Commentaire,* called by one historian "a veritable treatise of Restoration republicanism."[27]

The political orientation of the *Amis de la verité* appears to have been both republican and anti-Napoleonic, though these sentiments were rarely voiced in public.[28] Although all the philosophical currents that seemed to favor patriotic and liberal aspirations were represented in their discussions, the favored theorists were Rousseau, Kant, Tracy, and Bentham.[29] A *Déclaration des principes* was produced by the *Amis de la verité* around 1823 and gives some indication of the predominant concerns of the group. This document attempted to reconcile the strongest factions—the partisans of French "ideology" and the followers of German idealism—in a position that baptized itself *individualisme.*[30] The principal target of this document appears to have been Rousseau; i.e., the common ground of those who favored "ideology" and the Kantians excluded Rousseau, whom they interpreted as a theorist of centralization and dictatorship.

Certain features of the *Déclaration des principes,* e.g., its strong anticlerical tone and its advocacy of a utilitarian theory of law, indicate the dominant influence of the Idéologues and Bentham. Indeed, even the areas of compromise employ language more reminiscent of Cabanis and Tracy than of Kant. The main concern of the *individualistes,* whether "spiritualist" or "materialist," was to establish a scientific basis for rights. "Thus the principles of true morality must not be founded on opinions, whose form varies with the individual, but on bases that are firm and unassailable."[31] These bases were found in the laws of human organization. "Organization, either physical or moral, leads to faculties which, since they all desire satisfaction, resolve themselves into needs."[32] The phrase "moral organization" was probably an accommodation to the Kantians, but the list of needs that ought to have the character of rights in modern society appears to have come from Daunou. Daunou's influence, as well as that of Tracy, is also reflected in their conception of the function of legislation, which is seen as purely negative, as a *moyen de garantie.* Apparently the partisans of a Rousseauian view of the all-powerfulness of the general will were defeated by the majority, who maintained that the common interest was merely the sum of individual interests filtered through a series of express or tacit agreements made as human faculties developed in society.[33]

Despite the concentration on political conspiracies and projected coups, then, the first revival of radicalism in France after the Revolution was very ambivalent about the use of political power. This was largely the legacy of "ideology," as was the new radicals' desire to address the problem of social organization through a science of human intelligence based on the positive "facts" of human nature.

The decisive defeat of the Carbonari effectively brought an end to secret intrigues and aborted coups. Many of those involved in the plotting either entrenched themselves behind a liberal interpretation of the Charter, or turned more exclusively to theoretical studies. There was little further thought of insurrection until the turbulent months before the July days. But there was also little agreement on the bases and purposes of the liberal movement.

The nature of the link between "ideology" and political reform, and the peculiar problems that plagued French radicals in the late 1820s, are perhaps best illustrated by the early history of the *Tribune des départements,* a journal that was to become the fiery voice of the republican opposition to Louis Phillipe.

"Idéologue" Republican Reformers

By the end of the Restoration, republicanism was just slightly more respectable than it had been in 1814. The notion of a republic was usually praised only indirectly, as in the *Revue américaine,* a journal that appeared from 1826 to 1827 under the editorship of Armand Carrel, with the purpose of spreading information about the history and present governments of the American republics.[34] An article on the future of juries in South America shows how commonplace Tracy's and Daunou's distinction between national and special governments had become in the vaguely "republican" left. The *Commentaire* was clearly the basis of Charles Comte's distinction between those governments that owe their existence to an enlightened general will, place rights in the body of society, and depend on liberty, and those governments that owe their existence to conquest, exercise their power as though it were a right, and depend on slavery.[35]

In the final days of the Restoration, however, a more overtly "republican" current emerges in the press. The most important of these journals was the *Tribune des départements.* Funded by a group of businessmen, the *Tribune* was originally intended to preach fiscal restraint and decentralization; under the editorship of Auguste and Victorin Fabre and Armand Marrast, however, it became an organ for some younger followers of the Idéologues. Like the liberal writers of the *Censeur,* these republicans accepted the main themes of Idéologue social and political theory, but they too emphasized certain parts of the doctrine and deemphasized others to suit their purposes.

Victorin Fabre had developed an ardent admiration for the Idéologues and a permanent dislike for Napoleon upon his first visit to Paris in 1804. Returning to Paris during the Restoration, both Victorin Fabre and his brother Auguste became minor *hommes de lettres* with a firm belief in the philosophical and political correctness of "ideology." They edited a small literary journal and acquired some political experience in the liberal society *Aide-toi et le ciel t'aidera*.[36] When the increasingly intransigent government of Charles X broke with the Doctrinaires, the Fabres foresaw a crisis in which reason could "recover its empire."[37] They prepared for the fight in the *Tribune*.

The new journal soon distinguished itself from the other liberal journals by its running critique of the left in the Chamber. The feature article of the first issue was a critical attack on the constitutional opposition since 1815; the *Tribune* attributed the liberals' failure to their having heeded the salons rather than the interests of the masses. Indeed, the whole Restoration had been characterized by a contempt for the interests of nonvoting citizens. These charges were followed by an attack on the Martignac ministry.[38]

Although not explicitly republican, the *Tribune* argued that it was useless to attack the republican form of government. Soon several other vaguely republican papers appeared, each less important than the *Tribune,* but more strident.[39] The growing outspokenness of these militant papers frightened the *Tribune*'s backers, who withdrew their support in October of 1829. However, large contributions by Destutt de Tracy and Lafayette, as well as small amounts donated by students, allowed the journal to reappear in April of 1830.[40]

Auguste Fabre later stated the purpose of the *Tribune* to have been "to enlighten the French people gradually and prudently, about the hoax which had taken them in."[41] The French had a special government "adapted to the interests, prejudices, and vices of certain classes" that ought to be replaced by a national government "instituted for the needs and the progress of the whole society."[42] In 1833, Auguste Fabre published an account of a political program that would allegedly have been accepted by all the republicans in 1830, if victory had not been "snatched from their hands." Its proposals often sound the themes of the Idéologues. For example, Fabre argued that bizarre political slogans like *salut et fraternité* should always be avoided. Political language ought to leave figurative expressions to religion, and adopt only clear and precise terms, for linguistic corruptions confuse the understanding and may encourage a fevered emotional state in which the reasoning faculties are powerless.[43]

Fabre's *plan des républicains* called for a provisional government to convoke primary assemblies of all citizens to elect municipal magistrates and electors charged with creating a constituent assembly.[44] Any constitution would have to be ratified by the primary assemblies, but the "plan" strongly urged that the following be reflected in the new code: an independent jury system; complete liberty of the press; respect of existing property rights; abolition of much economic interference, especially taxes on beverages and salt; advancement in the army by election and democratization of the national guard;[45] strict separation of church and state; and official recognition of revolutionary patriots, the talented, and the great.

It is significant that this platform was published only after the Revolution of 1830. Of necessity, the *Tribune* had to be somewhat circumspect in its political pronouncements in 1829. Furthermore, there was at first only a tiny audience for republican ideas. Until the early days of the July monarchy, most of the common people tended to look on the constitutional liberals as their spokesmen. Even during the July Days, the republicans had little success in changing the street cries of "Vive la Chartre!" to "Vive la nation!"[46] Thus, the *Tribune* initially perceived its role as one of cautious education.

Moderate republicans like the Fabres were also constricted in their ability to define clearly a strategy of political reform by their relationships with other elements of the opposition. Throughout the 1820s, the prestige of Napoleon had been growing steadily, and Bonapartism was to provide the strongest single focus for popular resentment during the July Days.[47] Some of the military and patriotic themes sounded by the *Tribune,* especially the hatred of foreign domination and a call for expansion to national boundaries, appealed to the same sources of national pride as did Bonapartism. These themes were muted in the older generation of Idéologues who tended to stress schemes for international peace, but many of the younger radicals, including the Fabres, were openly hostile towards the "occupying powers." The *Tribune* remained bitter towards Napoleon, however, because of his suppression of civil liberties and his persecution of philosophy.[48]

The other important source of inspiration to the radical opposition was the growing legend of the Convention and of Robespierre. Most young republicans had little real knowledge of the First Republic. But Thiers had begun its rehabilitation in his *Histoire de la Révolution,* published in 1825. Danton especially appeared in a more favorable light.

Likewise, Robespierre emerged as a hero in the *Mémoires* of the *conventionnel* Levasseur, published by Achille Roche (1829–31) and in Laurent's *Réfutation de l'histoire de France de l'abbé Montgailard* (1828).

The *Tribune*'s editors were less hostile to this orientation, and even agreed on the need for a "glorious" foreign policy, democratization of the army, and abolition of certain taxes. Like many republicans, they thought that their success would have "caused the Machiavellian edifice of the Congress of Vienna to crumble" and would have touched off wars of liberation in Europe.[49] The Fabres, however, were haunted by the specter of the guillotine. They insisted that the Terror would be used to discredit republicans and all democratic reform, and that patriots who attempted to excuse terrorists were tragically mistaken. Nevertheless, the Fabres vacillated and extenuated. They held that some Jacobins were courageous, or that Jacobins suffered most under the royalist reaction, or that great patriotic accomplishments occurred under the Terror (although they were not *due* to the Terror), or even that the threat to France's independence had produced an emergency situation that called for "firmness."[50] Yet the Fabres insisted that the Terror represented an insane, hysterical version of firmness. To call oneself a neo-Montagnard was to become a dupe of the reactionaries. The Orleanists would see such views as insurmountable obstacles to the formation of a national party, while the Legitimists and Bonapartists would exploit this division gleefully in hopes that a coup would allow power to drop into their hands.[51]

These warnings seem to suggest that the Fabres wanted to build a broad coalition in favor of a liberal republic, and that they had some idea of the need to work out a *modus vivendi* with the dominant liberal opposition. In fact, if the first statement is true, the second is emphatically false. Not only did the Fabres have no sophisticated grasp of political tactics, but they continually displayed both moral and tactical inflexibility.

Auguste Fabre defined political "firmness" as selecting one's goal, and the proper means to that goal, and keeping to that program regardless of the passions that raged around or within. If a party (in "madness"), or the people (in "error") pretended that liberty could be reached by another route, one ought to repulse them or die in the attempt. One must above all avoid contamination: by fanatics, traitors, cowards, and the credulous.[52] And the most dangerous potential sources of contamination, according to the Fabres, were the influences of Eclecticism and romanticism, which they associated with the leadership of the constitutional opposition.

The Fabres' campaign against Eclectic philosophy and romantic literature was indeed more visible than their political program. This displacement of emphasis is understandable, not only because of their own biases, but because it was impossible to launch a program of public political agitation for their principles. Furthermore, it was proving very difficult even to formulate a joint political plan for the opposition without awakening slumbering antagonisms bequeathed by the Revolution. Nevertheless, the nature of the Fabres' attack on the Doctrinaires effectively isolated these moderate republicans from other liberal critics of the regime.

In the spring of 1830, for example, the liberal opposition was mustering a great effort to reelect the "221" deputies who had replied to a menacing royal speech with a vote of support for a constitutionalist interpretation of the Charter. The opposition wished to put pressure on the King with a show of liberal strength and solidarity in the parliamentary elections. The *Tribune,* however, urged the electors to vote only for true *patriots,* a term they preferred to *liberals.*[53] And, for the Fabres, *patriot* had philosophical and literary as well as political connotations. To understand the resonance of this use of *patriot,* we have to consider briefly the philosophical and aesthetic currents that were transforming French intellectual life during this period.

An often bitter rivalry divided the partisans of Tracy, Laromiguière, and Thurot from the new Eclecticism of Cousin and Royer-Collard, which borrowed elements both from German philosophy and from the Scottish school of Reid and Stewart. The technical issues involved were quite overshadowed by the emotion-laden charges of "spiritualist metaphysics" and "materialist atheism" that were hurled between the groups. This bitterness often carried over into politics, since the Eclectics tended to favor a carefully tempered constitutional monarchy, while the followers of "ideology" supported a more radical theory.

In 1824 the new journal *Le Globe* had appeared, directed primarily at the new generation that had come to maturity since 1815. At first largely an organ of independent (especially literary) criticism, the *Globe* soon became an effective organ for Guizot and Cousin.[54] In 1825 Jouffroy published a manifesto to French youth, "Comment les dogmes finissent," in which he announced that the new generation realized the emptiness of *all* the old doctrines, whether religious or revolutionary.[55] In May of the same year the *Globe* printed an article savagely attacking Tracy and *idéologie.*[56]

Cousin resumed his lectures at the Sorbonne in 1828. Although he assumed a respectful stance towards Tracy, he used the occasion of his first lecture to denounce the sensualism, materialism, and immoral atheism of the eighteenth century.[57] The publication of Broussais's *De l'irritation et de la folie* in the spring of 1828 further contributed to the polemic. Broussais's work was less a treatise on physiology than a declaration of war against Eclecticism.[58] Also in 1828, the Cousinist Jean Damiron published his *Essai sur l'histoire de la philosophie en France au dix-neuvième siècle,* which subjected Tracy's philosophy to merciless attack. The following year the ultra journal *Gazette de France,* worried over growing liberal opposition, printed a long and passionate attack on Tracy, accusing him of wishing to establish a rule of force and of ignoring spiritual liberty.[59]

The Idéologues felt themselves directly threatened and rallied to defend their philosophy.[60] In truth, "ideology" had continued to inspire a devoted following that repudiated the current developments in philosophy. Stendhal, for example, lauded Tracy and "ideology" in his articles for the British press. Stendhal insisted that Cabanis's *Rapports* and Tracy's *Elémens* and *Commentaire* were the foundation of all sound French education, despite official persecution.[61] Again and again, he upheld "ideology" against the so-called "dreams of Plato, Descartes, and the Germans" that were being rehabilitated by Jesuit mystics and the Eclectics.[62] François de Corcelles noted that even many in the new French historical school hesitated to disavow "ideology." "There is in our works a secret reluctance to disassociate ourselves from the philosophic school to which we owe the dignity of our new social regime."[63]

Related to the debate between Eclectics and Idéologues, although clearly a separate issue, was the antipathy between the "romanticists" and the "classicists." The romantic movement in France was at first largely identified with political reaction.[64] The liberals who published the *Constitutionnel,* as well as Idéologues like Tracy, Daunou, and Laromiguière, clearly preferred Voltaire to Chateaubriand for the former's style as well as for his opinions. In truth, style and substance were inextricably intertwined in the debate. When not seen as passionately unstable reactionaries, those sympathetic to romanticism (which was, in fact, increasingly favorable to the liberal cause) were mourned by some as misguided converts to obscure *sentiment,* and to a style that was *barbare* and *frénétique.*[65]

The editors of the *Tribune* deplored both Eclecticism and romanticism, which they portrayed as linked in a deadly conspiracy to poison French culture and to undermine the very foundations of a rational polity. The second issue of the *Tribune* carried a strong attack on Hugo and Dumas. Soon the theme was taken up again, and the editor did not refrain from criticizing the only other republican paper existing at the time, the *Jeune France.* "Without contesting the patriotism of many *new* citizens," the *Tribune* editor wrote, "the *Jeune France* ought to forbear scorning courageous patriots, i.e., those who prefer Racine to Shakespeare, Malherbe to M. Hugo, Voltaire to M. Nodier, and Condillac to M. Cousin."[66]

In three articles on Damiron, the editors attacked Cousinists as muddled, misguided, and fundamentally opposed to liberty and enlightenment. A review of Cousin's *Cours de philosophie* harshly criticized Cousin for slandering Tracy's work by calling it *sensualiste* in order to exploit the associations of *sensualité.* In an article repudiating the entire romantic movement, an editor noted that "politics, philosophy, literature, fine arts, everything must submit to the yoke of the conquerors."[67] Indeed, the pervasive theme of *Tribune* articles was that Doctrinaires, Eclectics, and romantics were anti-French—even traitors. They were speaking a new "patois of the invasion."[68]

These sharp divisions in the loose coalition of liberals and republicans who made up the opposition to Charles X were made manifest in the July Days. In January of 1830, many of the students who had helped to save the *Tribune* formed an armed association to prepare for the government coup that most political observers had been expecting from the very beginning of the Polignac ministry. They chose August Fabre as second in command and asked him to put them in touch with Lafayette, whom they named commander-in-chief. This association had a great many affiliated members (it was organized in *ventes* like the Carbonari) but never attained real power. It was Auguste Fabre, however, who gave the order on July 27, 1830, to begin tearing up the streets to form barricades.[69]

By the evening of July 29, Paris was in the hands of the insurgents, but it was at first unclear who would benefit from the victory in the streets.[70] A group of young republicans held the Hotel de Ville and hoped to make Lafayette the head of a provisional government, but they were easily outmaneuvered by the better-organized and more powerful Orleanists. When Lafayette acquiesced in the choice of Louis-Philippe as king of the French, the republican cause was lost.

Because the moderate republicans had been so strongly identified with Lafayette, his "capitulation" was especially damaging to their cause. Victorin Fabre died shortly after the Revolution of 1830. Melancholy over his brother's death, and politically disillusioned, Auguste soon retired as an editor of the *Tribune,* to be succeeded by Marrast and Sarrut. This change indicated the growing power of the "Robespierrist" republican faction. Marrast, an exuberant republican newly converted to the tactics of Jacobinism, mounted a furious assault on the government.[71]

Strengthened by disaffected liberals, the republicans regrouped as the most important opposition to the July Monarchy. By 1848, however, most of the republicans in France were admirers of a "Jacobinized" Rousseau or followers of Cousin, while others had embraced one of the various pantheistic creeds of the romantic age. Only much later, with the positivism of Gambetta and Ferry, did the scientific spirit of the Idéologues return to republican politics.[72]

The swiftness of the decline of a specifically "ideological" republicanism was undoubtedly due in part to its difficulties in finding common ground with other critics of the regime. The most resonant strands of resistance theory in France were Bonapartist or Jacobin, and the "neo-Idéologues" were loath to draw on either of these traditions because of their associations with either dictatorship or popular violence. They were also convinced, however, that the more successful defenses of liberalism of the Doctrinaires represented an opportunistic capitulation to the forces of privilege and reaction. The Fabres' fight with the Doctrinaires, a fight in which philosophical and literary differences were politicized, and in which politics had become the stuff of aesthetic debate, was in reality a struggle over the political and cultural definition of the French nation. This underlying rift inevitably made cooperation on common aims more difficult.

A more fundamental problem with the Fabres' use of "ideology" as a reform ideology, however, was their increasing difficulty in coping with a set of political actors who stubbornly refused to play their assigned roles. The premise behind social and political "ideology" was that factional struggle was a matter of intellectual myopia, that the universal interest, represented by the Idéologue program of economic and political reform, would be readily apparent if only society could be freed from the parasitic grip of anachronistic private interests. But there seemed to be few who would identify only with the universal interest and the (latent) general will. From their point of view, the middle classes, and especially its intellectual elite, whose interests so apparently coincided with the universal interest, had continually betrayed the forces of progress.

After the July Revolution, Auguste Fabre placed the greatest blame for the failure of the radical program on the ideological corruption of the bourgeoisie, which, he argued, had blindly confided the destiny of France to Doctrinaire intriguers.[73] His memoir on the Revolution makes it clear that the enlightened *classes aisées* were to be the dominant force in the new republic. The savagery of the Fabres' diatribe against Eclectic philosophy and romanticism can be explained only by their belief that these tendencies disqualified the bourgeoisie for political leadership in its partnership with *le peuple,* a term now often confined to artisans, workers, shopkeepers, and peasants.[74]

Fabre argued in 1833 that the essential parts of the republican program were the institution of a truly representative legislature and complete educational reform. But he treated the first only summarily; concentrating on a long reiteration of the dangers of the current trends in philosophy and art. Fabre noted that during the July Days the people had shown themselves more enlightened than the bourgeoisie by rejecting the politics and culture of the Doctrinaires. By their forebearance, and by their deference to middle-class leadership, the people had risen above the level of the masses of '89; unfortunately, the bourgeoisie had sunk below it.[75]

The people, then, appeared to represent an alternative to the bourgeoisie as the bearers of political reform. Fabre clearly believed, however, that they could shoulder this burden only temporarily. The alliance of the people with certain middle-class elements in the Revolution in fact offered a rare opportunity to the middle classes to take the lead in an age of regeneration based on real unity of interests.[76] The victory of the Doctrinaires indicated that this opportunity had been lost. And, since the middle classes were the most important conduit for enlightenment of the masses, what Fabre saw as the progressive corruption and elitism of the middle classes under the leadership of the Doctrinaires would necessarily have fatal consequences.[77]

Furthermore, Fabre became more and more disturbed by the direct "corruption" of the people by neo-Jacobinism and socialism. The immediate aim of many neo-Montagnards was to seize political control of Paris and to declare the Republic by force. But this would be to exchange "happy reform" for a "new barbarism."[78] Worse even than Jacobinism were those reformers who attacked property rights in a mistaken attempt to relieve the workers' misery. To refuse to accept inevitable inequality of fortunes was to deny the inevitable effects of civilization.[79] Fabre was discouraged by the spread of these socialist ideas not only among the working classes, but even among those he called "philosophic" republicans.[80] Indeed, many of the early followers of the Idéologues had turned away from their philosophy long before the period of working class activism in the early 1830s.

"Ideology" and Socialism

After 1830 the amalgam of industrialism and liberal democratic theory, and the battle to bring about the new age of *industrie et démocratie,* effectively collapsed.[81] The age of Louis-Philippe was one of growing political polarization between Jacobin social democrats and the conservative Doctrinaire liberals of the status quo. Insofar as it survived as a vision of social possibilities, the position of the Idéologues was transmuted into a variety of socialism. As "ideology" merged with socialism, however, it progressively lost its *political* program, thus indirectly contributing to the stark political confrontations of the mid-century. In the early Saint-Simonians, and in "individualist" socialists like Joseph Rey, the political legacy of "ideology" was largely forgotten.

From Individualisme *to Saint-Simon*

The youthful adherents of French Carbonarism had devoted themselves to the rather vague ideals of republicanism and liberalism as to an all-absorbing cause; the decisive shattering of their hopes for change, as well as the rapid disintegration of their organization, was a profound shock. The initial impulse of many ex-Carbonari to draw up a list of principles that could become the basis of a new phase of peaceful agitation was probably the reason behind the attempt to formulate a declaration of principles in the *Amis de la verité*. But many were not long content to acknowledge a short-term setback in an ongoing campaign. The most passionate and committed of the Carbonari, such as Buchez, Bazard, Duguid, and Leroux, soon began to doubt the aims of the war itself. Liberalism, and especially *individualisme,* must have failed not only because of deficiencies in practical organization, but also because of a radical defect in social theory. Hungry for a system, they scrutinized the bases of rational liberalism and began to explore those critics of liberalism who stressed the importance of a unified "organic" theory of society.[82]

At about this time two new members were introduced to the deliberations of the *Amis de la verité:* Olinde Rodrigues and Enfantin, disciples of Saint-Simon who were attempting to spread the ideas of their "master."[83] The ideas of Saint-Simon seemed to provide the disabused radicals with the sense of purpose and unity they had been seeking. The most influential of the young republicans were "converted," the journal *Le Producteur* was launched, and the phenomenon of Saint-Simonianism was born.[84]

Saint-Simon had been little concerned with some of the issues that passionately involved the Carbonari: the return of the Bourbons, military reverses in Spain, freedom of the press, or extension of suffrage. However, his claim to have found the key to the organization of industrial society in a positive science that would also serve a religious integrating function was enormously appealing. Saint-Simonianism filled a spiritual void; it became, according to Corcelle, a "nouvelle Charbonnerie."[85]

Saint-Simon's social science was congenial to the ex-Carbonari partly because Saint-Simon himself was in some ways an eccentric Idéologue.[86] The liberalism that they had learned from the Idéologues already slighted the political arena in favor of the laws of society. But now the Idéologue "republic of reason," with its popular base, representative institutions, and constitutional guarantees, appeared to the disillusioned radicals to be an admission—as indeed it was—that Idéologue science could not provide an ultimate "regulating" standard in social life. From Saint-Simon, the radicals learned that *individualisme* would always have to resort to "unnatural" coercion because it lacked the integrating *sentiment* that would supply true order and authority. Thus, it was futile to agitate for the individualist program of constitutional safeguards and democratic reform, or, indeed, to concern oneself with the conquest of political power. The new order would not depend on the traditional apparatus of public life at all, but on a proper identification with one's function in the "scientifically" organized society of the new organic age.

> If education attained what, according to us, should be its proper goal—if it prepared all men to contribute to social progress, each according to his passion, his intelligence, and his strength—then LEGISLATION [in its preventative character] would be pointless. [87]

The Saint-Simonians were surely turning away from the philosophy and politics of the Idéologues; yet this was not precisely a repudiation of a "bankrupt" approach.[88] For the Saint-Simonians of the *Producteur* and of the *Doctrine de Saint-Simon,* as for Saint-Simon himself, the Idéologues served a complex function as both a basis and a foil for a new version of social science.

Auguste Comte made one of the strongest attacks on the Idéologues' methodology. Tracy's exposure of an apparently unbridgeable gap between his rationalist presuppositions and the actual facts of social experience was used by Comte as incontrovertible evidence that the introspective method could not be the method of social science. According to Comte, Tracy's exact and discerning intelligence could be seen in the masterful critique of the vices associated with Condorcet's idea of social mathematics.[89] Tracy was a "metaphysician," but one who was "incontestably till now the closest to the positive state, and, moreover, one who always displayed an eminently progressive disposition and an admirable philosophical candor."[90] Even Tracy, however, was led radically astray by the persistence of the metaphysical in his approach. Thus, he could not make proper use of the principle that ideology was a part of zoology.[91] And his attempted deductions of the origins of property, wealth, and poverty by means of ideological analysis were patently contradictory.[92] "[In Tracy's work] metaphysics is radically discredited by a metaphysician who thought that he had escaped from it because he had the firm intention of doing so."[93]

If Comte saw the Idéologues as the last metaphysicians, others in the

Saint-Simonian school tended to see them as having made a more important break with the past. Thus Buchez could grant Cabanis the newly exalted status of a "synthetic" thinker: "This great man had generalized all previous studies, he had achieved an a priori work, a posteriori works necessarily had to come after him."[94]

In the *Producteur*'s stand on the debate between "ideology" and Eclecticism, the Saint-Simonians clearly displayed this ambivalence toward their erstwhile masters.[95] Laurent proclaimed the *Producteur*'s neutrality; its task was merely to remind the belligerent parties that social science ought not to concern itself with useless philosophical controversies whose answers would have little practical result. Laurent, however, was clearly more critical of Cousin's Eclecticism than of "ideology." After disclaiming any justifiable interest in the merits of *sensation transformée* beyond personal curiosity, he defended Tracy's position that the operation of the mind can be resolved into sensation. This view had advantages over "Platonic and Cartesian" psychology because of its precision, clarity, and accuracy. Furthermore, by making "ideology" a part of zoology, Tracy opened the way for the science of ideas to become positive.[96] Although the "Newto-Lockiste" school ought to be transcended, Cousin's philosophy was not transcendence but regression.

Buchez's series of articles "De la physiologie" also depicted the development of "ideology" as the critical departure from the conjectural past. Buchez, like Comte, wanted to explain the psychic by the physiological, thereby assuring the unity of physical and moral phenomena. In his historical sketch of the development of theoretical social science from the Greeks to the nineteenth century, he attributed to Cabanis and Tracy the most decisive advance since Locke.

> Cabanis and Destutt de Tracy, by relating apparent phenomena only to the sensory faculty—that is to say to the nervous system—established a basis for the doubt expressed by Locke in his essay. From that time forth, psychology disappeared; there remained only one science of man, physiology.[97]

For Buchez, it was the Idéologues who had established the scientific priorities of the new age.

> As for the science of intellectual and moral man, we have seen that, after having been divided by Catholicism into two branches, it was reunited into

a whole by the works of Cabanis and Destutt de Tracy. We conclude that these two men still preside over the research done today.[98]

Buchez had many of the same criticisms of the actual methodology of "ideology" as Comte; he insisted less, however, on the involuntarily metaphysical side of "ideological" analysis. Rather, Buchez argued that the tendency of both Cabanis and Tracy to see the mind and the human brain *en masse,* rather than to differentiate its coordinating functions, led to a disproportionate emphasis on the analysis of mental phenomena in isolation from the history of social interactions.[99] This criticism can be seen in his elaboration of Bichat's distinction between *vie organique* and *vie de relation.* Tracy had deduced the individual demands of *personnalité* from the priority of organic functions. Buchez agreed that the satisfaction of organic life is the root of industry, i.e., that man's *vie organique* indicated a general end for man, "that of modifying the environment to his advantage."[100] It was wrong, however, to try to deduce anything about man's economic and social life from the needs of organic life, conceived narrowly. All human acts were mediated through relational nervous impulses, and were thus social in implication. Buchez grew increasingly obsessed with the nature of the coordinating impulse behind man's "animal life."[101] Even during his most spiritual phase, however, Buchez did not surrender the opinion that human acts were necessarily determined by underlying physiological phenomena. Buchez called this process *logic;* extending Tracy's conception of a logic of the will to absorb the Saint-Simonian idea that human physiology yielded a tripartite series of activities: industrial, scientific, and emotional.[102] Buchez undoubtedly echoed Tracy's *Elémens* in his description of the "logic" of activities at the psychophysiological level.

> You will observe how need is converted into a desire by the discovery of its object or goal; then, you will find the rationale of the means necessary to achieve this goal, and finally, you will see the assemblage of organs that acts on the exterior world put into play, and the object assimilated by another organ, thus ending this sequence by satisfying the need.[103]

A similar perspective on the Idéologues emerged in Rouen's reviews of the works of Dunoyer and Comte, reviews that clearly announced the *Producteur*'s break with the "analytical" methodology of rational liberalism. Taking his argument from Auguste Comte's essays on positivism, Rouen asserted that:

> the most general idea of this system [liberalism] is the conception of individual man, of his needs and mental faculties as the unique bases of politics and as the principles that generate social laws.[104]

The attempted deduction of social laws from a psychological model, however, produced only excessively general notions because it avoided a direct study of social and historical activity.

Rouen criticized Dunoyer's conception of freedom as moral and industrial development by returning to Tracy's discussion of the generic sense of liberty. For Rouen, this discussion represented the point at which critical philosophy had reached the level of a truly general criticism, and had thus indicated the way to its own transcendence by "positive" notions. "In order to define liberty, one must first trace its history, then abstract the generic idea from all its varieties."[105] The most general idea of liberty was indeed negation, i.e., the notion of expressing one's will through the overcoming of obstacles. The proper conclusion to draw from this preliminary critique, however, was that liberty could be conceived only in opposition to something positive; it emerged in ages in which social forms were not in harmony with the needs of the population. Thus, liberty was a relative concept that could not be taken as an absolute normative end, or as a political goal.

Again, in the sphere of political economy, the Idéologues were regarded as having made a crucial reorientation in the theory of social science by recognizing the central role of the laws of material production resulting from the action of man on nature.[106] According to the then Saint-Simonian Adolphe Blanqui, only in the nineteenth century had the economic principles of the social body begun to be fixed, coordinated, and explained through rational analysis. As an example, he quoted from the "very remarkable" treatise of Destutt de Tracy—"commerce is the whole of society as labor is the whole of wealth"—while cautioning that this idea not be adopted in an absolute manner.[107]

The Saint-Simonians believed that the Idéologues and Economists had rightly placed the organization of industrial activity at the heart of social science, but that these writers had been seduced by faulty individualist premises into an overconfidence in current economic dogmas and a misguided suspicion of directive authority. One classic example of their errors was the defense of existing property and inheritance.

In the eighth session of the *Doctrine de Saint-Simon*, Bazard sought an answer to the following question: is there a theory of property that adequately justifies the transfer of property by birth in terms of the functional necessities of modern society? He then turned to an examination of the theories of Bentham and Tracy, and his criticisms of these two were fundamentally similar. Bentham's defense of property was based upon the prevention of the pains of disappointment, but he ignored the historical context in which property expectations were developed. Bentham, therefore, assumed that attitudes coincident with one level of historical activity were universal tendencies of human nature. Similarly, Tracy's justification of property through the etymological sense of *mine* and *thine* ignored the historical context of these words; thus, he would be unable to explain why one should no longer say *my* slave. Tracy's theory, however, as that of a positivistic philosopher, revealed its own insufficiency in a more pregnant fashion.[108] By defining property as the extension of the human will, and by recognizing in death the end of willing, Tracy implicitly denied inheritance. Furthermore, in spite of his explicit endorsement of the "naturalness" of inheritance, Tracy sensed this contradiction when he called inheritance a "worse" means of acquiring property than work.[109]

The passionate Saint-Simonian propaganda of the early 1830s was largely responsible for creating the notion of a monolithic system of liberalism that was to be transcended by an age of socialism. The Saint-Simonians, however, had found analytic philosophy, liberal economics, the morality of self-interest, and political democracy already combined in a "critical" form by the Idéologues and their followers. By changing the value signs on this system, by opposing it from a "higher" perspective, the Saint-Simonians helped to portray "ideology" as the first ideology in the modern sense.

It is perhaps important to note that most political radicals were not led to Saint-Simonian socialism by a reaction to the misery produced by the industrial revolution, or indeed, by any particular concern for the working classes. Both the social science of the Idéologues and that of Saint-Simon were predicated on the normative end of the greatest possible satisfaction of human needs, with a consequent bias towards the welfare of the "poorest and most numerous classes." In the five volumes of the *Producteur,* only two articles deal directly with the plight of the working classes, and these were probably based on reports of Joseph Rey on working conditions in England.[110] At that time, Rey had not yet detached himself from Idéologue orthodoxy. In truth, although most of those who called themselves *socialist* became progressively more interested in the evils suffered by the working classes under the competitive system, many utopian socialists stood aloof from the political organization of the working class, which was closely linked to resurgent political Jacobinism.[111]

Socialism Individualiste: *the Case of Joseph Rey*

Joseph Rey was both a sensitive barometer of socialist opinion in France and England and a good example of the transformation of "ideology" in the socialist speculation of the 1830s and 1840s. In his extensive writings, Rey commented on most of the important socialist thinkers in France and England, but always in an attempt to revise and complete Idéologue social science, without abandoning its original conceptions.[112]

When Rey began his political exile in 1821, he contacted Bentham, upon the recommendation of Lafayette. Bentham aided him financially and put his private library at Rey's disposal. While in England, Rey devoted much of his time to a comparative study of English and French legal institutions, a work which Bentham arranged to have translated into English.[113] But even as he wrote, he began to lose interest in the law as an instrument of social reform. He was growing increasingly aware of the evils attending industrialization, and became something of a disciple of Owen.[114] He also read Fourier's *Traité d'association domestique et agricole* and became acquainted with the Saint-Simonians through copies of the *Producteur* forwarded by Rodrigues. His gradual evolution away from political radicalism can be seen in the *Traité des principes généraux du droit et de la legislation* of 1828, revised and expanded as *Des bases de l'ordre social* in 1836, and, finally, recast as the *Théorie et pratique de la science sociale* in 1842. In these disorganized and rambling works, Rey transformed "idéologie" into his own peculiar version of utopian socialism.[115]

Rey retained all the basic tenets of "ideology": the sensationalistic the-

ory of mind based on pleasure/pain psychology, the morality of enlightened self-interest, the utilitarian theory of law (often supplemented
by Bentham), and, most important, the greatest happiness principle as
the goal of social science. In his method, and in his organization of the
subject matter of social science, Rey also followed Tracy closely. He first
analyzed the nature of man, then deduced general principles by placing
man in hypothetical social situations, and, finally, used this general
knowledge as the basis of a prescriptive theory of the laws of social happiness.[116]

Rey was certainly aware of the attacks made on this general conception
of social science, especially those of the Saint-Simonians, who criticized it
from the perspectives of both physiology and history. Consequently, in
Des bases, Rey added a preliminary section greatly expanding the account
of man's physical "organization."[117] His theoretical attitude toward this
material, however, was unchanged. Rey merely concluded that a legislator ought to take physiological and mental differences into account in his
attempt to maximize pleasure in its widest sense. Similarly, Rey carefully
considered the Saint-Simonian view of history, and even acknowledged
the theory of alternating critical and organic epochs. Nevertheless, his
view was fundamentally opposed to theirs. For Rey, history represented
the steady march of reason, with temporary reverses in times of ignorance and reaction. Social truth was not relative, but absolute; thus, in
Rey's view, social progress was not made because of the Middle Ages,
but despite them.[118]

If Rey was impervious to many of the methodological criticisms that
were leveled at "ideology" as social science, he was deeply troubled by
other aspects of the doctrine. In Rey's view, "ideology" had failed to live
up to its acknowledged normative end. He chided Tracy for this failure
only obliquely, but openly reproved theorists like Dunoyer, who had
insisted even more strongly on the distinction between "descriptive" and
"prescriptive" theory and on the dangers of moralistic exhortation.[119] Rey
correctly noted that, for the Idéologues, description and prescription were
never truly divorced. Indeed, according to Rey, their attempt to separate
"science" from "art" had been unfortunate in some ways, because it helped
to obscure the intimate connections (that is, the true chain of ideas) that
alone would have allowed men to discover the laws of social happiness.
Rey's critique of "ideology" had two major foci: 1) the role of the sym-

pathetic faculties in the individual and in society, and 2) the derivation of the laws regulating labor and the distribution of its fruits. If the positivists drew inspiration from "ideology's" empiricism and realism, Rey laid bare its implicit moralism.

The most disturbing charge against "ideology" was that the conjunction of an analytic or negative method with a perspective that stressed individual interests destroyed the *impulsion sympathique* necessary to any harmonic society. It was "dry," "egoistic," "unfeeling," "calculating," and "dessicated"—all devastating epithets in the romantic age. In answer to these charges, Rey reiterated the Idéologue position that pleasure involved expansion of all human power, including the faculties of sympathy and intellect. Rational self-interest was the opposite of exclusive egoism, because it necessarily entailed the development of sympathetic and intellectual pleasures, which required cooperation and harmony. Indeed, Rey argued that the affective pleasures (except for sex) were in a sense inexhaustible, because they increased indefinitely when shared.[120]

Rey's exposition insisted on the need for emotional satisfaction and sympathy in the new age "of love, of science, and of peaceful industry";[121] his distance from the other socialist schools on the role of love, however, is unmistakable. He noted that the "love" of the Christian socialists was based on an unnecessary hypothesis about first causes, whereas the Saint-Simonian notion that the social order was based upon a love for leaders and hierarchy and a common creed absorbed the individual in the mass, and was a mere "philosophical dream."[122] Rey resisted the idea that the social bond had anything to do with shared belief in ritual. Indeed, he remained devoted to absolute freedom of conscience and expression. The pleasure involved in the expansion of personality could come only through natural individual effort.

Rey commended Fourier for not confounding the individual with the social whole, but he found Fourier's *gamme passionelle* in its own way as problematical as the suggestions of Saint-Simon. Struck by the absurdity of the ascetic ideal, Fourier had gone to the other extreme and exalted the intensification of all the passions. He overemphasized purely material satisfactions, which could be corruptive, and relied too heavily on extravagantly external artifice, rather than on inner control, to maintain harmony.[123]

Rey, then, reiterated the Idéologue belief in the "naturally" sympathetic and rational individual. Nevertheless, he shared with the socialists the bitter condemnation of society as antagonistic, egoistic, and productive of misery. Unable to tolerate Tracy's pessimistic stoicism in the face of such evils, Rey sought the flaws in "ideological" reasoning.[124]

According to Rey, human reasoning goes astray whenever the *impulsion sympathique* is absent. When present, a judicious weighing of the sympathetic and material needs of personality leads to the moral law of the golden rule, which, in turn, leads to the principle of social equality. Rey sometimes called this enlightened self-interest working at a "synthetic" level, i.e., not occurring by analysis or calculation, but rather being suggested irresistibly to all men living in society.[125] Of course, this "synthesis" was also susceptible of analysis into parts. Rey elucidated the following "ideological" chain of ideas:

(1) Men are unequal in intelligence, passion, and energy.

(2) These men act so as to maximize their material and affective pleasures; therefore, the social state, which makes both of these kinds of pleasure possible, is the only imaginable social condition.

(3) All men equally have the right to expand their faculties as much as their natures allow and the end of society can only be the greatest possible satisfaction of the greatest number.

(4) However, *intérêt bien entendu* indicates that factual inequality does *not* rightly entail material inequality, for the following reasons. First, even a favored individual recognizes that chance could render him weak or disabled. Moreover, if men were to act as if they had an absolute right to develop their faculties, the stronger and more intelligent would usurp the greater part of all available resources. In effect, social inequalities would soon reflect inequalities *greater* than natural inequalities, because the life chances of some would be totally destroyed. The imbalance would weaken, even destroy, the sympathetic faculties among large portions of society, thus decreasing the affective pleasures of all. Hence, "there is *true equality* of legal protection only when each person is constantly aided and supported in the employment of his faculties."[126]

Rey, of course, had to explain the fact that society had followed the path of profound disequilibrium. He assumed that initially widespread ignorance led to carelessness about social organization. Then, intellectual progress occurred only among the rich elite, who were prevented from seeing their true interests by the atrophy of their sympathetic faculties.[127]

This general failure to perceive the utilitarian principles of organization was most pronounced in the current theories about economics. Even Destutt de Tracy had not truly looked at industrial society through the lens of the moral law; hence, he was led insensibly to accept the "naturalness" of an immoral system of distribution.

Like Tracy, Rey traced the origin of property to labor, i.e., to the fundamental tendency of movement to satisfy desire.

> If [man's] work incontestably belongs to him, it is because this work comes out of his own substance, bears the stamp of his personality, belongs to him in the same way that he belongs to himself.[128]

He noted, however, that Tracy had not realized the correct implications of this theory. Rey deduced from it the law of work, the law that labor is the only legitimate source of value and property, and that each producer ought to enjoy the fruits of his labor. "[A]ny possession not founded on this unique means of creating utility is not based on its true source."[129] Tracy had exploited the moral dimensions of the labor theory of value to condemn *les oisifs,* but his ostensible proof of the validity of the labor theory was that it provided the only intelligible measure of value. Rey, however, was convinced of its truth because it was consistent with the moral principle of equality.

> It is clear that, if it were not the quantity of labor that determined the value of things we no longer would exchange products on the basis of work, and it would then often happen that a few men, with little labor, would procure things that had cost their producers a great deal of fatigue, and as a consequence, the former would profit unjustly from the exertions of the latter. That would be exploitation of man by man.[130]

Thus, the law of work must be the fundamental law of distribution.

According to Rey, the moral law and the law of work, if applied absolutely, would guarantee optimum social happiness. With the abolition of classes, the primary source of social antagonism and disorder would vanish. Industry itself would become enormously more productive, easily supplying both necessary and useful articles to the entire population, especially since the jaded tastes fostered by excessive wealth would have disappeared. Society would be organized in regional communes, with common ownership of land and capital, distribution according to need, free education, and absolute personal freedom of speech and movement, and without government.[131]

Rey offered several detailed versions of this utopia. Yet he apparently never believed in its feasibility, but only in its attractiveness as a vision of human possibilities. *Théorie* was "scientifically" derived and absolute, but *pratique* was purely a matter of judgment and approximation.

In its final version, Rey's model is depicted as a pure utopia, unattainable because it would require not only universal education, but also absolute equality of intellect, passion, and energy. Having conceded its impossibility, however, Rey followed a bizarre procedure that he believed would answer his realistic critics. He progressively added imperfections to a theoretically perfect human being; based on these beings he projected six progressively less perfect societies.

His realistic goal was now what he called the "model social state" in which concessions were made to innate inequalities, but not to differences caused by faulty social organization. Since inequality implied inevitable disagreement on common policy, even a model society would need direction and leadership. In the economic realm, Rey advocated a mixed system of public and private ownership, with modified reliance on the profit motive. If all men could not be trusted to perform their economic tasks spontaneously, it would be better to rely on selfish interests as incentives than to introduce state coercion into the workplace.[132]

Rey also reintroduced positive law and, consequently, politics into the model state. With differences of opinion and passion, there would be the ever present possibility that those most gifted would begin to usurp resources. The safest guarantee of the general interest, then, would be representative democracy, with universal suffrage, and short terms in office. Under conditions of free debate and universal education in an almost classless state, the majority decision would be most likely to reflect the general interest, since the few antagonistic private interests would be canceled out. Such a system would also lessen the pain associated with direction from without, thus encouraging harmony.

Rey, then, retained the standard utilitarian and Idéologue position that rational self-interest and the greatest good of the greatest number were identical. Since political power had to be exercised in a less-than-perfect world, political democracy would lessen the chance that misperceptions of self-interest would become the ruling elements in the community, because it would provide a multiplicity of political actors. The issue of political rights, however, was clearly not a part of theory, but only of relative practice. And in Rey's view, the corruption of a society shot through with antagonisms made any excursion into practical politics highly dangerous.

As Rey depicted the successive corruptions of his ideal society, he generated an excessively mechanical triadic theory of class divisions (the "superior," "middle," and "inferior" classes), based on the hypothetical share of "original" capital retained by each family.[133] In his model state, differences between the extremes were slight, and the inferior class was hardly distinguishable from the middle class; however, as the middle class began to shrink, differences in consumption became more pronounced, bringing in their wake wholly different manners and tastes. Eventually, individuals of the inferior class had no space left in which to expand their personalities. Rey pictured them as stunted creatures, ground down by unremitting labor and toiling to support their oppressors. This, he thought, was the picture of his own society.

The proletarians clearly could not take advantage of such educational opportunities as were available; even had they developed their *rational* faculties to the fullest, however, Rey assumed that only the middle class could be fully trusted to see that the moral law and the law of work were in everyone's long-term interest. The sympathies of this class were not warped by excessive vanity or by hopeless envy, and its perceptions of immediate self-interest did not fundamentally contradict the long-term interest of society as a whole.

Therefore, Rey advocated universal suffrage only when the middle class was in the majority. For example, in the "secondary" social state, in which Rey assumed the middle class to be about half of the population, universal suffrage was feasible. But in the transitional social state in which the middle class dropped to about one-third and the lower class rose to over half, universal suffrage would assure the predominance of short-sighted passion. Rey then suggested weighted voting to give the middle class control of the government, to the detriment of the other classes.[134] Clearly, however, this situation would be highly unstable. In the actual state of France, Rey assumed that the ratio of superior to middle to inferior classes was approximately 1:1:17, with both the middle and inferior classes excluded from the suffrage.[135] If weighted voting was offered half-heartedly as an expedient in the transitional state, it was obviously completely impractical in a state with such a tiny middle class. Rey could only suggest the institution of juries to judge intellectual capacity for the suffrage, with the extension of a civil diploma to the qualified.

According to Rey, among the most important intervening steps between contemporary French society and the next stage of improvement were a progressive income tax, some social insurance against unemployment, and the establishment of a central bank. Given his assumptions about democracy, however, he could hardly rely on political mobilization of the working-class majority to achieve these limited reforms. Universal suffrage would merely bring ignorance and ungoverned passion to power. Rey feared that private property, which was a necessary condition of social happiness (albeit in a severely modified and regulated form) would be endangered. Furthermore, since the poor had real moral grievances, they could hardly be expected to refrain from violence if they met with opposition to their demands. Social violence, however, would further rend the already weakened fabric of social sympathies.

Rey, therefore, saw only two safe avenues of social activism: propaganda for complete freedom of information and universal education, and the launching of communal experiments that would encourage sympathy among classes.

> If, in the midst of this general confusion, you link men together, if you propose to them the attainment of a common purpose, you evidently draw men out of their isolation in that respect, you put an end, in part, to their antagonism; and you replace all these elements of disorder by a common sentiment, by a harmonious bond.[136]

For Rey, the route to socialism was through the gradual spread of voluntary socialist experiments. He remained interested in Owen's efforts, and was greatly attracted to certain aspects of Fourierism, which became influential in the late 1830s and early 1840s under the leadership of Victor Considérant, who was committed to the launching of experimental *phalanstères*.

Rey was never comfortable with the opinion that the political system made no difference to the progress of socialism. But his model of democracy was apparently useless as a guide to responsible practical action. In his theory, the rationalist assumptions of the Idéologue political tradition pass into utopia.

After the preternatural quiet of the Empire, the era of constitutional monarchy was a period of stormy verbal controversy: social, literary, and political. This chapter has argued that—in the school of the *Economistes,* in the revolutionary *ventes* of the Carbonari, in the republican agitation preceding the Revolution of 1830, and among disabused radicals who turned to socialism—the Idéologue theory of politics and society shaped the emerging contours of radicalism. Among all these groups (sometimes involving the same people either simultaneously or successively), there was an initial enthusiastic acceptance of the notion of a third level of civilization that would correspond to the scientific realities of man's nature and needs. A future, truly enlightened, representative system would transcend existing antagonisms that had an unnatural basis in misguided interests.

The school of the *Censeur* championed the laws of social production in society as the basis of the unity of all *industrieux;* this perspective provided an obvious rationale for a rejection of the Restoration alliance of throne and altar, whose pretensions seemed to contemporaries so at odds with the notion of a society based on *commerce.* As the chasm between the sweeping Idéologue claims for a normative social science and the realities of industrialization deepened, however, these thinkers retreated behind the necessity of the invariable laws of economics. It has been said that Comte and Dunoyer were, after all, "only economists." [137]

Moderate republicans like the Fabres hoped to bring about a "democracy of enlightened reason" by replacing the special government of the Restoration with a national republic under the tutelage of a middle class educated by "ideology" to see and act on the general interest. Yet their hopes appeared to dissolve as the middle classes, who in their view were corrupted by obscurantist philosophy and literary barbarism, failed to meet the challenge of leadership, and as the people consequently fell helplessly into error.

Finally, the young radicals of the *Amis de la verité* and the Carbonari, who initially had been inspired by the hopeful messianism implicit in "ideology's" invocation of a rational and harmonious society that needed only to be liberated from the yoke of reactionary political elements, rejected *individualisme* in the wake of the debacle of their revolutionary hopes. They criticized "ideology's" scientific pretensions and questioned its moral adequacy, using Tracy's own exposure of ambivalences and disjunctions as evidence for the prosecution. But, even as many radicals were absorbed into socialist movements, they often transmuted, rather than abandoned, the underlying themes of "ideology."

The assumptions behind Tracy's theory of society as the sum of rational individual *commerce* were challenged successfully, and "ideology" in its original form went into eclipse. With this eclipse, however, the vision of a society at once learned, liberal, and democratic tended to fade from French politics. The Idéologues had hoped to create a new republican spirit, composed of industry, rational simplicity, liberty, and love of peace and toleration.[138] They failed not least because they faced the problem of creating an "ethos" of republicanism quite ill-equipped to solve it. The rapid fractionalization of "ideology" reflected not only the inhospitable historical climate, but also the competing tendencies and ambiguities within the thought of the Idéologues themselves. Nevertheless, the passing of *idéologie*, which had at least aspired to create a neutral space in which parties and classes could come to agreement, had its unfortunate aspects. Its passing foreshadowed the increasing suspicion, intransigence, and divisiveness of French politics in the mid-nineteenth century. The significance of the end of "ideology" is perhaps best expressed in the telling comments of Guizot and Sainte-Beuve. Guizot replaced Tracy at the Académie française in 1836. In his maiden speech he argued that "ideology" had not recognized that men were evil, that they needed religion, and that the sovereignty of numbers was a rash illusion.[139] And in 1868 Sainte-Beuve was moved to remark, as he contemplated the proceedings of the Imperial Senate, "what a distance we have come from M. de Tracy."[140]

Conclusion

I N THIS ESSAY I have attempted to answer two related questions. In what way did the Idéologues' vision of society and politics define the message of revolutionary liberalism for postrevolutionary France? And what was the significance of their having expressed this message in the language of utilitarianism? Let me briefly address these questions again.

What seems to me most important about Idéologue liberalism is the extent to which it must be understood in the context of political and constitutional crisis, and the way in which it illuminates the nature of the nineteenth-century commitment to constitutionalism. The Idéologues re-acted to the French failure to establish effective liberal government with a repudiation of the figurative, the symbolic, and the flamboyant aspects of revolutionary speech. It is hard to overestimate—but easy to miscon-strue—the distaste the moderates felt for the "commotion" of revolu-tionary politics. In their view, zealous rhetoric had stimulated atavistic passions, encouraged a surrender to the dictates of short-sighted interests and permitted the evil flowering of monstrous ambitions. But if one in-terprets this disenchantment as an "intensifying elitism" and an "exclu-sion of the political," it is difficult to make sense either of the way the Idéologues were understood by the postrevolutionary generation or of their own preoccupation with the institutions of public liberty.[1]

The real counterpart of their recoil from the rhetoric of "sentimental liberalism" was an attraction to the elements in their intellectual milieu that seemed to offer the promise of solidity and stability: the claims to an empirical basis for knowledge and the defense of the rule of law, individual rights, and representative institutions on utilitarian grounds. There was a new effort, then, to reorganize their social and political theory around these elements. This new determination to remain close to the immediate data of the senses, the facts of experience, and the practical needs of man did not entail a rejection of the assumptions on which the epistemology, the economic thought, or the politics of the "philosophical party" rested. But it did introduce a number of obvious contradictions that would be resolved by succeeding generations in very different directions. I have argued that the Idéologues helped to transform the universe of political discourse in France, but that their new synthesis was ultimately unstable; *idéologie* fell victim to its own internal incoherencies as well as to concerted outside attacks.

Cabanis's closer attention to physiology, for example, undermined the existing scientific basis for liberty and equality, and ipso facto exposed the Idéologues' own faith in these ideals to the charge of ungrounded utopianism. Tracy's inability to distinguish between the true and false evidence of the senses apparently branded his own economic and political views as mere opinion. Nevertheless, perhaps to overcome his own doubts, and certainly to console himself in political defeat, Tracy's claims for his "logic of the will and its effects" became more sweeping. If his conception of reality bore little relation to his time, it would nonetheless be vindicated triumphantly in the future. A new civilization would be marked by patterns of individual activity close to the lucid logic of the will.

What in fact lay at the heart of Tracy's logic of willing was a model of society that had been implicit in the works of many of the Idéologues' eighteenth-century progenitors, but that was made explicit in the works of writers like Say, Daunou, and especially Tracy himself. No longer expressed in the language of natural right, this economic model of society clearly revealed the assumptions about the utility and rationality of social cooperation made by such theorists as Turgot, Condorcet, and Sieyès. Inequality of rights was inefficient because the resulting insecurity prevented some people from entering the productive process and thus reduced the total amount of social happiness. Since government was to be justified only by its utility, it ought above all to promote equal security and economic freedoms. And, finally, monopolies and corporate privileges directly and indirectly menaced civil equality and were, consequently, disutilitarian. Thus, the greatest possible happiness of the human species (seen most concretely in the production of material goods) was paralleled by a series of individual gains that would occur "naturally" if individuals were given basic assurances of security.

Natural rights theorists had insisted on the claims for legal protection that an individual could legitimately make on society. These claims were now defended on the safer ground of their utility. But the moral dimension of the individual right to pleasure remained; it emerged clearly in Tracy's "ideological" definitions of right, labor, property, liberty, and happiness. To the extent that Tracy could not successfully integrate these assumptions about the increase in individual happiness into his analysis of contemporary society, he exposed the difficulty at the very marrow of utilitarian "social science." Its assumption of a coincidence of interests was fundamentally at odds with the developing social and political antagonisms of the early nineteenth century.

The Idéologues' own belief in what Tracy termed the "logic of the will" was not undermined by the doubtful applications of "ideology." Indeed, they had developed this side of the revolutionary legacy precisely because it seemed to make sense out of their understanding of the Revolution, and because it provided a polemical weapon against the newly emerging ideology of conservatism. Their view of society as *commerce* allowed them to begin to connect existing theories of the stages of civil society more explicitly to corresponding political "types," thereby justifying the necessity of the civil reforms of the Revolution. And it led them to state a rationale for democratic reform based almost solely on the need to neutralize perceived threats to the bases of society as *commerce*. Tracy and Daunou thought that this program of reform—justified in terms of utility rather than rights—could provide progress without disorder. But the notion of "happiness" would prove to be as explosive as, and perhaps more unmanageable than, any appeal to the natural rights of man.

The initial effect of "ideology" in France was to give younger followers a sense of liberation from existing politics, without invoking the forbidden *formule sacramentelle* of revolution. The neglect of the compromising language of political principle, the stress on the essential modernity and promise of postrevolutionary society, and the identification of the Restoration political elite with those who were impeding the emergence of the "French era" in world history would characterize the rebirth of radicalism in France. The Idéologues' commitment to liberal constitutionalism, then, did not survive the active political involvement of its disciples, who were rapidly transformed into revolutionary republicans, socialists, economists, physiologists, positivists, or merely disillusioned optimists, rather than "ideologists."

Perhaps the animal least likely to be found in France after 1830 was the liberal "ideological" democrat. Democratic reform had appeared to republicans like the Fabres to be the fundamental answer to the "hoax" that had been perpetrated on the French public, but soon the prescription seemed not to fit the disease. The Fabres transformed the Idéologues' hopes for a public life based on reason into an obsession with "true philosophy," an obsession that made cooperation with other liberals virtually impossible, and that encouraged a fatal blindness to important currents in the "new France." French society, with its enthusiasms for idealism, romanticism, religion, and new forms of egoism, appeared to them to be exhibiting tendencies toward the grotesque that left them bereft of their moorings. This disorientation was perhaps the most striking anticipation of the plight of the modern ideologue whose faith in reality is mocked by events.

I have argued that the social and political philosophy of British utilitarianism—and the movement it inspired—can be understood as occasioned by a similar impatience and weariness with existing political rhetoric, in conjunction with a similar displacement of attention to the conditions necessary for the operation of a society based on exchange. These conditions—in the economy and in civil society generally—included closer attention to the sanctions that would ensure that the rational course of action would become the basis of individual action, but the expectation was that interests would be identified at once "naturally" and "artificially."

The democratic politics of the Philosophic Radicals, like those of the Idéologues' followers during the Restoration, were designed to meet a situation in which there was thought to be only one politically significant threat to the emergence of this rationalized polity: that of the unenlightened aristocracy. The acceleration of economic class formation in England soon made this analysis obsolete. If utilitarianism had appealed originally because of its apparent ability to transcend the rhetoric of party, it rapidly lost this appeal as the lines between middle-class and working-class radicals hardened into barricades.

My discussion of philosophic radicalism as part of a broad intellectual shift toward utilitarian argument within liberalism tends to support those interpretations which have stressed the importance of its intellectual continuity with the Enlightenment. The Philosophic Radicals were inspired, I have argued, by a notion of the public good first articulated in a preindustrial world. If one takes their expressed belief in this conception seriously, and there seems to be no reason to doubt it from their actions, it helps to explain why neither the standard liberal view of them (as the successful modernizers of British law and institutions in the nineteenth century) or the Marxist view (as geniuses of bourgeois ignorance) fits the facts.[2] Like the followers of the Idéologues, the Philosophic Radicals seem to have been ineffectual as reformers at least partly because they suffered from collective illusions at odds not only with the temper of the age, but with the emerging realities of economic and political life.[3]

A second conclusion that emerges from considering philosophic radicalism as a variant of classical utilitarianism, rather than as its type, is the peculiarity of its pretensions to certainty. An irrepressible sense of self-confidence is often taken as a characteristic feature of classical utilitarianism, and is usually explained by referring to its roots in sensationalist and associationist psychology, a psychology purged of Locke's anxieties about the activity of "reflexion." It has been said that utilitarianism "is essentially the drawing-out of the practical implications of the empiricists' analysis of human nature and the human mind."[4] I have suggested, however, that Bentham's and Mill's use of psychology, like that of the Idéologues, was not essential to their social philosophy. Their passion for the data of sensory pleasures and pains and the use of these data as talismans to ward off obscure philosophical fictions resembled the Idéologues' insistence on the positive evidence of the senses. Although there were certainly differences in emphasis and style, both the French and the English hoped that the scientific authority of psychology would provide a standard of judgment in a world in which people disagreed "about everything which has a name."[5] But they could not convincingly demonstrate the link between empiricist psychology and their prescriptive judgments.

If Bentham and Mill turned to sensationalist psychology for a sense of certainty, there is no intrinsic reason why they should have found it. A similar project led Tracy, for example, to skepticism and an incipient critique of his own methodology. In fact, the belief in a rationalized ego that would act according to the dictates of utility based on universal experience, was particularly vulnerable to new doubts about the methodological status of experience. Comte's attack on naturalistic psychology, an attack which seemed to John Stuart Mill so persuasive as a critique of his own Benthamite heritage, was partially developed in response to the problematical issues presented by *idéologie*.[6]

The reasons for Bentham's and Mill's convictions of methodological certainty are undoubtedly much too complex to be explored here. But two preliminary suggestions can be made. First, the associationist tradition in England—with the significant exception of Hume—was informed by a deeply religious sense of nature's intentions. Condillac's religious references could easily be read as irrelevant to his philosophy, but David Hartley's *Observations on Man* (which was an important source for both Bentham and Mill) displayed an unshakeable confidence that the association of ideas carried out "the benevolent designs of him who is *all in all*."[7] In many ways, the utilitarians took over the religious conviction without the deity. Second, and more important, neither Bentham nor Mill focused seriously on epistemological questions. For them, questions about the bases of knowledge were almost always secondary to the intense practical motives with which they approached the study of psychology. Among the Idéologues, on the other hand, these questions were fundamental. And their inability to find satisfactory answers had significant implications for their conception of the political.

What is often seen to be central to the Idéologue position—and I have insisted on it in this essay as well—is their polemical tendency to deflate the pretensions of politics, to view public life instrumentally, as a means of assuring private happiness.[8] Their concern to find the laws governing social rather than political phenomena, as well as their predictions of a transcendence of irrationality in the future, apparently illustrate what has been called the nineteenth century's inexorable "sublimation of politics."[9] But what is less noticed is their equally strong tendency to represent the abstractions of "reason" in the concrete apparatus of the constitutional state.

Tracy and Daunou remained committed to restraints on the use of power, to inviolable safeguards for rights, to legal procedures for apportioning authority, and to regular processes for calling officials to account. Sheldon Wolin has argued that one should see these basic elements of modern constitutionalism as variants of the organizational, scientific, and technocratic tendencies of the age.

> Constitutionalists have been especially susceptible to the lures of scientific method because of an assumption that a constitutional system provides a field of phenomena, so to speak, which is uniquely receptive to scientific methods.[10]

But my reading of the Idéologues, who can plausibly be credited with having advanced all of these tendencies in western culture, suggests that their constitutionalism was not simply an application of their scientism, but a compensation for their realization of the limits of science. It was precisely because the phenomena ordered by a constitutional system were unreceptive to scientific methods that one needed to establish human rules to produce agreement. This point of view may not be the "art of politics" in Wolin's sense, but I would argue that it was and is a large part of any recognizably liberal politics. The real division between the Idéologues and some of their followers, then, was the latters' abandonment of the commitment to constitutionalism as the imperfect instantiation of reason in an irrational world.

NOTES

INTRODUCTION

1. See Michel Foucault, *Les mots et les choses: une archéologie des sciences humaines* (Paris: Gallimard, 1966), pp. 13-16, 249-56.

2. Sergio Moravia's works now provide the most comprehensive history of this period in France. See *Il tramonto dell'Illuminismo: Filosofia e politica nella società francese (1770-1810)* (Bari: Laterza, 1968) and *Il pensiero degli Idéologues: scienza e filosofia in Francia (1780-1815)* (Florence: La Nuova Italia, 1974). Overviews of the period can also be found in George Gusdorf, *Les sciences humaines et la pensée occidentale*, vol. 8, *La conscience révolutionnaire: les Idéologues* (Paris: Payot, 1978) and in Thomas Kaiser, "The Idéologues: From Enlightenment to Positivism" (Ph.D. dissertation, Harvard University, 1976).

The fragmentary published information concerning the life and intellectual development of Destutt de Tracy has been superseded by a recent intellectual biography of Tracy that relies heavily on unpublished archival materials. See Emmet Kennedy, *A Philosophe in the Age of Revolution: Destutt de Tracy and the Origins of "Ideology"* (Philadelphia: The American Philosophical Society, 1978). There is also a recent study of Tracy's social and political thought in English by B.G. Garnham, "The Social, Moral, and Political Thought of Destutt de Tracy" (Ph.D. dissertation, University of Durham, 1974). Garnham's study is premised on a view of Tracy directly opposed to the one I am urging here; Garnham argues that Tracy was relatively isolated from his historical milieu, and that his work was unified and deductive, if not always consistent. More useful is Pierre Henri Imbert, *Destutt de Tracy: Critique de Montesquieu, de la liberté en matière politique* (Paris: A. G. Nizet, 1974), although this study is limited to Tracy's *Commentaire sur l'Esprit des lois de Montesquieu*. On Condorcet, see Keith Michael Baker, *Condorcet: From Natural Philosophy to Social Mathematics* (Chicago: University of Chicago Press, 1975). On Cabanis, see Martin Staum, *Cabanis: Enlightenment and Medical Philosophy in the French Revolution* (Princeton: Princeton University Press, 1980). There have also been relatively recent monographs on Roederer, J. B. Say, and Maine de Biran.

3. George Burdeau notes that three names are attached to the transmission of the revolutionary legacy: Destutt de Tracy, Daunou, and Madame de Staël. *Traité*

de science politique (Paris: R. Pichon & R. Durand-Auziat, 1971), 6:194. Madame de Staël, however, has received much more critical attention. M. Girard, *Le libéralisme en France de 1814 à 1848: doctrine et mouvement* (Paris: Centre de Documentation Universitaire, 1966), pp. 65–120, also discusses Tracy and Daunou together as a separate category. Sergio Moravia has called attention to the need to study the relationship between the thought of the Idéologues—in particular that of Say, Daunou, and Tracy—and the beginnings of nineteenth-century liberalism and constitutionalism. See Moravia, "Les idéologues et l'âge des Lumières," *Studies on Voltaire and the Eighteenth Century* 154 (1976):1473. This is essentially what I have attempted.

4. In general, the analogy between English utilitarians and Idéologues has gone unremarked except in passing references. See, e.g., Gusdorf, *La conscience révolutionnaire,* pp. 545–546. But see a book of readings on French liberalism that translates small selections from Tracy and Daunou as an example of "utilitarian liberalism" under the Restoration: William Simon, ed., *French Liberalism 1789–1848* (New York: John Wiley, 1972).

5. See, for example, John Plamenatz, *The English Utilitarians* (Oxford: Basil Blackwell, 1966), p. 2.

6. The view that utilitarianism was the quintessential bourgeois philosophy was of course stated by Marx; one modern restatement can be found in George Lichtheim, *A Short History of Socialism* (New York: Praeger, 1970), pp. 12–15. Lichtheim also argued that utilitarianism was an extrapolation from a unique set of British experiences. For an attempt to explain why utilitarianism was not successfully transplanted to the United States, which had a thoroughly bourgeois civilization, see P. A. Palmer, "Benthamism in England and America," *American Political Science Review* 35 (1941):855–71.

7. See below, p. 241n22.

CHAPTER ONE: THE REVOLUTIONARY LEGACY

1. The term *parti philosophique* is used by Moravia, *Il tramonto,* p. 7 and passim, to refer to the Auteuil circle. It was probably first used during the Directory to refer to the group of moderate republicans in the *Institut national.*

2. Antoine Guillois, *Le salon de Madame Helvétius: Cabanis et les idéologues* (Paris: Calmann Levy, 1894), p. 76, notes that there were three daily meeting places for this group: Mirabeau's in the morning, the Assembly during the day, and the salon of Madame Helvétius in the evening. Condorcet, Sieyès, Tracy, Cabanis, and Chénier are listed among the members of the Society of 1789, originally an alliance of public figures and commercial interests dedicated to extending knowledge of *"l'art social."* See Augustin Challamel, *Les clubs contre-révolutionnaires* (Paris: L. Cerf, 1895), p. 392, for bylaws of the society and pp. 391–443 for a list of membership. For a discussion of the Society of 1789, see also Keith M. Baker, "Politics and Social Science in Eighteenth-Century France: The Société de 1789,"

in *French Government and Society (1500–1850). Essays in Memory of Alfred Cobban,* ed. J.F. Bosher (London: Athlone Press, 1973), pp. 208–30, and Moravia, *Il tramonto,* pp. 152–60.

3. This salon was the only important eighteenth-century salon to persist without a break through the revolutionary period. Winfred Stephens, *Women of the French Revolution* (New York: E. P. Dutton, 1922), p. 54. Guillois's *Le salon de Madame Helvétius* still contains the most complete account of the salon of Madame Helvétius. See also Moravia, *Il tramonto,* pp. 45–87, for an analysis of the growing politicization of the salon during the prerevolutionary period.

4. Baker, *Condorcet,* p. 330.

5. *Vindiciae Gallicae* (London: G.G.J. & J. Robinson, 1791), p. 207. See Plamenatz, *English Utilitarians,* pp. 85–86.

6. Lafayette, who introduced the motion calling for such a declaration, was clearly looking toward the declarations of the American states, especially that of Virginia. In his *Souvenirs sur Mirabeau et sur les deux premières assemblées législatives* (Paris: Charles Gossalin, 1832), p. 138, Etienne Dumont recalls that the idea of a declaration of rights was explicitly recognized as American in origin, and thought to be indispensable to the new constitution by almost everyone. For a recent discussion of the "American dream" in eighteenth-century France, see Durand Echeverria, *Mirage in the West: A History of the French Image of American Society to 1815* (Princeton: Princeton University Press, 1968), pp. 116–74. There has been considerable scholarly debate over the American influence on the French Declaration. For references to the controversy, see G.P. Gooch, "The Study of the French Revolution," in *Maria Theresa and Other Studies* (London: Longmans, Green, 1951), p. 278. Most modern accounts stress the importance of French antecedents and French revolutionary experience, e.g., George Lefebvre, *The Coming of the French Revolution,* trans. R.R. Palmer (Princeton: Princeton University Press, 1971), pp. 169–81. R. R. Palmer recently upheld this view in "The Declaration of Independence in France," *Studies on Voltaire and the Eighteenth Century* 154 (1976):1569–79.

7. F.V.A. Aulard, *The French Revolution, A Political History, 1789–1804,* 4 vols., trans. Bernard Miall (New York: Russell & Russell, 1965) 1:155.

8. See, e.g., the speeches of Montmorency, Desmeuniers, Castellane, and Target, *Archives parlementaires de 1787 à 1860, Recueil complet des débats législatifs et politiques des chambres françaises, première série (1787 à 1799),* 82 vols. (Paris: Imprimerie administratif de Paul Dupont, 1875; Washington, D. C.: Microcard Editions, 1967), 8:320, 321, 334; hereafter cited as *A.P.*

9. *A.P.,* 8:322. The quote is from Barnave.

10. Ibid., p. 323.

11. See speeches by the Duc de Levis and La Luzerne, Bishop of Langres, *A.P.,* 8:322. The conservatives rejected the example of the American declarations, arguing that social equality was already a reality in America, whereas France was burdened with a feudal past and extremes of wealth and poverty. See speeches

by Champion de Cicé and Malouet, *A.P.*, 8:322. They argued that the Americans ran little risk in proclaiming the inalienable rights of man, but that such a course would be very imprudent for the French.

12. At the beginning of the Revolution, "popular" and "national" sovereignty were used interchangeably. See, for example, Emmanuel-Joseph Sieyès, *Prélimi-naire de la constitution française, Reconnaissance et exposition raisonnée de droits de l'homme et du citoyen* (Versailles: Bibliotèque Royale, 1789), p. 39, "all public powers . . . come from the people, that is to say the nation. These two terms must be synonymous." Later, national sovereignty was interpreted in a more conservative fashion. For the text of the Declaration of Rights and of the Constitution of 1791, see Jacques Godechot, *Les Constitutions de France depuis 1789* (Paris: Garnier-Flammarion, 1970), pp. 33–67.

13. Besides the theories of Volney, Condorcet, and Sieyès, discussed below, see also J. Duhamel, "Essai sur la langue française, considerée dans la morale et la politique," *Journal d'instruction sociale* 2 (June 8, 1793), and Pierre Louis Roederer, *Cours d'organisation sociale,* in *Oeuvres,* 8 vols. (Paris: Firmin Didot, 1853–59), 8:136–38; 228–305.

14. Condillac never questioned the prior ontological status of natural law as the eternal decree of God, but he insisted that man's discovery of this law is based on sense experience. Furthermore, he found the analytical abstractions of the state of nature and the social contract a particularly congenial way to explain the political order as based on psychological "facts." For Condillac's use of contract theory, see *Histoire ancienne* in Etienne Bonnot de Condillac, *Oeuvres philosophiques,* 3 vols. (Paris: Presses Universitaires de France, 1947), 2:16–17, 122–25. Isabel F. Knight, *The Geometric Spirit: The Abbé de Condillac and the French Enlightenment* (New Haven: Yale University Press, 1968) focuses on the Cartesian structure underlying Condillac's sensationalism and empiricism. See chap. 2, "Metaphysics en géometre," pp. 17–51 and passim. For a more general treatment of this theme in other thinkers of the French Enlightenment, see Ernst Cassirer, *The Philosophy of the Enlightenment,* trans. Fritz C.A. Koelln and James P. Pettegrove (Boston: Beacon Press, 1965), pp. 243–53.

15. Jacques Godechot, *Les Institutions de la France sous la Révolution et l'Empire,* 2nd ed. (Paris: Presses Universitaires de France, 1968), p. 30. With the publication of Mercier de la Rivière's *L'ordre naturel et essentiel des sociétés politiques* in 1767, the terms property, liberty, and security were united into a *"formule sacramentelle"* that constituted the political slogan of the school. Georges Weulersse, *Le mouvement physiocratique en France,* 2 vols. (Paris: Felix Alcan, 1910), 2:31. For a discussion of the Physiocratic conception of natural law and rights, see Weulersse, *Le mouvement physiocratique,* 2:1–119; John Arthur Mourant, *The Physiocratic Conception of Natural Law* (Chicago: University of Chicago Press, 1943); and Elizabeth Fox-Genovese, *The Origins of Physiocracy: Economic Revolution and Social Order in Eighteenth Century France* (Ithaca, N.Y.: Cornell University Press, 1976), esp. pp. 47–49.

16. Mourant, *Physiocratic Conception of Natural Law,* p. 36. The quote is from Mercier de la Rivière.

17. Constantin-François Chasseboeuf (1757–1820) published under the name of Volney; his writings touched on history, philosophy, and medicine, as well as the study of antiquity. A memoir on Herodotus brought him to the attention of Franklin and Holbach, who introduced him to the Auteuil salon. From 1783 to 1785 Volney travelled extensively in Syria and Egypt, and, on his return, wrote the *Voyages en Egypte et Syrie* (1787), still regarded as a pioneering work in anthropology and geography.

18. *Les ruines, ou méditation sur les révolutions des empires, Oeuvres complètes,* 2nd ed., 8 vols. (Paris: Parmentier, 1826), 1:28. See also *La loi naturelle ou principes physiques de la morale déduits de l'organization de l'homme et de l'univers,* ibid., pp. 260–61.

19. *La loi naturelle,* ibid., p. 294. In his pamphlet *Conditions nécessaires de la legalité des Etats Généraux* (n.p.:1789), Volney gives an explicit account of the French attempt to regenerate the political order. He states that the people retain the natural right to change the constitution (the "political contract") to conform with the essential rights of man. The Estates General is composed of representatives freely elected to contract for the nation. To be *legal,* the Estates must 1) be freely elected from all parts of the nation by as wide a suffrage as possible, 2) deliberate freely and vote by head rather than by order, and 3) take no measures that will not promote the will and interest of the people, who retain the ultimate constituent power.

20. Baker, *Condorcet,* p. 198, identifies three coexistent and overlapping conceptions in Condorcet's idea of social science: 1) the empirical study of the factors affecting social existence, 2) an abstract science comprising the first principles of social organization and moral conduct as derived from sensationalist psychology, and 3) a practical science or art that would implement these principles in the light of actually existing conditions. It is the second approach that underlies Condorcet's constitutional theory.

21. *Lettres d'un bourgeois de New-Haven à un citoyen de Virginie* (1787), *Oeuvres de Condorcet,* 12 vols., ed. A. Condorcet-O'Connor and François Arago (Paris: 1847–49) 9:14; hereafter cited as *O.C.*

22. See especially *Lettres d'un citoyen des Etats-Unis à un français sur les affairs présentes* (1788), *O.C.,* 9:97–123; *Sentimens d'un républicain sur les assemblées provinciales et les Etats Généraux* (1788), *O.C.,* 9:127–43; *Lettre d'un gentilhomme à Messieurs du Tiers-Etat* (1789), *O.C.,* 9:215–59; *Déclaration des droits* (1789), *O.C.,* 9:181–211. *Idées sur la despotisme* (1789), *O.C.,* 9:147–73.

23. *Idées sur le despotisme* (1789), *O.C.,* 9:166.

24. *Plan de Constitution présenté à la Convention nationale les 15 et 16 février 1793, O.C.,* 12:385.

25. *O.C.,* 6:176.

26. Condorcet was well acquainted at least with the works of Hume and Smith.

However, he probably adopted a version of the four-stage theory held by Turgot. For a discussion of Turgot's theory, see Ronald Meeks, "Smith, Turgot, and the 'Four Stages' Theory," *History of Political Economy* 3 (Spring 1971):9–27.

27. *O.C.*, 6:177.

28. *Réflexions sur les pouvoirs et instructions à donner par les provinces à leurs députés aux Etats Généraux (1789)*, *O.C.*, 9:266. Cf. *O.C.*, 9:165, 167, 182, 183, 206, 221, 230, and 266.

29. *O.C.*, 12:417.

30. For a discussion of this point, see Baker, *Condorcet*, p. 224.

31. *Lettres d'un citoyen des Etats-Unis (1789)*, *O.C.*, 9:103.

32. *O.C.*, 8:5.

33. Ibid., p. 8.

34. *O.C.*, 6:180.

35. Sieyès's analysis of the foundations and development of rights seemed to many to be the clearest expression of constitutional principles. It was adopted, in large part, by Roederer in the *Cours d'organisation sociale*. Roederer notes, "This analysis is perfectly illustrated in the *Reconnaissance et l'exposition raisonée des droits de l'homme et du citoyen* presented by Sieyès in 1789 to the Constituent Assembly. . . ." *Oeuvres*, 8:137.

36. *Préliminaire*, p. 19.

37. In the standard work on Sieyès's life and thought, Bastid notes that, although Sieyès was never particularly preoccupied with theories of knowledge, he undoubtedly accepted the principles of the philosophers of the sensationalistic school as demonstrated truths. Paul Bastid, *Sieyès et sa pensée* (Paris: Hachette, 1970), p. 299.

38. *Préliminaire*, p. 22. In an article for the *Journal d'instruction sociale* 2:35, Sieyès expresses his position succinctly, "Needs! There you have the prime mover of the human machine, the true origin of the rights of man, the inventive principle of the arts, etc. etc."

39. *Préliminaire*, p. 28.

40. Ibid., p. 24.

41. Ibid., p. 26.

42. Ibid., p. 32.

43. Ibid., p. 23.

44. Ibid., p. 38; see also p. 22.

45. J.P. Bélin, *La logique d'une idée-force: l'idée d'utilité sociale et la Révolution française (1789–1792)* (Paris: Hermann & Cie, 1939), p. 86, notes that, for Sieyès, the natural rights belonging to the individual are "not in contradiction" to this order, but Bélin does not explore the connection between the two conceptions.

46. *Préliminaire*, p. 6.

47. Sieyès, *What is the Third Estate?*, trans. M. Blondel, ed. S.E. Finer, intro. Peter Campbell (New York: Federick A. Praeger, 1963), pp. 167–72.

48. *Préliminaire*, pp. 27, 28–29.

49. *Third Estate*, p. 122.

50. Ibid., p. 151. Sieyès begins the *Préliminaire* by noting, "The Representatives of the French nation, reunited in national assembly, recognize that they have, by their mandates, the special responsibility of regenerating the constitution of the state. Consequently, in this capacity, they will exercise the constituent power," p. 17.

51. On the interaction between the language of right and that of utility in democratic theory, see Halévy, *The Growth of Philosophical Radicalism*, pp. 157–84. See also Basil Willey, *The Eighteenth Century Background: Studies on the Idea of Nature in the Thought of the Period* (London: Chatto & Windus, 1940), pp. 168–239.

52. Joseph Priestley, *Letters to the Right Honorable Edmund Burke Occasioned by his Reflections on the Revolution in France*, 3rd ed. (Birmingham: n.p., 1791), p. 13.

53. *Vindiciae Gallicae*, pp. 207, 211

54. Ibid., p. 116.

55. The first article of the second issue of the *Journal* ("Des intérêts de la liberté dans l'état social et dans le système représentatif") begins on an anxious note, "I see with pain that there is an effort to discredit the representative system in the name of liberty. This is a great evil. If it succeeds, we will begin the most disastrous era for the human race." *Journal d'instruction sociale* 2:33. He goes on to quote verbatim from the *Préliminaire* on the increase of liberty acquired with social control (p. 40). See also Bastid, *Sieyès*, p. 342.

56. For a contemporary account of Mirabeau's changing position on the issue of the Declaration of Rights, see Dumont, *Souvenirs sur Mirabeau*, pp. 139–49.

57. *A.P.*, 8:462–63.

58. Ibid.; see Jean Gaulmier, *L'Idéologue Volney (1757–1820): Contribution à l'histoire de l'orientalisme en France* (Beyrouth: Imprimerie Catholique, 1951), pp. 174–76.

59. See Kennedy, *A Philosophe in the Age of Revolution*, pp. 14–37.

60. Although never an important leader in the Assembly, Tracy is listed by Aulard in *Les orateurs de la Révolution: l'Assemblée constituante* (Paris: Edouard Cornely & Cie, 1905), p. 47, as among the eighty deputies who "left a name and played a role."

61. *Translation of a Letter from Monsieur de Tracy, Member of the French National Assembly, to Mr. Burke, in Answer to His Remarks on the French Revolution* (London: J. Johnson, 1790), p. 4. Tracy was commenting on Burke's February 9, 1790, House of Commons speech on England's military budget and on France. The printed letter to Burke anticipated Burke's *Reflections* by seven months. I would like to thank Emmet Kennedy for pointing out to me that no one else had responded to Burke's attacks this early.

62. Ibid., p. 21.

63. Ibid., p. 4.

64. Ibid., pp. 7–8.

65. Ibid., p. 6.

66. Ibid., p. 22.

67. Carl Ludwig Lokke, *France and the Colonial Question: A Study of Contemporary French Opinion 1763–1801* (New York: Columbia University Press, 1932), pp. 119–60; Godechot, *Institutions de la France,* pp. 56–58. Condorcet states this position clearly in his *Au corps électoral, contre l'esclavage des noirs:* "Indeed, how can one be so bold as to claim without blushing these declarations of rights, these inviolable bulwarks of the liberty, of the security of citizens, if everyday he himself takes the liberty of violating the most sacred articles?" *O.C.,* 9:471. Cf. also his *Sur l'admission des députés des planteurs de Saint-Domingue dans l'assemblée nationale, O.C.,* 9:479–85.

68. *A.P.,* 25:750. Tracy also signed a list of those willing to sacrifice the French colonies to England, rather than to sacrifice the rights of man. Kennedy, *A Philosophe in the Age of Revolution,* p. 26.

69. *Opinion de M. de Tracy sur les affaires de Saint-Domingue, en septembre 1791* (Paris: Imprimerie de Laillet, 1791). The *Opinion sur Saint-Domingue* was the reprint of a speech; it may also be found in *A.P.,* 31:259–63. Tracy takes no clear position on slavery here. While deploring both slavery and the slave trade, he also expresses unwillingness to face the economic upheaval of sudden emancipation. He presumably favored a policy of gradual emancipation.

70. The other issue that posed this dilemma was the question of universal suffrage. Bélin, *Logique d'une idée-force,* pp. 156–57.

71. *Opinion sur Saint-Domingue,* p. 18.

72. While recent historical scholarship on the role of the crowds in the French Revolution has tended to debunk the image of a bribed and manipulated mob serving the interests of power-hungry opportunists, it reiterates that this view was widely held by contemporaries and by hostile nineteenth-century historians. See George Rudé, "The Motives of Popular Insurrection in Paris during the French Revolution," *Bulletin of the Institute of Historical Research* 26 (1953):53–74; idem, *The Crowd in the French Revolution* (London: Oxford University Press, 1971), p. 196.

73. Rudé, *The Crowd,* p. 197.

74. Ibid., p. 197*n*27.

75. Albert Soboul, *Les sans-culottes parisiens en l'an II* (Paris: Librairie Clavreuil, 1958), p. 505. On the political ideology of the sans-culottes in general, see ibid., pp. 505–45.

76. George Lefebvre, *The French Revolution,* vol. 2: *From 1793 to 1799,* trans. John Hall Stewart and James Friguglietti (New York: Columbia University Press, 1964), p.64. Robespierre often castigated intellectuals as tepid supporters of the Revolution, while eulogizing the lower classes as its heart and soul. "Petty vain men, blush if you can. The marvels that have immortalized this epoch of human history were brought about without you and in spite of you. . . . While the artisan proved himself an expert in knowledge of the rights of man, the scribbler of books, almost republican in 1788, was stupidly defending the cause of kings in 1793." *Sur les rapports des idées religieuses et morales avec les principes*

républicains, et sur les fêtes nationales. Rapport présenté au nom du Comité de Salut public (18 floréal an II, May 7, 1794), in Maximilien Robespierre, *Discours et Rapports à la Convention* (Paris: Union Générale d'Editions, 1965), p. 270.

77. *Sur la nouvelle déclaration des droits* (April 24, 1793), *Discours,* pp. 119–20.

78. *Liberté, égalité ou la mort. Section des Sans-Culottes. Adresse à la Convention nationale,* in Paul H. Beik, ed. and trans., *The French Revolution, Documentary History of Western Civilization* (New York: Harper and Row, 1970), p. 264. The pamphlet was the product of the sectional deliberations of September 2, 1793. It was printed, but apparently never presented to the Convention.

79. *Moniteur universel. Réimpression de l'ancien Moniteur; seule histoire authentique et inaltérée de la Révolution française, depuis la réunion des Etats-généraux jusqu'au Consulat (mai 1789–novembre 1799),* 32 vols. (Paris: 1858–63), 16:747; hereafter cited as *Moniteur.*

80. *Sur les principes du gouvernement révolutionnaire. Rapport présenté au nom du Comité de Salut public* (5 nivose an II, December 25, 1793), *Discours,* p. 190.

81. *Sur les principes de morale politique qui doivent guider la Convention nationale dans l'administration intérieure de la République. Rapport présenté au nom du Comité de Salut public* (18 pluviose an II, February 5, 1794), *Discours,* p. 222.

82. *Le contrat social des français* (n.p.: July 23, 1789), p. 2.

83. *Observations sur la manière de discuter la constitution* (Paris: Imprimerie nationale, n.d.), p. 5.

84. Ibid.

85. *Essai sur la Constitution* (Paris: Imprimerie nationale, 1793), p. 2.

86. Ibid., p. 1.

87. Ibid., p. 9.

88. *Dictionnaire des sciences philosophiques* (1844–1852), s.v. "Idéologie," by D. Henne.

89. Cabanis also had a long-standing liaison with Charlotte de Grouchy (Condorcet's sister-in-law), whom he later married. See Staum, *Cabanis, pp.* 148–49.

90. Joanna Kitchin, *Un journal "philosophique": La Décade (1794–1804)* (Paris: n.p., 1966), p. 35. Kitchin characterizes the attitude of the Idéologue journal *La Décade* during the Terror as one of limited collaboration with the Committee of Public Safety. She argues that the *Décade's* editors apparently concluded that only the Montagnards had the energy and patriotism to fight against counterrevolutionaries.

91. François Picavet, the first historian of the group, included in his study, *Les idéologues* (Paris: Félix Alcan, 1891), almost every thinker who continued to acknowledge the influence of the Enlightenment. He sorted these out somewhat artificially into three generations. Sergio Moravia also uses the term very inclusively, as the subtitles of his two volumes on the Idéologues indicate ("Filosophia et politica nella societate francese 1770–1810," "Scienza e filosophia in Francia 1780–1815"). Kaiser tends to follow Moravia in "From Enlightenment to Pos-

itivism." In contrast to this broad use of "Idéologue," some scholars have used the term to refer only to those who were more strictly "followers of Condillac." See, e.g., Charles van Duzer, *The Contribution of the Idéologues to French Revolutionary Thought* (Baltimore: Johns Hopkins Press, 1935) and Jay Stein, *The Mind and the Sword* (New York: Twayne Publishers, 1961). I think that Picavet, Moravia, and Kaiser construe "Idéologue" too loosely, since they occasionally include figures (such as Condorcet, Madame de Staël, and Benjamin Constant) whose links with "idéologie" are tenuous. On the other hand, to limit the term to "followers of Condillac" is misleading, since it ignores important philosophical differences (both from Condillac and among the Idéologues). Furthermore, this narrow use tends to slight the social and political connotations of the term that were so important to contemporaries and to the post-Revolutionary generation. The rough and relative criteria I use in the text (some adherence to Cabanis's and Tracy's view of the scope and function of "idéologie," a loose web of social connections, and moderate political opinions) would include (at least) Cabanis, Tracy, Volney, Garat, Dégerando, Maine de Biran, Laromiguière, Roederer, Say, Jacquemont, Thurot, Ginguené, Chénier, Andrieux, and Lakanal. This view approximately corresponds to the way the word is used by Georges Gusdorf, Martin Staum (who, however, excludes some figures because they did not author major works) and Emmet Kennedy. See Martin Staum, "The Class of Moral and Political Sciences, 1795–1803," *French Historical Studies* 9 (Spring 1980), p. 372.

92. Among those who met regularly in the rue du Bac were Garat, Cabanis, Tracy, Thurot, Gallois, Jacquemont, Laromiguière, Chénier, Andrieux, Ginguené, Daunou, and Benjamin Constant. Picavet, *Les idéologues,* p. 30. For a discussion of the Idéologues in the Institute, see below, pp. 33–35.

93. *La Décade philosophique, littéraire et politique par une société des républicains,* ed. Andrieux, Duval, Ginguené, J.B. Say, et al., 54 vols. (Paris: 1794–1807) [From 1804 to 1807 published as *La Revue philosophique littéraire et politique.*] There is a five-volume unpublished thesis on the *Décade,* Marc Regaldo's *Un milieu intellectuel: la Décade philosophique (1794–1807)* (Thesis, Lille-Paris, 1976), which, unfortunately, could not be consulted for this study. Other journals in which Idéologues published regularly include *Le Conservateur, Journal politique, philosophique et littéraire,* ed. Garat, Daunou, Chénier, et al., 3 vols. (Paris: 1797–98); *Journal d'économie politique,* ed. Roederer, 5 vols. (Paris: 1796–97); *Clef du cabinet des souverains,* ed. Garat, Peuchet, Pommereuil, et al., 32 vols. (Paris: 1797–1804).

94. For the relations between the Idéologues and the circle around Madame de Staël, see R. G. Carey, "The Liberals of France and their Relation to the Development of Bonaparte's Dictatorship 1799–1804" (Ph.D. dissertation, University of Chicago, 1947), pp. 11–16; Adrienne Gobert, *L'Opposition des assemblées pendant le consulat, 1800–1804* (Paris: Sagot, 1925), pp. 18–22; Guillois, *Le salon de Madame Helvétius,* pp. 123–25, and Gusdorf, *La conscience révolutionnaire,* pp. 354–355.

95. In a letter to Tracy, Madame de Staël noted, "You tell me, sir, that you

follow me neither into the heavens nor into the tomb. It seems to me that a mind as superior as yours, detached from everything material by the nature of its tasks, must take pleasure in religious ideas, for they perfect all that is lofty, they assuage all that is sensitive, and, without this hope, I would be seized with a nameless, insurmountable terror of life and death." Madame de Staël to M. de Tracy, 31 May 1807. *Société des Amis des Livres, Annuaire* (1881), pp. 97–98.

96. *Moniteur,* 25:150.

97. Ibid.

98. *Discours prononcé par le Cen Daunou, président de la Convention nationale, 23 thermidor an III, jour anniversaire du 10 août* [August 10, 1795] (n.p.: 1795), p. 3. See also his *Rapport au nom des Comités de salut public et de sûreté générale, 11 vendémiaire an IV* [October 3, 1795] (Caen: Le Roy, 1795); and *Rapport au nom des Comités de salut public et de sûreté générale, 21 fructidor an III* [September 7, 1795] (Caen: Le Roy, 1795), pp. 1–2.

99. *Discours au Conseils des cinq-cents pour l'anniversaire de la fondation de la République, 1 vendémiaire an VII* [September 22, 1798] (Paris: Imprimerie nationale, n.d.), p. 3.

100. Kitchin, *La Decade,* p. 39.

101. See, e.g., the article by Ginguené, *Décade* 15 (10 vendémiaire an VI, October 1, 1797):18. See also Kitchen, *La Décade,* p. 43.

102. "Prospectus," *Conservateur* 1 (September 4, 1797).

103. *Conservateur* 1 (September 4, 1797):45.

104. *Décade* 6 (20 messidor an III, July 8, 1795):80.

105. *Lectures on History Delivered in the Normal School of Paris,* trans. anon. (Philadelphia: J. Bioren, 1801), p. 9.

106. Aulard, *The French Revolution,* 3:320; for an analysis of the plebiscite vote on the Constitution and the Two Thirds decree, see pp. 319–22.

107. See, e.g., Maurice Deslandres, *Histoire constitutionelle de la France de 1789 à 1870* (Paris: Armand Colin, 1932), p. 301; J.J. Chevallier, *Histoire des institutions et des régimes politiques de la France moderne (1789–1958),* 3rd ed. (Paris: Librairie Dalloz, 1967), p. 96; and Prélot, *Les institutions politiques,* p. 112.

108. In 1790 Cabanis had prepared four discourses on public education for Mirabeau; these were later published as *Travail sur l'education publique, trouvé dans les papiers de Mirabeau.* Other reports had also been submitted; e.g., by Talleyrand (September 1791), by Condorcet (April 1792), and by Lakanal (November 1794, March 1795). Lakanal's proposals were adopted by the Convention, but never implemented. See Charles Van Duzer, *Contribution of the Idéologues,* pp. 101–2.

109. For an analysis of the organization and operation of this educational system, see ibid., pp. 84–142.

110. Jules Simon, *Une Académie sous le Directoire* (Paris: Callman Levy, 1885), p. 65. For a general treatment of the Institute, see also Moravia, *Il tramonto,* pp. 410–25.

111. For a full list of the membership of the Second Class, see *Notices Biographiques et Bibliographiques*. Institut de France. Académie des Sciences Morales et Politiques (Paris: Librairie d'Argences, 1960), pp. 367–407. Among those assigned to the section "Analysis of Sensations and Ideas" were Volney, Garat, Cabanis, and Ginguené; Tracy, Laromiguière, Jacquemont, and Dégerando were associates. For a recent consideration of the Second Class as a whole, see Martin Staum, "The Class of Moral and Political Sciences."

112. For the lectures of Cabanis and Tracy, see *Mémoires de l'Institut national, Classe des sciences morales et politiques*, 5 vols. (Paris: Baudouin, 1798–1804), 1:37–208, 284–450; 3:491–551; 4:544–606. Cabanis's lectures appeared in 1802 as the *Rapports du physique et du moral de l'homme*. Future citations are to the critical edition in *Oeuvres Philosophiques de Cabanis*, ed. Claude Lehec and Jean Cazeneuve, 2 vols. (Paris: Presses Universitaires de France, 1956). Tracy refined and greatly expanded his lectures in the *Elémens d'idéologie*, which was published in four volumes from 1801 to 1815. *Elémens d'idéologie. Première partie: Idéologie proprement dite* (first published as *Projet d'élémens d'idéologie à l'usage des écoles centrales de la République française* in 1801; second revised edition, 1804); *Seconde partie: Grammaire* (1803); *Troisième partie: Logique* (1805); *Quatrième et cinquième parties: Traité de la volonté et de ses éffets* (1815). The third French edition of the *Traité de la volonté* (1823) was published under the title *Traité d'économie politique*. Hereafter, I will cite the complete edition of the *Elémens d'idéologie* published in 1817 (Paris: Courcier) by volume and page.

113. *Mémoire sur la faculté de penser*, *Mémoires de l'Institut* 1:324. The *New Monthly Magazine* 3 (January–June 1797):285 gave an accounting of Tracy's coining of the word to the English public.

114. *Mémoire sur la faculté de penser*, p. 287.

115. Simon, *Académie*, p. 111. Tracy prefaced his introductory remarks to the Institute with this question, ". . . in the last analysis, what is the end of all research if not utility?" *Mémoires de l'Institut*, 1:285. Simon is clearly hostile to this spirit: "The utilitarians, for the name was created for them, imagined, for example, that they were doing something very intelligent when they transformed the palace of Saint-Germain into a penitentiary." *Académie*, p. 111.

116. Deslandres, *Histoire constitutionelle*, p. 345.

117. Jean Bourdon, "Le mécontentement public et les craintes des dirigeants sous le Directoire," *Annales historiques de la Révolution française* 18 (1946), pp. 227–33, examines the directors' fears of the right and left opposition. In *Jacobin Legacy: The Democratic Movement under the Directory* (Princeton: Princeton University Press, 1970) Isser Woloch argues that the neo-Jacobins in reality formed the nucleus of a party of democratic, but constitutional, opposition. In Woloch's view, it was largely the excessive reaction of the ruling oligarchy that "broke the fragile evolution of a certain kind of democracy" (p. 398).

118. For details of the Idéologue role in government, see Picavet, *Les idéologues*, pp. 20–28; Moravia, *Il tramonto*, pp. 223–315.

119. *Décade* 6 (20 messidor an III, July 8, 1795):79; 6 (10 messidor an III, June 28, 1795):21.

120. Alphonse H. Taillandier, *Documents biographiques sur P.-C.-F. Daunou,* 2nd ed. (Paris: Firmin Didot, 1847), p. 76. Roederer also strongly objected to the organization of the executive power in the *Journal de Paris.* He would have preferred a prime minister and a more strongly centralized administration. See *Oeuvres,* 7:24–45.

121. Quoted in Vermeil de Conchard, "Cabanis homme politique (coups d'état du 18 fructidor an V et du 18 brumaire an VIII, d'après des lettres inédites)," *Société scientifique, historique et archéologique de la Correze, Bulletin (Brieve)* 35 (1913):688.

122. See *Décade* 18 (10 germinal an VI, March 30, 1798):63–64; 18 (20 germinal VI, April 9, 1798):127, 18 (30 floréal an VI, May 19, 1798):377.

123. Albert Meynier, *Les coups d'états du Directoire,* 3 vols. (Paris: Presses Universitaires de France, 1927–28), 2:96. For a discussion of the Floréal purge, see *ibid.,* pp. 68–109; Lefebvre, *The French Revolution,* vol. 2: *From 1793–1799,* pp. 207–8.

124. *Moniteur* 19 (29, 30 brumaire an VII, November 19, 20, 1798): 240–41.

125. Sieyès's proposals dismayed some of his supporters, since he largely abandoned the electoral principle in favor of lists of notables. Daunou's proposal reinstated two-tiered elections. The split in the Sieyès faction helped Bonaparte to outmaneuver those who had helped elevate him to power. Carey, "The Liberals of France," pp. 96–119.

126. *Quelques considérations sur l'organisation social en général et particulièrement sur la nouvelle constitution, Oeuvres philosophiques,* pp. 460–61. In a review of this pamphlet for the *Décade,* Say seconds Cabanis's opinion. *Décade* 24 (10 nivôse an VIII, December 31, 1799): 9–17. See also Cabanis's *Discours prononcé à suite du Rapport de la Commission des Sept* (19 brumaire an VIII, November 11, 1799), *Oeuvres philosophiques,* p. 455: "you must pull the Republic out of this state of anguish, or perish with her."

127. Quoted in Conchard, "Cabanis homme politique," p. 694.

128. This attitude was clearly articulated in an article that appeared in *Le Messager des relations extérieurs* (22 nivôse an VIII, January 12, 1800), quoted in F.V.A. Aulard, *Paris sous le consulat. Recueil de documents pour l'histoire de l'esprit public à Paris,* 4 vols. (Paris: L. Cerf, 1903–1909), 1:89.

129. For a discussion of this protest, see Gobert, *L'Opposition des Assemblées,* pp. 40–183; Carey, "The Liberals of France," pp. 119–251; Moravia, *Il tramonto,* pp. 445–62, 480–89.

130. From a conversation between Napoleon and Lucien Bonaparte reported in *Lucien Bonaparte et ses Mémoires, 1775–1840,* ed. Jung, 3 vols. (Paris: 1882–1883), 2:208, quoted in Maxime Leroy, *Histoire des idées sociales en France,* vol. 2: *De Babeuf à Tocqueville* (Paris: Gallimard, 1962), p. 160.

131. The rapprochement with Rome alienated Volney, who had until then been one of Napoleon's staunchest supporters. The story is often told of a conversation between the first consul and Volney, in which Napoleon allegedly explained that he sought to restore the Church only because ninety-eight percent of Frenchmen were religious. Volney is supposed to have retorted that Napoleon ought then to restore the Bourbons, since ninety-eight percent of the people wanted Louis XVIII. Napoleon's response has been variously reported: from a cold stare, to a violent kick. Guillois, *Le salon de Madame Helvétius,* pp. 171–72.

132. *Décade* 31 (30 vendémiaire an X, October 21, 1801):156–69.

133. *Observations sur le système actuel d'instruction publique* (Paris: Panckoucke, an IX, 1801), p. 2.

134. Tracy's conception of education was clearly elitist, but it does not seem that his position was fundamentally inconsistent with that of earlier liberal reformers, or with his own later emphasis on the link between education and political equality. (For a different view, see Kennedy, *A Philosophe in the Age of Revolution,* pp. 91–92, 174.) Most liberals accepted the class nature of society; Tracy was merely more frank in recognizing its implications, "Habits, needs, resources (*moyens*), everything is different between the two kinds of men" (p. 5). However his concept of a shortened and simplified education for the *classe ouvrière* was consistent with the intent of Sieyès and Condorcet in the *Journal d'instruction sociale,* which was meant to provide the masses with the rudiments of sound reasoning in social and political affairs. Tracy's educational scheme was meant to provide the masses with the minimum basis for citizenship. Furthermore, he did suggest scholarships that would help to discover talent in the working classes (pp. 37–38).

135. See *Décade* 35 (20 frimaire an XI, December 10, 1802):466–71; 38 (30 thermidor an XI, August 17, 1803):328–34, (20 fructidor an XI, September 6, 1803):470–77; 39 (30 vendémiaire an XII, October 22, 1803):143–53, (10 brumaire an XII, November 1, 1803):198–208. On the *Décade*'s favorable response to foreign literature, see Paul Hazard, *La Révolution française et les lettres italiennes 1789–1815* (Paris: Hachette, 1910), p. 436.

136. Louis de Villefosse and Janine Bouissonouse, *The Scourge of the Eagle: Napoleon and the Liberal Opposition,* trans. and ed. Michael Ross (New York: St. Martin's Press, 1972), p. 238.

137. Ibid., p. 211. Private letters of Andrieux and J.B. Say, for example, show a scornful hostility to the Empire. Kitchin, *La Décade,* p. 93. Tracy, the born aristocrat, disdained Napoleon's pretensions to grandeur. However, although he may have engaged in "parlor conspiracy," he was too cautious to become involved in any serious attempt to overthrow the regime. See Kennedy, *A Philosophe in the Age of Revolution,* p. 190.

138. For an analysis of the changing temper of the age, see Richard Fargher, "The Retreat from Voltaireanism," in *The French Mind: Studies in Honor of Gustave Rudler* (Oxford: Clarendon Press, 1952), pp. 220–38.

139. François Furet, *Penser la Révolution française* (Paris: Editions Gallimard,

1978), esp. pp. 77–80. One can accept Furet's brilliant description of the power of this ideology, without, I think, acceding to his view that it was the implicit democratic "logic" of the ideology that "explains" the events of the Revolution.

140. Tracy completed the *Elémens d'idéologie* and composed the *Commentaire sur l'Esprit des lois de Montesquieu*. Too prudent to attempt to publish the *Commentaire* (written between 1805 and 1808) or the final volume of the *Elémens* (completed by 1811) in France, Tracy instead sent them to Thomas Jefferson, who superintended their translation and publication in the United States. See *A Commentary and Review of Montesquieu's Spirit of Laws. Prepared for press from the original manuscript . . . To which are annexed, Observations on the thirty-first book by the late M. Condorcet; and two letters of Helvétius, on the merits of the same work* [trans. William Duane] (Philadelphia: William Duane, 1811); *A Treatise on Political Economy; to which is prefixed a supplement to a preceding work on the Understanding or Elements of Ideology, with an Analytical Table, and an Introduction on the Faculty of the Will* [trans. T. Jefferson] (Georgetown, D.C.: Joseph Milligan, 1817). For the extensive correspondence dealing with these publications, see Gilbert Chinard, *Jefferson et les idéologues d'après sa correspondance inédite avec Destutt de Tracy, Cabanis, J.B. Say, et Auguste Comte* (Baltimore: Johns Hopkins Press, 1925), pp. 47–93 and passim. In fact, the fourth volume of the *Elémens* appeared in France before it appeared in the United States. Hereafter I will refer to the French versions of these texts. Daunou contributed to the rethinking of the liberal revolutionary heritage in his influential *Essai sur les garanties individuelles que réclame l'état actuel de la société*, which was first published in 1818. Future citations are to the third edition (Paris: A. Bobée, 1822) to which are appended his speeches in the Chambres des Députés; Daunou also lectured on history at the Collège de France from 1819 to 1830 and his lectures were gathered into the twenty-volume *Cours d'études historiques* (Paris: Firmin Didot, 1842–49).

CHAPTER TWO: *IDÉOLOGIE* AND SOCIAL SCIENCE

1. The scientists of the French Institute were at the center of scientific research during this period, a period in which the foundation was laid for many of the theoretical and practical advances in nineteenth-century science. See H. Guerlac, "Some Aspects of Science during the French Revolution," *The Scientific Monthly* 80 (1955):99; C.C. Gillispie, *The Edge of Objectivity: An Essay in the History of Scientific Ideas* (Princeton: Princeton University Press, 1960), p. 117; George Rosen, "The Philosophy of Ideology and the Emergence of Modern Medicine in France," *Bulletin of the History of Medicine* 20 (1946):328–29; and Sergio Moravia, "Philosophie et médicine en France à la fin du XVIIIe siècle," *Studies on Voltaire and the Eighteenth Century* 89 (1972):1089–1151.

2. Staum, *Cabanis*, pp. 72–93, and Moravia, *Il pensiero*, pp. 187–226, stress the predominant influence of vitalism in Cabanis's work. A recent article on the relationship between Cabanis and La Mettrie, on the other hand, notes the continuing presence of mechanistic concepts in Cabanis's thought. See Aram Vartan-

ian, "Cabanis and La Mettrie," *Studies on Voltaire and the Eighteenth Century* 155 (1976):2158–65. Vartanian's analysis is closer to my own reading of Cabanis.

3. *Rapports, Oeuvres philosophiques,* 1:239.

4. Ibid., p. 527.

5. Ibid., p. 360*n*, 528–32.

6. However, see his later "Lettre à F* sur les causes premières," *Oeuvres philosophiques,* 2:256–98, in which he indicates a rapprochement with a more spiritual point of view. This letter was not published until 1824, and has been held by many commentators to be inconsistent with the rest of his theory. See ibid., editor's note, p. 256.

7. *Rapports, Oeuvres philosophiques,* 1:251. See also ibid., pp. 272, 277, 291, and 617.

8. Ibid., p. 260.

9. Ibid., p. 357. See also "Préface," pp. 109–22, passim.

10. Ibid.

11. Ibid., p. 115.

12. Ibid., p. 619.

13. Ibid., p. 159.

14. Ibid., p. 121.

15. Ibid., p. 165.

16. Ibid., p. 167.

17. "But is not this temperament a true abstraction, a purely ideal model? Has it ever really existed in nature? Probably not." Ibid., pp. 353–54.

18. Ibid., pp. 175–77.

19. Ibid., p. 257.

20. Roussel was a doctor of the Montpellier school, and author of the influential *Système physique et moral de la femme* (1775).

21. *Rapports, Oeuvres philosophiques,* p. 291. Cabanis further specifically states that women lacked the energy, reason, and character for civil or public functions; that, although acute observers of social relations, they were unfit to undertake scientific research or any profound meditation; and that "the happiness of women will always depend on the impression that they make on men." Ibid., p. 299. These opinions on women are certainly not unusual for the time, but are rather surprising, in view of Condorcet's radical views on women, and Cabanis's own freindship for Madame de Staël and Madame Condorcet, the editor and translator of the French edition of Smith's *Theory of Moral Sentiments.* For a discussion of Cabanis's views on women, see Staum, *Cabanis,* pp. 213–17. Cabanis's arguments could certainly be used to undermine the ideology of revolutionary feminism. Advocacy of rights for women, like rights for blacks in the colonies, was based on a natural rights argument. In 1791 Olympe de Gouges had published a *Déclaration des droits de la femme et de la citoyenne.* A year earlier, Condorcet had unambiguously stated the logic of this argument in an article advocating women's suffrage: since women, like men, were sensitive and reasonable creatures, they necessarily had equal rights.

22. Xavier Marie François Bichat, *Physiological Researches Upon Life and Death,*

trans. Tobias Watkins (Philadelphia: Smith and Maxwell, 1809), pp. 107–9.

23. *Rapports, Oeuvres philosophiques*, p. 618.

24. Occupation has a particularly great effect on character and intelligence, which depend on the types of tools employed, the variety of the work, etc. Ibid., pp. 449–54. In an interesting anticipation of Marx, Cabanis notes that working together in a close space may increase social feeling: "all else being equal, the particular physical dispositions on which the social instinct apparently directly depends are more highly developed and acquire more intensity." Ibid., p. 452.

25. Ibid., p. 468.

26. See Frank Manuel, "From Equality to Organicism," *Journal of the History of Ideas* 17 (1956):61–69.

27. *Elémens*, 1:212–13.

28. Jean François La Harpe, *Du fanatisme dans la langue révolutionnaire* (Liège: J.A. Latour, 1797), p. 165. The quote is from p. 162.

29. Ibid., p. 122. See also pp. 48–49, 72, and 117.

30. *Elémens*, 2:390–91. In a characteristic blend of the attitudes of the new "ideologist" and the *ci-devant* noble, Tracy adds that such rhetoric consists of "tricks reproved by good taste" (p. 391). See also Volney's *Discours sur l'étude des langues, Oeuvres*, 1:416. Volney uses the rhetoric of the revolutionary Convention as an example of the alteration of a language by "impoverishment from within."

31. Tracy's philosophy shares with that of Condillac an extremely rationalistic, even formalistic, quality. It is significant that Tracy had a singular admiration for Hobbes. He translated the introduction to Hobbes's *De Corpore*, "Computatio sive Logica," and appended it to his own treatise on logic. Tracy's was apparently the first French translation of this work. See *Elémens*, 3:515–85.

32. *Elémens*, 1:223–25; 3:215.

33. *Elémens*, 1:40. At the end of his discussion of the intellectual faculties, Tracy adds a characteristic note: "But it should never be forgotten that the things which we have separated theoretically in this way are often confounded and united in the same fact, and that we must always begin from the actual facts." Ibid., p. 152. One commentator notes that Tracy tended throughout his work to "contrast immediate, concrete observation with the more or less arbitrary results of [Condillac's] reductive analysis." Emile Bréhier, *The History of Philosophy*, vol. 6: *The Nineteenth Century: Period of Systems, 1800–1850*, trans. Wade Baskin (Chicago: University of Chicago Press, 1968), p. 31.

34. *Elémens*, 1:xiii.

35. Ibid., p. 34. Tracy asserts that Cabanis "is the first to have distinguished quite clearly the different effects of our sensibility, and developed all their circumstances and consequences." *Elémens*, 3:175n.

36. *Elémens*, 1:234. Tracy's understanding of the analogy between biology and chemistry is perhaps more simplistic than is the more nuanced position of Cabanis.

37. In the introductory fragment to the unfinished Part Five of his *Elémens d'idéologie*, "De nos sentimens et de nos passions, ou morale," Tracy begins from

the physiologist Bichat's distinction between organic (interior) and animal (exterior) life. See below, p. 74.

38. Tracy notes that Condillac's theory relies on the ideas of extent and mass but does not explain how these notions arise. *Mémoire sur la faculté de penser,* p. 299.

39. Ibid., pp. 308, 315. This theory of the significance of movement was repeated by Thomas Brown, the successor to Dugald Stewart in the chair of moral philosophy at Edinburgh, in Brown's *Lectures on the Philosophy of the Human Mind,* 4 vols. (Edinburgh: Adam and Charles Black, 1861), 2:1–22. (Brown's lectures were originally delivered in 1810–1811; they were published posthumously in 1820.) Through Brown, the theory influenced the two Mills. Thomas Brown's theory is so close to Tracy's that he was accused by William Hamilton of having plagiarized the French Idéologue. In comparing the texts, the conclusion of direct influence appears to me inescapable. This conclusion is strengthened by what is generally known of Brown. He was apparently a voracious reader, who possessed an almost photographic memory, and who read French as easily as English. See David Welsh, "Memoir of Dr. Brown," *Lectures,* 1:57–58. Brown frequently quotes from French authors, and is obviously familiar with Condillac and his followers. Leslie Stephen notes the similarity between Brown and Tracy on the significance of movement, but leaves open the question of plagiarism. He also points out that Brown did not publish his own lectures, which may excuse his failure to mention Tracy as a source. *The English Utilitarians,* 3 vols. (New York: Peter Smith, 1950), 2:277–78. There is other textual evidence to suggest that Brown was almost certainly familiar with Tracy's *Elémens.* His frequent analogy between the analysis of thinking and the science of chemistry; his insistence on the importance of the science of mind to other sciences; his analysis of thinking as a sequence of interrelated "feelings"; his refutation of the logic of the syllogism—all these arguments closely resemble those of Tracy. See, e.g., *Lectures,* 1:511, 548; 2:182, 433–560, passim; 3:13–15. It is understandable that Brown might not have wanted to acknowledge Tracy as a source for these discussions. Brown was a friend and disciple of Stewart, who disliked the reductionism associated with Hartley. Brown accuses Condillac and his followers of a similar over-eagerness to reduce everything to sensation (although he himself adopts a remarkably analogous position in his reference to intellectual operations as feelings). Furthermore, Brown is always careful to avoid any attack on religion, and he obviously thought the Idéologues veered dangerously toward atheism.

40. *Mémoire sur la faculté de penser,* pp. 309–12; *Elémens,* 1:155–209.

41. *Mémoire sur la faculté de penser,* pp. 311–12.

42. For Tracy's initial position, see *Mémoire sur la faculté de penser,* pp. 333, 348–55. For the later position, see *Elémens,* 1:121–55. Biran accused Tracy of abandoning his own principles and falling into the same error as had Condillac: "I am astonished and a bit chagrined that you abandon or at least very much circumscribe your principle relative to motility, by drawing nearer to the theory of exclusive sensation proposed by Condillac." Biran, *Oeuvres,* ed. Pierre Tisser-

and (Paris: Félix Alcan, 1920–49), 6:231. On the relationship between Tracy and Maine de Biran, see René Lacroze, *Maine de Biran* (Paris: Presses Universitaires de France, 1970), pp. 41–44; F.C.T. Moore, *The Psychology of Maine de Biran* (Oxford: The Clarendon Press, 1970), pp. 81–82, 82–104 passim; and Kennedy, *A Philosophe in the Age of Revolution*, pp. 120–31.

43. *Elémens*, 1:112. Tracy dismisses Berkeley and the skeptics rather lightly, as if the matter were of little importance. On this point, see Colin Smith, "Destutt de Tracy and the Bankruptcy of Sensationalism," in *Balzac and the Nineteenth Century*, ed. D.G. Charlton, J. Goudon, and Anthony Pugh (Leicester: Leicester University Press, 1972), p. 200.

44. *Elémens*, 3:280.

45. *Elémens*, 1:25.

46. Ibid., pp. 81–106.

47. *Commentaire*, p. 21.

48. Ibid., p. 219.

49. Ibid., p. 128.

50. Ibid., p. 4.

51. *Elémens*, 4:429. Cf. ibid., pp. 172 173, where Tracy notes that it is said to be just that an entrepreneur should receive compensation for his labor, risk, and investment. Tracy agrees with this sentiment; nevertheless, the word *just* is here badly applied. Since the entrepreneur has no legally enforceable contract to receive this compensation, there is technically no injustice if he does not receive it.

52. On a few occasions, Tracy uses the expression "natural rights" or the "rights of man" to refer to civil liberties. See, e.g., *Commentaire*, p. 249, where Tracy notes that monopoly is "odious, tyrannical, contrary to the natural right to buy and sell as one pleases." See also ibid., pp. 26, 43, 72, 132, 215. These are all casual references, uncharacteristic of Tracy's later caution in using these terms.

53. *Elémens*, 4:108.

54. *Mémoire sur la faculté de penser*, p. 357.

55. *Elémens*, 4:79.

56. *Mémoire sur la faculté de penser*, p. 356.

57. *Elémens*, 4:113. Tracy never directly examines the genesis of moral values; he seems to take for granted that the general process of curbing desire in the spirit of enlightened self-interest is at the heart of social morality. His scattered comments on sympathy, however, indicate that he viewed this passion as a natural instinct whose satisfaction is of considerable importance in creating human happiness. See *Elémens*, 3:200–1; 4:72–73, 133–34; 5:514. In his unfinished treatise on morality, Tracy speculates on the roots of sympathy. Influenced by his reading of Gall, whose *Discours . . . sur la physiologie du cerveau* appeared in 1808, Tracy locates physiological centers of moral activity: the spinal column is the center of the life of *conservation*, the brain the center of the life of *relation*. Ibid., pp. 510–11. See Kennedy, *A Philosophe in the Age of Revolution*, p. 218.

58. *Elémens*, 4:117–18.

59. "It would be superfluous, having principally in view the human species, to concern ourselves any longer with beings who feel and will, but live in isolation." Ibid., p. 128. Tracy's discussion of the four hypothetical situations is an expansion and restatement of the derivation of rights and duties presented in the *Mémoire sur la faculté de penser,* pp. 380–81.

60. *Commentaire,* p. 233.

61. *Elémens,* 4:427.

62. *Essai sur l'origine des connaissances humaines, Oeuvres,* 1:39.

63. *Mémoire sur la faculté de penser,* pp. 382–84; *Elémens,* 3:54–55, 139.

64. Ibid., p. 138.

65. Ibid., p. 321.

66. *Elémens,* 4:16; cf. *Elémens,* 3:180, 194.

67. Tracy speculates that original sensations may be the result of a reaction that goes from nerves to brain, while remembrance goes from brain to nerves. However, "these are but conjectures; the mechanical action of our nerves has hitherto escaped all observation." *Elémens,* 1:38–39.

68. *Elémens,* 3:186, 218.

69. Ibid., pp. 182–83.

70. *Essai sur l'origine des connaissances humaines, Oeuvres,* 1:11–13.

71. *Extrait raisonné du Traité des sensations, Oeuvres,* 1:326. See Knight, *The Geometric Spirit,* pp. 107–8.

72. For Helvétius's discussion of attention, see *De l'esprit,* 2 vols. (Paris: Durand, 1758), 1:368–94.

73. *Elémens,* 1:243.

74. *Mémoire sur la faculté de penser,* pp. 346–47. Cf. *Elémens,* 1:219: "Attention is the state of a man who wishes to surmount a difficulty; it is a mode of being produced by the energy of the will."

75. Ibid., p. 253.

76. "Thus the more a memory reoccurs, the more easily it stirs up collateral memories." Ibid., p. 262.

77. Ibid., p. 266.

78. Ibid., p. 258*n.*

79. Ibid., p. 273.

80. *Elémens,* 2:ix. Tracy first deals with the nature of language in his *Mémoire sur la faculté de penser,* pp. 400–17, and in the *Réflexions sur les projets de pasigraphie* (read to the Institute in March 1800), *Mémoires de l'Institut,* 3:535–51. He later expanded this treatment in the *Elémens,* 1:302–8, and in the second volume of the *Elémens,* entitled *Grammaire.*

81. Speculation on the natural origins of language was greatly influenced by Bernard Mandeville's *The Fable of the Bees* (1714) and William Warburton's *The Divine Legation of Moses Demonstrated* (1737). See F.B. Kaye, "Mandeville on the Origin of Language," *Modern Language Notes* 39 (1924):136–42. In the 1750s and 1760s a flood of quasi-anthropological accounts of the origins of language were published, including Condillac's *Essai sur l'origine des connaissances humaines*

(1746), Diderot's *Lettre sur les sourds et muets* (1751), Rousseau's *Discours sur l'origine de l'inégalité* (1754), Maupertuis's *Réflexions philosophiques sur l'origine des langues et la signification des mots* (1756), Nicholas Sylvestre Bergier's *Les éléments primitifs des langues* (1764), Charles de Brosses's *Traité de la formation méchanique des langues et des principes physiques de l'étymologie* (1765), Nicholas Boulanger's *L'antiquité devoilée* (1766), Claude François de Radonvillier's *De la manière d'apprendre les langues* (1768); and l'Abbé Copineau's *Essai synthétique sur l'origine et la formation des langues* (1774). See Paul Kuehner, *Theories on the Origin and Formation of Language in the Eighteenth Century in France* (Philadelphia: University of Pennsylvania, 1944), pp. v–viii, 20–50.

82. H.B. Acton, "La philosophie du langage sous la Révolution française," *Archives de philosophie* (July–December 1961):445. Then, as now, ideas discussed included: that to think is really to speak, that language is a sort of calculation, and that many philosophical problems are pseudoproblems to be unmasked by linguistic reform.

83. *Elémens*, 1:318; 2:18–20. Unlike Condillac and Brosses, however, Tracy did not think that signs were determined by the nature of the things designated, but rather by the constant relations between actions and thoughts or sentiments. *Elémens*, 1:305–6. On this point, see Guy Harnois, *Les théories du langage en France de 1660 à 1821* (Paris: Société d'Edition "Les Belles-Lettres," 1929), p. 60.

84. *Mémoire sur la faculté de penser*, pp. 410–13.

85. *Elémens*, 2:21.

86. *Elémens*, 1:103–4; 2:41.

87. Ibid., pp. 182–84.

88. Ibid., p. 379. See also *Elémens*, 1:384–86.

89. *Réflexions sur les projets de pasigraphie*, p. 584.

90. "A language, whether erudite or vulgar, is never established by express conviction and by premeditated design." *Elémens*, 2:371. See also ibid., pp. 284, 359.

91. Ibid., p. 369.

92. *Réflexions sur les projets de pasigraphie*, p. 584. Cf. *Elémens*, 2:369: "Indeed, I firmly believe what I have always said, that a universal language is as impossible as perpetual motion."

93. Ibid., p. 375.

94. Tracy approvingly refers to Biran's work on the close links between hearing, speaking, and memory. Ibid., p. 384. A pervasive theme of Tracy's *Grammaire* is the superiority of western languages based on the Phoenician alphabet to hieroglyphics. The latter relies too heavily on unaided memory and prevents the spread of knowledge beyond a small learned caste. Ibid., pp. 67–74, 281.

95. *Elémens*, 3:423.

96. For a detailed structural analysis of Tracy's effort to use language analysis to establish the possibility of truth, see François Rastier, *Idéologie et théorie des signes: Analyse structurale des Eléments d'Idéologie d'Antoine-Louis-Claude Destutt de*

Tracy (The Hague: Mouton, 1972). Rastier uses Tracy's work as an illustration of an epistemological break between universal grammar and historical linguistics.

97. *Mélanges de littérature, Oeuvres de Stendhal,* ed. Henri Martineau, 46 vols. (Paris: Le Divan, 1927–1938; repr. Nendeln, Liechtenstein: Kraus, 1968), 39:417.

98. Tracy deals with this issue in the "Supplément à la première section des Elémens d'idéologie," *Elémens,* 4:22–46. Reservations about the applicability of probability theory to the human sciences had already been expressed in similar terms by Cabanis. See *Révolution et réforme de la médicine, Oeuvres philosophiques,* 2:150–54, 242–46. On the general debate over the place of mathematics in social science, see Moravia, *Il pensiero,* pp. 729–62. Moravia claims that François Thurot, in his 1797 lectures at the *Lycée des Etrangers,* had already attacked Condorcet's concept of social mathematics in a discussion very similar to Tracy's. Ibid., pp. 736–38, 740–41. The language is indeed similar, but there is no indication that Thurot's "Sixième Leçon," in which his discussion of probability appears, was written in 1797. The editor of Thurot's posthumously published lectures gives dates only for the first four lessons, and notes that the lectures were frequently revised and rewritten up to Thurot's death in 1832. François Thurot, *Oeuvres posthumes* (Paris: L. Hachette, 1837), p. v. The actual text of the Sixth Lesson must have been revised at least as late as 1813, since it refers to a study by Laplace that appeared "last year [1812]" (p. 339). Tracy's discussion of probability was most probably written in 1805. See Kennedy, *A Philosophe in the Age of Revolution,* p. 49. It seems apparent that Thurot, an acknowledged disciple of Tracy, based his discussion on the latter's work. This seems even more likely since Thurot's Seventh Lesson on Logic is clearly based on Tracy's *Traité sur la volonté.* See pp. 360–71, in which some passages are obviously lifted from Tracy's text.

99. *Elémens du calcul des probabilités, et son application aux jeux de hasards,* ed. Joseph Marie Fayolle (Paris: an XIII [1805]), p. 91, quoted in Baker, *Condorcet,* p. 188.

100. *Elémens,* 4:37.

101. Ibid., p. 38.

102. Ibid., p. 34.

103. *Elémens,* 1:199; 4:44.

104. On this point see Henry G. Van Leeuwen, *The Problem of Certainty in English Thought: 1630–1690* (The Hague: Martinus Nijhoff, 1963).

105. Volney, *Lectures on History,* p. 55.

106. Ibid., p. 183.

107. Ibid., p. 56.

108. Daunou, "Analyse des opinions diverses sur l'origine de l'imprimerie," *Mémoires de l'Institut,* 4:543.

109. *Elémens,* 3:87.

110. Hobbes, *De Corpore, The English Works of Thomas Hobbes,* ed. William Molesworth (London: John Bohn, 1839; repr. Scientia Aalen, 1962), 1:30.

111. *Elémens,* 3:555. Thomas Brown repeats Tracy's attack on syllogistic rea-

soning in remarkably similar terms. Cf. Ibid., pp. 86–91, 135–36, and Brown, *Lectures,* 3:535–40.

112. *Elémens,* 4:79–80.

113. *Elémens,* 3:145.

CHAPTER THREE: POLITICAL ECONOMY AND THE LOGIC OF THE WILL

1. *The Selected Work of Tom Paine,* ed. Howard Fast (New York: Random House, The Modern Library, 1945), pp. 192–98 and passim. See Halévy, *Philosophical Radicalism,* p. 188 on this point.

2. Roederer, *Oeuvres,* 8:130.

3. On the growing interest in economics in France, see Emile Levasseur, *Histoire des classes ouvrières et de l'industrie en France de 1789 à 1870,* 2nd revised ed., 2 vols. (New York: AMS Press, 1969), 1:676 ff.

4. See Joseph Schumpeter, *A History of Economic Analysis* (New York: Oxford University Press, 1974), p. 454.

5. *A Treatise on Political Economy,* trans. from the fourth edition by C. R. Princeps, intro. trans. Clement C. Biddle (Philadelphia: Grigg & Elliot, 1832), pp. xix–xx. Unless otherwise noted, references to Say's *Treatise* will be to this edition.

6. Say, *Treatise,* pp. xxxviii–xliv.

7. Ibid., p. lv.

8. See "Ce que c'est qu'une nation eclairée," *Oeuvres diverses de J.B. Say,* ed. Ch. Comte, E. Daire, and Horace Say (Paris: Guillaumin et Cie, 1848), pp. 280–83.

9. *Treatise,* p. lv. In the first edition of the *Traité sur l'économie politique* (Paris: Deterville, 1803), p. iv., Say argues that particular and general facts result from the action of the law of nature. However, in later editions, he suppresses the phrase "law of nature" in favor of the more neutral phrase "the results of the nature of things."

10. *Treatise,* p. xlvi. This criticism of Ricardo echoes Tracy's discussion of the limitations of the scientific method in social theory. Say's remarks were added to the second edition (1814); therefore, he may have been influenced by Tracy's discussion, which was written by 1811.

11. Ibid., p. xxi.

12. Ibid., p. 72. As an editor of the *Décade,* Say had usually deferred to Tracy and Cabanis in matters of philosophy. Kitchin, *La Décade,* p. 135. In the *Treatise,* he continues to refer approvingly to their work. See *Treatise,* pp. xxx, lv.

13. For a discussion of the probable French influence on the developing notions of an economic science in England, see Halévy, *Philosophical Radicalism,* pp. 266–76, 333. On the theory of markets developed by Say and James Mill, see Thomas Sowell, *Say's Law—An Historical Analysis* (Princeton: Princeton University Press, 1972), pp. 17–28.

14. On his return, Say submitted the report, *De l'Angleterre et des Anglais*. See *Oeuvres diverses*, pp. 205–31. His correspondence with Ricardo, much of which concerns their long-standing dispute over the definition of value, can be followed in ibid., pp. 406–29, and in David Ricardo, *Works and Correspondence*, 12 vols., ed. Piero Sraffa (Cambridge: Cambridge University Press, 1951–53), vols. 6–9. Say published a famous series of letters to Malthus and also corresponded privately with him. See *Oeuvres diverses*, pp. 439–520. It was with Say that John Stuart Mill stayed on arriving in France for the first time. See Anna Jean Mill, ed. *John Mill's Boyhood Visit to France* (Toronto: University of Toronto Press, 1960), pp. 5–8.

15. D'Hauterive, *Elémens de l'économie politique* (1818); Heinrich von Storch, *Cours d'économie politique ou exposition des principes qui déterminent la prosperité des nations* (1823). Storch first published his work in St. Petersburg in 1817 for the benefit of the future Czar Nicholas. It was reprinted in Paris in 1823, with notes by Say. Storch apparently resented this edition and accused Say of theft. In reply, Say accused Storch of having copied three fourths of his work textually from Tracy, Bentham, Sismondi, and Say. See Say, *Commentaire sur le Cours d'économie politique d'Henry Storch, Oeuvres diverses*, p. 287.

16. Robert Goetz-Girey, *Croissance et progrès a l'origine des sociétés industrielles* (Paris: Editions Montchrestien, 1966), p. 108. Comte and Dunoyer edited the liberal journal, *Le Censeur européen, ou Examen de diverses questions de droit public et de divers ouvrages littéraires et scientifiques* (Paris: February 1817–April 1819).

17. See, e.g., *Elémens*, 4:289–90. The expression was later adopted and popularized by Sismondi. Leroy, *Histoire des idées sociales*, 2:168. It was also adopted by J.B. Say in the later editions of his works, as a more precise description of his theory. See Say, *Oeuvres diverses*, ed. n., p. 136.

18. *Elémens*, 4:131.

19. *Elémens*, 3:380–81. Cf. also *Commentaire sur l'esprit des lois de Montesquieu . . . suivi d'observations inédites de Condorcet sur le vingt-neuvième livre du même ouvrage et d'un mémoire sur cette question: quelles sont les moyens de fonder la morale d'un peuple?* (1819; repr. Geneva: Slatkine, 1970), pp. 95, 280; hereafter cited as *Commentaire*. Tracy intended to continue the *Elémens d'idéologie* in order to treat moral and political questions. He never finished the fifth part, partly because of failing health. See his letters to Jefferson of 24 December 1816 and 8 January 1824, in which he says that his philosophical work is finished. Chinard, *Jefferson et les idéologues*, pp. 166, 219. In the introduction to the *Commentaire* (p. vii), Tracy notes that the collection of political opinions scattered through this work forms a "complete treatise of politics or *social science*." The rambling discursive form of commentary had disadvantages, but it allowed him to develop and present his opinions while refuting some of the still influential ideas of Montesquieu.

20. *Commentaire*, p. 285.

21. *Elémens*, 4:258, 440.

22. Edgard Allix, "Destutt de Tracy, Economiste," *Revue d'économie politique* 26 (1912):425.

23. Karl Marx, *Capital,* 3 vols., trans. Samuel Moore and Edward Aveling, ed. Frederick Engels (New York: International Publishers, 1967), 1:648. The only work by Tracy to which Marx refers is the fourth volume of the *Elémens,* the *Traité sur la volonté.* Marx apparently read Tracy in the early 1840s, since he refers to him in the *German Ideology.* See below, n. 32. The particular Marxian use of the term *ideology,* i.e., to mean a set of ideas justifying a particular economic, social, and political order in terms of universal truths, certainly owes something to Marx's reading of Tracy. Nevertheless, Marx also cites Tracy with approval—on the labor theory of value, the process of exchange, and the benefits of cooperative labor—judging him to be "to a certain extent a luminary among the vulgar economists." Ibid. For other references to Tracy, see *Capital,* 1:80, 325, 327–28, 2:480–88. On the transformation of the term "ideology" from Tracy to Marx, see Kennedy, *A Philosophe in the Age of Revolution,* pp. 339–46.

24. *Elémens,* 4:507. Tracy does not seem to realize the extent to which Bichat's dualism had broken with the assumptions of "ideology" as exemplified, for example, in the work of Cabanis. In Bichat's theory, organic life is largely exempt from the influence of habit. See Bréhier, *History of Philosophy,* 6:42.

25. *Elémens,* 4:513.

26. Sieyès, *Préliminaire,* p. 42.

27. *Elémens,* 4:55–56.

28. Ibid., p. 61. Tracy suggests that, instead of saying, "I can walk," we could say more precisely, "the faculty of feeling, which constitutes the moral person who is speaking to you, has the property of making its legs react in such a way that its body walks." Ibid., p. 62.

29. Tracy speculates that a limited notion of self-consciousness might arise without the willing faculty, but not the full notion of self, which necessarily includes the ideas of circumscription and individuality. Ibid., pp. 65–66.

30. Ibid., p. 67–68.

31. *Quels sont les moyens de fonder la morale d'un peuple?* in *Commentaire,* p. 449. This short pamphlet was originally published in 1798, and later appended to the French edition of the *Commentaire.* In a forward to this work, Tracy says that he is reprinting it to show that he held the same general views in 1798 as in 1806, when he composed the *Commentaire.*

32. *Elémens,* 4:70–71. In the *German Ideology,* Marx notes that this defense of property was used by "Saint Sancho" (Max Stirner) as though it were novel, although, in fact, Tracy (among others) had said the same thing much better thirty years earlier. Marx then quotes all the relevant passages from Tracy's *Traité sur la volonté.* See Karl Marx and Frederick Engels, *Collected Works,* vol. 5: *Marx and Engels: 1845–47,* trans. Clemens Dutt, W. Lough, and C.P. Magill (London: Lawrence and Wishart, 1976), pp. 228–29. Proudhon also indignantly denied that Tracy's theory of property was an adequate defense of privately owned capital. See Pierre-Joseph Proudhon, *Qu'est-ce que la propriété?* (Paris: Garnier-Flammarion, 1966), pp. 100–4.

33. "There's already one great source of divagations and declamations com-

pletely dried up." *Elémens,* 4:259. In the *Moyens de Fonder,* p. 450, Tracy identifies the subjects of this refutation of communism as the ancients—Plato and the Spartans—but he clearly has in mind also the more recent critics of property such as Rousseau, Mably, and Babeuf. Commenting on Rousseau, in a manner uncommonly perceptive for the time, he notes that the "Genevan" was more consistent than the Greeks in his view of property. While Rousseau called property the source of all crime, he also called society the cause of all vice, thereby simply underlining a truth that cannot be denied: "where there is no moral relationship there can be no moral evil."

34. *Elémens,* 4:70.

35. Ibid., p. 89.

36. *Treatise,* p. 2. See also *Catéchisme d'économie politique* (Brussels: P.J. Hanicq et Cie, 1836), pp. 19–23. Unlike Adam Smith, Say was careful to note clearly that economics is not concerned with real needs, or what is useful "to the eye of reason" but with actual needs, i.e., whatever men happen to value. Tracy also makes this distinction, albeit in a more confused manner, by distinguishing between effective or present needs, which are synonymous with conscious desires, and real or true needs, which seem to be synonymous with our long-range interest in maximum well-being. *Elémens,* 4:79–82. Elsewhere he states the position unambiguously. "In general it can be said that whatever is capable of procuring any advantage, even a frivolous pleasure, is *useful,* . . . for, in the end, all that we desire is to increase our enjoyments and diminish our sufferings; and certainly the feeling of pleasure and of satisfaction is a good: all goods are even nothing more than that variously modified." Ibid., pp. 156–57.

37. *Treatise,* p. 2. Halévy incorrectly states that Tracy followed Say in deriving value from utility. See *Philosophical Radicalism,* p. 320.

38. *Treatise,* pp. 235–44. For Say's struggle to use utility as an adequate tool of analysis, see Marian Bowley, *Studies in the History of Economic Theory before 1870* (London: Macmillan, 1973), pp. 143–44.

39. In the third edition of the *Principles of Political Economy* (1821), Ricardo inserted several paragraphs on Tracy's theory of value in support of his own position against that of Say. According to Ricardo, Say's position is contradicted by "a very distinguished writer, M. Destutt de Tracy" who has shown that a thing can be measured only by a determinate quantity of the same thing. For Ricardo, the only common measure of value is labor. He adds, "This also, I am happy to say, appears to be M. Destutt de Tracy's opinion." *Works and Correspondence,* 1:284. In 1822, Ricardo was introduced to Tracy in Paris. In a letter to Malthus, he notes, "I was very much pleased with Mons. Gallois, who made me acquainted with M. Destutt Tracy, a very agreeable old gentleman whose works I had read with pleasure. I do not entirely agree with him in Political Economy—he is one of Say's school—there are nevertheless some points of difference between them." Ricardo to Malthus, 16 December 1822, ibid., 9:248.

40. *Elémens,* 1:132.

41. *Elémens,* 4:95.

42. Ibid., p. 96. Tracy is a bit troubled that the changes in human needs over time render the labor theory of value less certain, and speculates that we might be able to use probability theory to assess the limits of the variability of human nature. However he immediately qualifies his own suggestion: "But this observation must teach us how delicate and skilful is the calculation of all moral and economic quantities, how much it requires caution, and how imprudent it is to wish to employ the rigorous gradation of numbers inconsiderately." Ibid., p. 97.

43. Ibid., pp. 160–65. Cf. ibid., p. 282: "Mr. Say understands by production, *production of utility*. It is . . . following him that I have given this idea of it."

44. *Commentaire*, pp. 262–63. See also *Elémens*, 4:396. For a careful discussion of Tracy's theory of value, see Allix, "Tracy, Economiste," pp. 440–43.

45. *Elémens*, 4:95.

46. Tracy was wrong about Smith, who did speculate on the cause of man's propensity to "truck" in *The Theory of Moral Sentiments*. On this point, see Robert D. Cumming, *Human Nature and History: A Study of the Development of Liberal Political Thought*, 2 vols. (Chicago: University of Chicago Press, 1969), 2:215–16.

47. *Elémens*, 2:68–71; see also *Elémens*, 4.143.

48. Ibid. See also ibid., pp. 131, 145 and *Commentaire*, pp. 313–14.

49. *Elémens* 4:133.

50. Ibid., p. 145. "Concurrence of forces, increase and conservation of enlightenment, and division of labor, these are the three great benefits of society." Ibid., p. 146. Allix argues that Marx clearly used Tracy's discussion of cooperative labor as a basis for the thirteenth chapter of volume one of *Capital*, Allix "Tracy, Economiste," p. 451.

51. See, for example, Diderot's article on *pauvreté* in the *Encyclopédie*.

52. *Elémens*, 4:320.

53. Ibid., p. 135.

54. Ibid., pp. 141–142. See also ibid., p. 320, where Tracy notes that "it must be admitted that when it [society] completely loses sight of its end, the reproaches of its most bitter detractors are justified."

55. For the origins and implications of *industrie* in Say's work, see the article by Michael James, "Pierre-Louis Roederer, Jean-Baptiste Say, and the Concept of *industrie*." *History of Political Economy* 9 (1977):455–75, which the following discussion of Say follows quite closely.

56. Say, *Treatise*, p. 4.

57. Ibid., pp. 20–21. James argues that Say's use of *industrie* reflected peculiarly French social experience and thought, in particular the revolutionary consciousness of an opposition between the *industrie* of the small entrepreneur—to which the poor and unskilled aspired—and the idleness of landed interests. See "Roederer, Say, and the Concept of *industrie*," p. 470.

58. Say, *Treatise*, pp. 363–73.

59. Ibid., pp. 74, 360–67.

60. *Commentaire*, pp. 290–92; *Elémens*, 4:169. This theory is quite close to

Ricardo's theory of rent. In commenting on the theory of MacCulloch, Say argued that MacCulloch was wrong to attribute this theory solely to Ricardo; it had already been put forth by Tracy in the *Commentaire*. See Say, *Examen critique du Discours de M. Macculloch sur l'économie politique, Oeuvres diverses*, pp. 275–77.

61. *Elémens*, 4:183.

62. Ibid., p. 201.

63. Ibid., p. 338.

64. Ibid., p. 341.

65. Ibid., p. 155.

66. Ibid., p. 183.

67. Ibid., p. 156.

68. *Commentaire*, pp. 75–76; *Elémens*, 4:316. Following Smith, he distinctly excludes the employment of domestic servants, doctors, lawyers, soldiers and public officials, as well as expenditures for entertainments such as theater or concerts. Ibid., p. 343.

69. Ibid., p. 336; *Commentaire*, p. 81.

70. Ibid.; *Elémens*, 4:345.

71. Ibid., p. 356.

72. Occasionally, Tracy recognizes this distinction. See ibid., p. 348; *Commentaire*, p. 87.

73. *Elémens*, 4:154.

74. Ibid., p. 368.

75. Ibid., p. 366n. Tracy was himself one of France's largest proprietors, an absentee landlord who derived most of his income from the rent of his properties (although he may have reinvested some of it). Kennedy suggests that Tracy's sense of persecution and futility led him to praise the role of "ideologist" as an unmasker, and to denounce mercilessly the pretentions of his own class. See Kennedy, *A Philosophe in the Age of Revolution*, pp. 206–7. There is certainly a bitter flavor to Tracy's comments on the nobility: "The degree to which arrogance can deceive and cause one to exaggerate his individual importance is incredible. I have seen men, compelled to abandon their estates because of revolutionary disturbances, who believed in good faith that the whole village would lack work, without noticing that it was not they, but their tenant farmers, who paid out most of the wages. These men sincerely convinced themselves that even if their peasants were to divide their property or to buy it dirt cheap, [these same peasants] would only become more destitute." *Elémens*, 4:354–55n.

76. Ibid., p. 446.

77. Ibid., p. 319.

78. Ibid., p. 174.

79. Ibid., p. 269.

80. Ibid., p. 140.

81. Ibid., pp. 287–88.

82. See Joseph J. Spengler, "French Population Theory since 1800," *Journal of Political Economy* 44 (1936):579; Allix, "Tracy, Economiste," p. 534. Tracy's

celebration of production and the benefits of the division of labor is so striking that a neglect of his treatment of distribution leads to the mistaken characterization of him as even more optimistic than Say. See, e.g., L.H. Haney, *History of Economic Thought* (New York: Macmillan, 1911), p. 277*n*.

83. *Elémens*, 4:283. Tracy was familiar with the 1809 French translation of Malthus's *Essay on Population*. See Kennedy, *A Philosophe in the Age of Revolution*, p. 197. His adoption of a Malthusian perspective did much to popularize these ideas in France. See Spengler, "French Population Theory," pp. 581–82 and Allix, "Tracy, Economiste," p. 450. Tracy was apparently dismayed at Malthus's defense of wealthy landowners in the later *Principles of Political Economy* (1820). In a letter to Jefferson, Tracy reports that Malthus had contradicted his earlier work in deference to the defenders of privilege. According to Tracy, Malthus attempted to prove that men who do nothing are the most useful, and that the "poor devils who die of hunger" are pleased to see wealthy idlers multiplying next to them. Tracy to Jefferson, 24 October 1820, Chinard, *Jefferson et les idéologues*, pp. 197–99.

84. *Elémens*, 4:283.

85. Ibid., pp. 273–75, 289–94.

86. Ibid., p. 286. Tracy's view of the population problem is not quite as pessimistic as that of Malthus because of his position on birth control. Since it is not numbers of individuals, but rather their well-being, that is the true end of society, it is not always desirable to multiply men in a country like "rabbits in a warren." *Commentaire*, p. 384. Tracy states that to prevent a birth is often an act of prudence and that religious precepts and positive legislation have wrongly forbidden this practice.

87. *Elémens*, 4:265.

88. Say, *Treatise*, p. 245.

89. *Elémens*, 4:261.

90. Tracy is inconsistent on this point. At times he stresses the utter debasement of wage laborers: "disgraced by fate [they] become almost as unhappy as if they were still savages." Ibid., p. 267. He notes that machinery is beneficial to the species but not to individual workers. Ibid., p. 162. Finally, he notes the paradox that in poor countries, people live comfortably, while in rich nations the people are poor. Ibid., p. 328. (Marx says that Tracy blurts this out "brutally." *Capital*, 1:648.) However, Tracy sometimes argues that everyone is better off in society. See, e.g., *Elémens*, 3:149. This is proved by the fact that the population does not die out. *Elémens*, 4:407. This optimism, however, is elsewhere contradicted by Tracy's argument that numbers do not prove happiness, because they only mean an increase of *misérables*. The increase of numbers is but a "symptom," not a "*bonheur*." Ibid., p. 358. Perhaps Tracy's most characteristic statement on this question is that "the elements of this calculation are so numerous that it is very difficult, and perhaps impossible, to make it directly." Ibid., p. 164.

91. Ibid., p. 329.

92. Ibid., pp. 269, 295.

93. Ibid., p. 294.

94. Ibid., p. 302. For a discussion of the perceived consonance of interests between prince and people in French thought, see Nannerl O. Keohane, *Philosophy and the State in France* (Princeton: Princeton University Press, 1980), esp. pp. 155–56.

95. In Tracy's view, to deny workers the opportunity to emigrate is particularly criminal: "it is as if, having shut two men up in a box in which there was only enough air for one, it was determined that one or even both should suffocate, rather than that either be allowed to go out." Ibid., p. 303.

96. *Elémens*, 4:446.

97. Ibid., pp. 304, 308. See also *Commentaire*, p. 275.

98. *Elémens*, 4:262. Cf. ibid., p. 514; "It is thus that we are constituted by nature, which, if it had any purpose at all in making us as we are, could hardly have been concerned with the happiness of individuals. . . . Assuredly [nature] is much less a mother than a *marâtre* ['harsh stepmother'] to us."

99. Ibid., p. 371; *Commentaire*, p. 242.

100. *Elémens*, 4:420.

101. Cf. Say, *Treatise*, pp. 280–83, 477–87 and Tracy, *Elémens*, 4:425–39, 215–57. Influenced by the disastrous revolutionary inflation associated with the issuing of assignats, as well as by the inflation of 1810, Tracy concludes by quoting Mirabeau, "Tout papier-monnaie est un orgie du despotisme en délire." Ibid., p. 241.

102. Ibid., p. 432.

103. Tracy analyzes the effects of particular taxes in Book Thirteen of the *Commentaire,* and repeats his discussion, often verbatim, in the *Traité sur la volonté.* Cf. *Commentaire*, pp. 237–94 and *Elémens*, 4:376–420. Allix notes that Tracy's discussion of taxation is one of the most interesting parts of the work for an economic historian, since Tracy clearly formulated the classical theory of *incidence*, a theory usually attributed to H. Passy. "Tracy, Economiste," p. 446.

104. *Elémens*, 4:403–4.

105. Ibid., p. 413.

106. *Commentaire*, p. 366.

107. Ibid., p. 247.

108. *Elémens*, 4:419.

109. For a discussion of these characteristics of eighteenth-century economics, see Harry C. Payne, "*Pauvreté, misère,* and the aims of Enlightened Economics," *Studies on Voltaire and the Eighteenth Century* 154 (1976):1581–92.

110. Tracy, *Elémens*, 4:514.

111. See below, pp. 171–85.

CHAPTER FOUR: "IDEOLOGICAL" POLITICS

1. *Cours d'études,* 1:6, 2:77. Throughout his historical lectures, however, Daunou clearly accepts the psychological and moral presuppositions of *idéologie.*

See ibid., pp. 63–130. To the extent that he directly considers the implications of human psychology and physiology for political theory, he merely suggests that the innate inequalities in sensitivity discussed by Cabanis and Bichat are reflected in differing political talents. Ibid., pp. 47–48.

2. David Hume, "Of the Original Contract," *Political Essays* (New York: Library of Liberal Arts, 1953), p. 48.

3. Cabanis, *Quelques considérations sur l'organisation en général et particulièrement sur la nouvelle constitution, Oeuvres philosophiques,* 2:463.

4. *Elémens,* 4:130. See also ibid., pp. 119–20, 128–29, 259.

5. Ibid., p. 105.

6. Ibid., p. 371. See also *Mémoire sur la faculté de penser,* p. 363.

7. *Essai sur les garanties,* p. 6.

8. Ibid., pp. 86–87. Daunou's lectures on public law avoid the direct discussion of either legitimacy or sovereignty. The term *puissance souveraine* refers to that power actually exercised by any existing government. See, e.g., *Cours d'études* 2:234.

9. *Cours d'études* 2:77.

10. Tracy does not directly integrate his general view of the economic stages involved in the growth of civil society into this three-stage theory, which is elaborated in the context of his rejection of the typology of governments found in the sixth book of Montesquieu's *Esprit des lois. Commentaire,* pp. 62–78, 223–24. His longest discussion of the religious culture of the aristocratic period can be found in the introduction to his *Analyse raisonée de l'Origine de tous les cultes, ou religion universelle; Ouvrage publié en l'an III par Dupuis, Citoyen français* (Paris: Courcier, 1804).

11. *Commentaire,* p. 67.

12. Imbert makes this suggestion in *Tracy: Critique,* p. 42.

13. *Analyse raisonée,* p. xxxix.

14. *Elémens,* 1:302–3.

15. *Commentaire,* p. 357.

16. For a sketch of the history of the notion that commerce breeds peaceful men, see Albert O. Hirschman, *The Passions and the Interests* (Princeton: Princeton University Press, 1977), pp. 78–87.

17. Picavet already saw this connection clearly in 1891. See *Les idéologues,* pp. 453–54.

18. Ibid., p. xli. In a similar way, Tracy notes that the establishment of monasteries may once have been useful. *Commentaire,* p. 209. He consistently argues that institutions bad in themselves may be suited to the times. Ibid., p. 148.

19. "I consider theology the philosophy of the childhood of the human race, ready to cede to the philosophy of its age of reason." *Analyse raisonée,* p. xliv.

20. *Commentaire,* p. 219.

21. *Elémens,* 1:199–200.

22. *Commentaire,* p. 162.

23. Ibid., p. 10.

24. Ibid., p. 66.
25. Ibid., p. 16.
26. *Commentaire*, p. 11. Tracy refers to some famous letters on the *Esprit des lois* widely attributed to Helvétius in the eighteenth and nineteenth centuries, but now believed to be forgeries. See R. Koebner, "The Authenticity of the Letters on the *Esprit des lois* attributed to Helvétius," *Bulletin of the Institute of Historical Research* 24 (1951):19–23.
27. *Commentaire*, p. 12.
28. Ibid., p. 8.
29. Ibid., pp. 13–14.
30. Ibid., p. 14.
31. Ibid., p. 15.
32. *Elémens*, 5:428.
33. *Commentaire*, pp. 26, 43, 56 (emphasis added).
34. Ibid., p. 109.
35. Ibid., p. 18; see also p. 52. The only long quotations from the *Esprit des lois* cited by Tracy are those on the corruption of the *Ancien Régime*. See ibid., pp. 19–20, 197. For a discussion of the debate over the meaning of "honor" during the Restoration, see Imbert, *Tracy: Critique*, pp. 49–52. Imbert argues that Tracy's *Commentaire* should be placed in this context. Although the *Commentaire* in fact contributed to this debate, Tracy's original fears were probably centered more on the increasingly aristocratic pretensions of the Napoleonic regime, than on the attempts of returned emigrés to reestablish the status quo ante.
36. *Commentaire*, pp. 196–97. Tracy equivocates on this point in the French version of the *Commentaire*. See below, p. 111.
37. Ibid., pp. 22–23.
38. Ibid., pp. 111–12, 133.
39. See Bourdon, "Le mécontentement," p. 21.
40. See, for example, Volney's discussion in his *Lectures on History*, pp. 169–84. Volney compares the Greeks and Romans to the Vandals and Huns (p. 174). For the Idéologues' rejection of the model of ancient republicanism, see Mouza Raskolnikoff, "Volney et les Idéologues: le refus de Rome," *Revue historique* 267 (April-June 1982):357–73.
41. "Eloges de Franklin," *O.C.*, 3:372, 374, 382–83, 402–3; "Sur l'instruction publique," *O.C.*, 7:197–98, 202–3, 268–69, 278–79, 374–75, 417–18.
42. See *A.P.*, 11:684–85, 28:250. On this point, see Harold T. Parker, *The Cult of Antiquity and the French Revolutionaries* (New York: Octagon Books, 1965), pp. 80–88, 139–77.
43. *Commentaire*, p. 304.
44. Ibid., p. 70. See also, pp. 21–22, where Tracy characterizes modern social relations as both "tighter and more diverse," and pp. 42, 70 and 115. Most eighteenth-century thinkers considered direct democracy to be impractical in Europe because of the size of modern nations, but this was only a minor consideration for Tracy. The notion that the economy was an intricate and complicated

mechanism had been clearly stated by the Physiocrats, and Sieyès had earlier suggested that the modern economy precluded direct democracy as a viable form of government. See Bastid, *Sieyès,* p. 352. Tracy is probably expanding on Sieyès's argument.

45. *Commentaire,* pp. 31, 216.

46. Ibid., pp. 8–9, 51, 64, 66, 70–71. Tracy argued that despotism as Montesquieu described it had never existed, even in the Orient.

47. Ibid., p. 38.

48. *Commentaire,* p. 7.

49. *Cours d'études,* 2:249, 255. Daunou criticizes both Montesquieu and Helvétius's letter on Montesquieu in almost the same terms used by Tracy, indicating that he was probably using Tracy's *Commentaire* as the basis of his lecture. See ibid., pp. 236–49.

50. Ibid., p. 251.

51. Ibid., p. 259.

52. Ibid., p. 252.

53. "Above all, it is necessary to know if resistance will cause more evil than obedience." *Commentaire,* p. 5. Cf. ibid., p. 31, where Tracy argues that it is not necessarily just to resist an unjust law. This is a decision that must be made by calculating the probable results of one's actions.

54. Ibid., pp. 130–31.

55. *Cours d'études,* 2:117.

56. Ibid., p. 119; *Garanties,* pp. 182, 244.

57. *Commentaire,* p. 211.

58. Ibid., p. 197.

59. Tracy to Jefferson, 22 February 1821, Chinard, *Jefferson et les idéologues,* p. 209.

60. This theme was central to the Restoration liberals' defense of the French Revolution. There was, however, relatively little discussion of the economic roots of the Revolution. Most liberal writers were concerned with reestablishing the theme of a political struggle for liberty in French history. For a discussion of the political aspects of historical writing during the Restoration, see Stanley Mellon, *The Political Uses of History: A Study of Historians in the French Restoration* (Stanford, California: Stanford University Press, 1958). Mellon's book is very useful, although many of the themes that he asserts were "introduced" under the Restoration had been standard fare in liberal circles much earlier.

61. During the revolutionary period, economic interpretations of the Revolution were not unknown, but were not very significant. The works of Harrington were very popular, along with the works of Locke and Sidney. But it was largely Harrington's republicanism that was attractive, not his economic approach to history. See Condorcet, *Esquisse, O.C.,* 6:154. A clear exception to the widespread theory of revolution based exclusively on natural rights can be found in the work of Joseph Barnave. The materialist conception of history contained in his posthumously published papers was eagerly rehabilitated by Jean Jaurès in

his *Histoire socialiste de la Révolution française*. A good discussion of Barnave in English can be found in Emanuel Chill, ed. and intro., *Power, Property, and History: Joseph Barnave's Introduction to the French Revolution and Other Writings* (New York: Harper Torchbooks, 1971). Chill stresses the influence on Barnave of Montesquieu, and his relative isolation from the mood of other revolutionaries.

62. *Commentaire*, p. 88.

63. *Elémens*, 4:363.

64. *Commentaire*, p. 95.

65. *Elémens*, 4:357.

66. *Cours d'études*, 2:165–66.

67. Ibid., p. 163. Cf. ibid., p. 230, where, following Tracy, Daunou defines society as ". . . wherever there are men who divide their labor in order to reap, exchange, and conserve its fruits."

68. Ibid., p. 145. Daunou's lectures on political economy were directly based on the works of Say and Tracy.

69. Ibid., p. 273.

70. *Elémens*, 2:10.

71. *Commentaire*, p. 60.

72. *Commentaire*, p. 57; see also p. 22.

73. Equality, of course, may also refer directly to the distribution of material and social goods. It is in this sense that Tracy uses it when he states that the laws should "tend to diminish *inequality* as much as possible because it imperils *liberty*." Ibid., p. 306.

74. Ibid., pp. 60, 210.

75. Ibid., pp. 212–17, 227.

76. Ibid., p. 387.

77. Ibid., p. 72.

78. Tracy to Fauriel, 12 December [1807], quoted in Kennedy, *A Philosophe in the Age of Revolution*, p. 177.

79. *Elémens*, 4:98.

80. Ibid., p. 99.

81. *Commentaire*, p. 145.

82. Ibid.

83. The chapter "De l'amour" was long considered to consist of an incomplete fragment. In reviewing the Tracy-Jefferson correspondence, however, Gilbert Chinard noticed a reference to a more complete essay, which had been published only in an Italian translation. Chinard then retranslated the complete chapter into French, and published it as *De l'amour* (Paris: Société d'édition "Les Belles-Lettres," 1926). While Tracy did not publish "De l'amour" in French, he showed it to close friends. Its influence can be seen in Stendhal's work of the same name. See Albert Harry Berrian, "Stendhal and the Idéologues" (Ph.D. dissertation, New York University, 1954), pp. 63–70.

84. *De l'amour*, p. 49. Chinard speculates that Tracy may have been acquainted with Fourier's *Théorie des quatres mouvements* (1809), since Tracy liked to keep

abreast of advanced ideas. Chinard, Introduction to *De l'amour,* p. xxii. There are
some similarities between the two theorists, e.g., the stress on physical passion as
the source of love, and the criticism of marriage as practiced in nineteenth-century
society.

85. *De l'amour,* p. 14. See also *Commentaire,* p. 299.

86. *De l'amour,* p. 36.

87. Ibid., p. 20.

88. Ibid., p. 56. Tracy does consider that divorce—if frequent—might have
bad social effects, but he thinks that divorces would remain relatively rare because
most people take drastic action only in intolerable situations.

89. See Tracy to Jefferson, 22 February 1821, in Chinard, *Jefferson et les idéologues,* pp. 208–11.

90. *Commentaire,* p. 148.

91. Ibid., p. 208.

92. Ibid. Imbert argues that this passage can be explained only by a lingering
ambivalence toward Napoleon. See *Tracy: Critique,* p. 71. But Tracy is clearly
hostile to Napoleon throughout the *Commentaire.* His seeming equation of despotism with liberty in this passage is more probably due to his persistent failure
to fit existing realities within his categories.

93. *Commentaire,* p. 149. Cf. also p. 7: the despotic impulse occurs everywhere "because all human institutions are imperfect like their makers."

94. Ibid., pp. 149–50. In this quotation the phrase "many ways to manifest
their will" apparently refers to ways of manifesting public opinion. See ibid., p.
156.

95. *Commentaire,* p. 194.

96. *Moyens de fonder,* p. 453; cf. *Commentaire,* p. 158.

97. Ibid., p. 61.

98. Ibid., p. 166. Tracy weighs this option against an appeal to existing authorities or an appeal to a strongman like Napoleon.

99. Ibid., p. 176.

100. Ibid., pp. 176–77.

101. Ibid., p. 175.

102. Tracy undoubtedly refers to Condorcet, and probably to Sieyès (who
had no theoretical objections to women's suffrage), as the "respected authorities."
Among the Idéologues, Condorcet, Sieyès, and Tracy himself held exceptionally
liberal views regarding women. A more common opinion was that of Roederer,
who denied women any place in public life on the basis of incapacity. See his
Cours d'organisation social (1793), *Oeuvres,* 8:159–63. It has been suggested that
it is evidence of Tracy's radicalism even to have discussed this question when the
Commentaire appeared. Girard, *Le Libéralisme en France,* p. 73.

103. The indirect election of deputies is usually regarded as a patently anti-
democratic measure. See, e.g., Norman Hampson, *A Social History of the French
Revolution* (Toronto: University of Toronto Press, 1974), p. 114; Albert Ma-
thiez, *The French Revolution,* trans. Catherine Alison Phillips (New York: Alfred

A. Knopf, 1956), p. 87: Prélot, *Les institutions politiques,* pp. 65–66, 106. However, although the demand for direct suffrage had been part of the revolutionary democratic program, by 1795 the question no longer took this form. The debate was between those favoring indirect elections and those favoring the English model, i.e., direct elections with a high property qualification for the vote. See *Moniteur* 25:252–56. The latter was not necessarily more "democratic" than universal, but indirect, suffrage. Furthermore, by 1795 the arguments about how best to organize the electorate tended to turn on practical matters relating to the actual conditions under which primary and secondary assemblies operated. See Deslandres, *Histoire constitutionelle,* pp. 324–26, and Aulard, *The French Revolution,* 3:290. Tracy preferred indirect elections partly because he assumed that voters would in normal times naturally choose as electors their social and intellectual superiors. But he also appreciated the mechanical advantages of primary assemblies in a system without parties, and argued that this system would be less open to corruption. See *Commentaire,* p. 180.

104. This third principle represents a distillation of Tracy's views on the proper characteristics of a nation-state and the scope of its powers. His consideration of these issues was prompted partly by Montesquieu's discussion of geographical and sociological influence. Cf. *L'Esprit des lois, Oeuvres complètes* (Paris: Editions du Seuil, 1964), pp. 570–85, 613–41, and *Commentaire,* pp. 105–37, 296–306. Tracy concludes by dismissing most of Montesquieu's climatic determinism, arguing that a legislator need not be bound by geographic considerations. Tracy's discussion also reflects the recent period of revolutionary war. On his account, national stability requires sufficient territory, undisputed and defensible borders, and an efficient defensive force; however, he condemns expansion beyond "natural" borders and the keeping of overseas colonies, and hopefully anticipates peaceful European federation.

105. *Commentaire,* pp. 184, 366.

106. Ibid., p. 185.

107. Tracy himself felt strongly bound by the *cahier* of the Bourbonnais nobility, which forbade its delegates to join the Third Estate. See *Cahier de l'ordre de la Noblesse du Bourbonnais. Et pouvoirs remis à Mm. Denis-Michel-Philibert Dubuisson . . . Antoine-Louis-Claude de Stutt . . . et Henri Coiffier . . . députés au Etats-généraux,* p. 16. Only after Louis had capitulated and ordered the First and Second Estates to join the Third did Tracy submit his credentials. Even then he restricted himself to a "consultative voice" until he had heard the opinion of his constituents. *Procès verbal des séances de la Chambre de la Noblesse aux Etats généraux de 1789* (Paris: n.p., 1789), p. 335.

108. *Commentaire,* p. 33.

109. Ibid., p. 46.

110. Ibid., p. 32.

111. Ibid., pp. 75–76.

112. Ibid., p. 69.

113. Ibid., p. 394.

114. Ibid., p. 182.
115. Ibid., pp. 121–22. See also Tracy to Jefferson, 21 October 1811, Chinard, *Jefferson et les idéologues*, p. 90.
116. *Commentaire*, p. 185.
117. Ibid., pp. 184, 366.
118. In the *Commentaire*, pp. 187–88, Tracy gives a de-historicized account of Louis XVI's role in the Revolution, concluding that monarchical authority exists only uneasily with popular government. See also p. 196, where he uses similar language to condemn Napoleon: "We have seen [the authority of a single executive] limited to a few years, necessarily extended for life, and then made hereditary. This latter stage is only the complete development of its continuously active nature."
119. Ibid., p. 186.
120. Jefferson to Tracy, 26 January 1811, Chinard, *Jefferson et les idéologues*, pp. 75–79.
121. *Commentaire*, p. 207.
122. Ibid., p. 267. Tracy was probably thinking of Daunou's criticisms. Daunou argued that such a body would become a mere tool for the continual amendment of the constitution, and would become hardened to the just claims of others because of its privileged, isolated position. *Garanties*, p. 241.
123. See Girarde, *Le Libéralisme*, p. 74.
124. *Essai sur les garanties*, p. iii.
125. Daunou, however, also adopts (as subsidiary arguments) several themes more typical of the historical liberal movement in the Restoration, e.g., 1) the Old Regime was not a period of stability and tranquillity, but one of constant struggle and upheaval; 2) the Revolution must be seen as part of a centuries-old struggle between a newly emerging society and the remains of the institutions of the Middle Ages; 3) the Revolution was not a conspiracy and could not have been made without the cooperation of most of the people. Ibid., pp. 151–55. He also indirectly contributes to the politicized Gallican/Ultra-montane dispute with his attack on the pretensions of the papacy. On this point see also his *Essai sur la puissance temporelle des papes, et sur l'abus qu'ils ont fait de leur ministère spirituel* (Paris: Bureau Censeur européen, 1818).
126. *Essai sur les garanties*, p. i.
127. Ibid., p. 6.
128. Ibid., p. 26.
129. See ibid., pp. 50–51. Daunou's real grievance seems to have been that the restored nobility was reaping a large share of public revenues.
130. *Essai sur les garanties*, p. 67. Daunou also defends property on the basis of its necessary link to personality. "The civilized man is master of his person and understands that to include being master of the fruits of his labor." Ibid., p. 37. Property is necessary for the exercise and development of personal talents because it confers independence. The best laws ought to aim at enabling everyone to achieve this independence (admittedly an impossible goal).

131. Many of the speeches that Daunou delivered in the *Chambre des députés* dealt with the issue of freedom of the press. See, e.g., "Discours sur le projet d'assujeter les journaux à des cautionnemens" (1 May 1819), ibid., pp. 269–88; and "Discours contre le projet de soumettre les écrits périodiques à une censure préalable" (21 and 23 March 1820), ibid., pp. 326–49.

132. Ibid., p. 79.

133. Ibid., p. 76.

134. Ibid., p. 123; *Cours d'études,* 2:208–9.

135. *Essai sur les garanties,* p. 153; see also pp. 26, 167, and 191 where he speaks of the "germ of revolution" and reminds the reader of the consequences of past governmental obduracy ("dethronemens" and "revolutions").

136. *Cours d'études,* 2:269.

137. *Essai sur les garanties,* p. i.

138. Ibid., p. 240.

139. Ibid., pp. 169–202 passim.

140. Ibid., p. 201.

141. "Discours sur les élections" (20 May and 8 June 1820), ibid., p. 357.

142. Ibid., p. iii. Daunou also argued that there were French precedents for local juries. Thus, the institution of juries would not technically be an innovation. Ibid., pp. 30–31.

143. Ibid., pp. 207, 251–52. Daunou's conception of the function of a representative assembly differs from that of Tracy, in part because he is addressing more directly the situation in France under the *Charte.* In his view, the assembly is primarily a body that protects civil liberties and defends the constitution. Thus, it should act as a tribunal that accepts or rejects measures initiated by the government.

144. Ibid., p. 248.

145. Ibid., p. 225.

146. "Discours sur les élections," ibid., p. 372.

147. Ibid., pp. 206–7.

148. Ibid., pp. 351–401 passim.

149. For Daunou's opposition to the trial of Louis XVI, see *Considérations sur le procès de Louis XVI* (n.p., n.d.), pp. 5–6. Daunou's position was close to that of Condorcet and many Girondins. For a sympathetic analysis of this position, see Michael Walzer, *Regicide and Revolution: Speeches at the Trial of Louis XVI* (Cambridge: Cambridge University Press, 1974), pp. 55–59, 69–86. For Daunou's position on the Eighteenth Brumaire, see Taillandier, *Documents sur Daunou,* p. 162.

150. *Essai sur les garanties,* pp. 242, 246.

151. Ibid., pp. 91–92.

152. Ibid., pp. 165–67.

CHAPTER FIVE: FRENCH AND ENGLISH UTILITARIANS

1. The term *social science,* which had been current in Idéologue circles at least since the early 1790s, made its way into England by way of a Spanish translation

of Bentham's works, entitled *Espiritu de Bentham: Sistema de ciencia social* (Salamanca, 1920). The Spanish translator was familiar with the works of Destutt de Tracy and apparently used the latter's term to characterize Bentham's work. Bentham approved this use of *social science* and it was probably introduced to his followers in this way. See Keith Michael Baker, "The Early History of the Term 'Social Science,' " *Annals of Science* 20 (1964): 211–26. The term had earlier been introduced into America through translations of Tracy's works.

2. The Idéologues and the growing circle of reformers around Bentham certainly knew of each other and were aware of similarities in their approaches. James Mill was a philosophical disciple of Thomas Brown, who, in turn, was greatly influenced by the Idéologues. See above, p. 214. Mill was also an admirer of Helvétius, Condillac, Cabanis, and the Physiocrats. See Leslie Stephen, *The English Utilitarians,* 3 vols. (New York: Peter Smith, 1950), 2:268–78, 289. See also a projected introduction to Bentham's *Théorie des peines et des récompenses:* "When an Englishman and a Frenchman agree upon any point . . . there is a strong presumption that they are right." Quoted in Elie Halévy, *The Growth of Philosophical Radicalism,* pp. 435–36. The English were not particularly anxious to publicize their agreements with the French school because they did not want to provoke charges of being influenced by French "Jacobinism." As it was, the English Tories reproached the radicals with taking their morality from Helvétius, their psychology from Condillac, their political philosophy from Condorcet, and their political economy from J.B. Say. See Burdeau, *Traité de science politique,* p. 172. The Whig *Edinburgh Review* was consistently hostile in its references to the Idéologues; see e.g., 2:60, 5:318–24; 31:368ff., 35:158–90, 49:446ff.

Frederick B. Artz states that Tracy and Daunou were disciples of Bentham, and spread his ideas on the continent, *Reaction and Revolution: 1814–1832* (New York: Harper Torchbooks, 1963), p. 84. I can find no direct evidence for this, other than the general similarity in approach. Undoubtedly, the Idéologues were aware of Bentham, and regarded him as an enlightened legal reformer and valuable ally in the battle against "reaction." Roederer published a very favorable review of the *Principes de législation,* in the *Journal de Paris,* 25 August 1802, *Oeuvres,* 8:62. See also Say's favorable reviews of the *Tactique des assemblées législatives* and the *Plan of Parliamentary Reform* in the *Censeur européen* 4 (1818):74–96; 5 (1818):105–28. However, it is not necessary to postulate Benthamite influence to make sense of the Idéologue position, which continues specifically French political traditions.

3. See William Thomas, *The Philosophic Radicals: Nine Studies in Theory and Practice 1817–1841* (Oxford: Clarendon Press, 1979), pp. 1–13.

4. For a good recent discussion of this point, see Nancy Rosenblum, *Bentham's Theory of the Modern State* (Cambridge: Harvard University Press, 1978), pp. 55–56. See also J.H. Burns, "Bentham's Critique of Political Fallacies." In *Jeremy Bentham: Ten Critical Essays,* ed. Bhiku C. Parekh (London: Cass, 1974).

5. *Anarchical Fallacies, The Works of Jeremy Bentham,* ed. John Bowring, 11 vols. (Edinburgh: William Tait, 1843), 2:500–2. Hereafter cited as *Works.*

6. Ibid., pp. 496–524 passim.

7. Ibid., p. 530. The specific reference is to Sieyès. It is interesting to note that Bentham's French disciple Dumont (at that time not yet fully Bentham's collaborator) was part of the circle of advisors surrounding Mirabeau. Dumont's reaction to the debates on the first French Declaration of Rights can be found in *Letters Containing an Account of the Late Revolution in France* (London: J. Johnson, 1792) which he published under the pseudonym Henry Frederic Groenvelt. Dumont criticized the debates as "tedious and uninteresting," ibid., p. 228. His final position was quite close to that of the more cautious French moderates. "Instead of a declaration of the rights of man, I would merely have prefixed to the constitution a few *social maxims,* founded upon general utility, and pointing out precisely the object of society, and the duties of government." Ibid., p. 240. Dumont concludes that he is not an enemy of the rights of man, and that he understands why many enlightened men rejoiced at the declaration of rights as the symbol of a revival of liberty. On the relations between Dumont and Mirabeau, see Charles Blount, "Bentham, Dumont and Mirabeau: An Historical Revision," *University of Birmingham Historical Journal* 3 (1952):153–67. Blount initially thought that he might find (through Dumont) some Benthamite influence on the debates over the Declaration of Rights, but concluded that there was none.

8. From a manuscript note added by Bentham in 1819, quoted in Burns, "Bentham's Critique of Political Fallacies," p. 157.

9. Bentham's reluctance to reprint his earlier work was probably increased by the fact that he had himself made use of certain "fallacies of the right" in attacking natural rights, for example, that of "imputing bad character." Cf. also his later exposure of the Snail's-Pace Argument with his earlier objections to Sieyès. The Snail's-Pace Argument "consists in holding up to view the idea of graduality or slowness as characteristic of the course which wisdom would dictate. . . . This is neither more nor less than a contrivance for making out of a mere word an excuse for leaving undone an indefinite multitude of things, which, the arguer is convinced, and cannot forbear acknowledging, ought to be done." *The Book of Fallacies, Works,* 2:433. Bentham had earlier objected to Sieyès's phrase that prejudices should be "instantly abolished" in the following terms: *"Instantly* is a term suitable to the meridians of Algiers and Constantinople. *Gradually* is the language of justice and prudence." Ibid., 2:533.

10. *The Theory of Legislation,* trans. from the French of Etienne Dumont by Richard Hildreth, ed. C.K. Ogden (London: Routledge & Kegan Paul, 1931), pp. 82–83. See also University College Collection Box 69, p. 102, *Preparatory Principles,* quoted in Mary Peter Mack, *Jeremy Bentham: An Odyssey of Ideas 1748–1792* (New York: Columbia University Press, 1963), p. 188: "It is the nature of a command when backed by punishment to produce uniformity among actions: Men love to know the causes of things: and when they do not know them to talk as if they did. Seeing uniformity anywhere else they must also have a cause for it, and the cause must be a law."

11. *Works,* 1:iv.

12. Mack, *Bentham: An Odyssey,* p. 161.

13. *An Introduction to the Principles of Morals and Legislation,* ed. J.H. Burns and H.L.A. Hart (London: Athlone Press, 1970), Preface, p. 3.

14. "Nomographie," *Works,* 3:270. Cf. *The Theory of Legislation,* ed. Ogden, p. 87: "The language of truth is uniform and simple. The same ideas are always expressed by the same terms. Everything is referred to pleasures and pains."

15. See especially the chapters on "Belief," "Reflection," and "Will." *Analysis of the Phenomena of the Human Mind,* 2 vols. (1869; repr. New York: Augustus M. Kelley, 1967), 1:341 –423; 2:176 –83, 327 –95.

16. From a letter, James Mill to Francis Place, 6 December 1817, quoted in Thomas, *Philosophic Radicals,* p. 121.

17. *Mémoire sur la faculté de penser,* pp. 379 –80.

18. See, for example, John Rawls, *A Theory of Justice* (Cambridge, Mass.: The Belknap Press, 1972), pp. 22 –23, and H.L.A. Hart, "Between Utility and Rights," in *The Idea of Freedom,* ed. Alan Ryan (Oxford: Oxford University Press, 1979), pp. 77 –98.

19. *Introduction to the Principles of Morals,* ed. Burns and Hart, Preface, p. 3. The new preface was written in 1789. On the increasing closeness between Bentham's views on political economy and civil law, see Douglas G. Long, *Bentham on Liberty: Jeremy Bentham's Idea of Liberty in Relation to his Utilitarianism* (Toronto: University of Toronto Press, 1977), pp. 181 –82, 189 –98. Long argues (against Halévy) that the idea of a natural harmony of interests has no real place in Bentham's theory. S.R. Letwin makes the same argument in *The Pursuit of Certainty* (Cambridge: Cambridge University Press, 1965), p. 146*n*1. I also question Halévy's distinction between Bentham's "natural identification of interests" in economics and "artificial identification of interests" in politics and law; however, I argue that it is the former, rather than the latter, that is most fundamental to his political position. See below, pp. 143 –44.

20. *Theory of Legislation,* ed. Ogden, pp. 100 –1.

21. From an unpublished Bentham manuscript, Box 99, p. 47, headed "Civil Ordo., 12 Oct. 1795," quoted in Long, *Bentham on Liberty,* p. 164. Cf. *Theory of Legislation,* ed. Ogden, p. 96: "They approach each other at different points, and mingle together."

22. Bentham, *Of Laws in General,* ed. H.L.A. Hart (London: Athlone Press, 1970), pp. 200 –2.

23. *Jeremy Bentham's Economic Writings,* ed. W. Stark, 3 vols. (Leicester: Blackfriars Press Limited, 1952), 1:109.

24. *Theory of Legislation,* ed. Ogden, pp. 100 –1.

25. *Economic Writings,* ed. Stark, 3:77, 339.

26. Long, *Bentham on Liberty,* p. 55.

27. *Economic Writings,* ed. Stark, 1:129.

28. James Mill, *Essays on Government, Jurisprudence, Liberty of the Press, and Law of Nations* (1825; repr. New York: Augustus M. Kelley, 1967), *Jurisprudence,* p. 3.

29. See Bentham, *Theory of Legislation,* ed. Ogden, p. 48. On this point, see David Lyons, *In the Interest of the Governed: A Study in Bentham's Philosophy of Utility and Law* (Oxford: Clarendon Press, 1973), pp. 132–33.

30. Bentham, *Of Laws in General,* ed. Hart, pp. 119–20. Charles Dunoyer, a follower of Tracy and Say, noted in his *L'industrie et la morale considerées dans leurs rapports avec la liberté* (Paris: Sautelet, 1825), pp. 42–44, that Bentham's apparently strict view of the antithesis between law and liberty was close to the traditional "state of nature" theory that viewed political society as a *sacrifice* of liberty. He rejected Bentham's view, therefore, as inexact because it apparently could not clearly account for Bentham's recognition of an *increase* of liberty gained through laws guaranteeing security.

31. For Halévy's position, see *Philosophical Radicalism,* pp. 15–33. David Lyons, who is mostly concerned with the philosophical problem of a divergence between individual and community ethics, offers an interpretation similar to mine, i.e., he argues that Bentham assumes a natural harmonization of interest as the basis of his *legal* theory. See *In the Interest of the Governed,* pp. 1–49 and passim.

32. *Theory of Legislation,* ed. Ogden, p. 102. Cf. *Works,* 4:450: "Pleasure itself not being ponderable or measurable, to form an estimate of its dimunition, take the general source, and thence representative of pleasure, viz. *money."*

33. See, e.g., Currin V. Shields, "The Political Thought of the British Utilitarians," in James Mill, *Essay on Government,* ed. Shields (Indianapolis: Liberal Arts Press, 1977), pp. 38–39.

34. Alan Ryan, "Two Concepts of Politics and Democracy: James and John Stuart Mill," in *Machiavelli and the Nature of Political Thought,* ed. Martin Fleisher (New York: Atheneum, 1972), pp. 76–113.

35. See Kaiser, "From Enlightenment to Positivism," pp. 66–67, 165, 210–32.

36. Cf. Tracy, *Commentaire,* pp. 53–56, and Bentham, *Plan of Parliamentary Reform, Works,* 3:435–57. Bentham's characteristically roundabout way of expressing the difference between short and long-term interests is: "The good which constitutes the ground of the prohibitory measure, the reason that operates in favor of it, is comparatively prominent; the evil not equally so; its place is comparatively in the background. Hence it is [that], as in too many other instances, a good, however small, is by its vicinity to the eye enabled to eclipse and conceal the evil, however large." *Economics Writings,* ed. Stark, 3:411.

37. See Bentham, *Plan of Parliamentary Reform, Works,* 10:511, and Mill, *Analysis of the Human Mind,* 2:227–29. Daunou argues that the existence of parliamentary factions and parties is caused by ambition, and will disappear when a representative system is soundly established: "In truth, if the representative system can exist only in a miserable game of intrigue, it is hardly worth exhausting ourselves to establish it." *Essai sur les garanties,* p. 217.

38. *Plan of Parliamentary Reform, Works,* 3:452; see also *Constitutional Code, Works,* 9:107.

39. *Commentaire,* pp. 176–77.

40. See Joseph Hamburger, "James Mill on Universal Suffrage and the Middle Class," *Journal of Politics* 24 (1962):167–90, for a good refutation of the view of Mill as a defender of the middle class. From the textual evidence of the *Essay*, as well as from a consideration of Mill's polemical purposes, Hamburger argues that Mill was a proponent of universal suffrage. My reading of Mill supports this interpretation on slightly different premises.

41. James Mill, *Essay on Government*, pp. 4–5.

42. Ibid., p. 22.

43. Ibid., pp. 12–13: "Not one item in the motives which had led English Gentlemen to make slaves of their fellow-creatures (in the West Indies) can be shown to be wanting, or to be less strong in the set of motives, which universally operate upon the men who have power over their fellow-creatures."

44. See, e.g., the argument in Ryan, "Two Concepts of Democracy," pp. 90–92.

45. Bentham, Mill, and especially the Philosophic Radicals also demanded the secret ballot to prevent corruption. Tracy and Daunou do not insist on this. The Constitution of 1795, however, provided for a secret ballot. Although neither the Charter nor the electoral law of 1817 established the principle of secret voting, some in the Chamber attempted to do so. See Charles Ferté, *Le secret du vote* (Montpellier: G. Firmin, Montane, et Sicardi, 1909), pp. 26–33.

46. *Constitutional Code, Works,* 9:452–60.

47. Ibid., p. 58.

48. *Commentaire,* p. 213.

49. *Plan of Parliamentary Reform, Works,* 3:450.

50. *Commentaire,* p. 185.

51. E. P. Thompson, *The Making of the English Working Class* (New York: Vintage, 1963), pp. 604, 631, 736.

52. On the Philosophic Radicals as a political movement see Thomas, *Philosophic Radicals* and two studies by Joseph Hamburger, *James Mill and the Art of Revolution* (New Haven: Yale University Press, 1963) and *Intellectuals in Politics: John Stuart Mill and the Philosophic Radicals* (New Haven: Yale University Press, 1965). This brief sketch largely follows Hamburger.

53. See Thompson, *Making of the Working Class,* pp. 768–73.

54. In public, the Philosophic Radicals most often blamed their failures in the reformed Parliament on the dishonesty of the Whigs. Thomas, *Philosophic Radicals,* p. 446.

CHAPTER SIX: DIASPORA AND DISSOLUTION

1. See Mellon, *The Political Uses of History*, pp. 1–30.

2. For a discussion of the attempts to avoid the issue of sovereignty during the Restoration, see Dominique Bagge, *Les idées politiques en France sous la Restauration* (Paris: Presses Universitaires de France, 1952), pp. 56–60, 102–5, and Charles Merriam, *History of the Theory of Sovereignty since Rousseau* (New York:

Columbia University Press, 1900), pp. 73–78. On the differences between extreme royalist conceptions of legitimacy and the more *politique* conceptions of other supporters of the regime, see Stephen Holmes, "Two Concepts of Legitimacy: France after the Revolution," *Political Theory* 10 (May 1982): 165–83.

3. "Discours sur les élections" (20 May and 8 June 1820), *Essai sur les garanties*, p. 352.

4. See Edgar Leon Newman, "Republicanism during the Bourbon Restoration in France, 1814–1830" (Ph.D. dissertation, University of Chicago, 1969), p. 144: "To praise the Republic or to be linked with republicanism or the old republicans in any way, it seems, was suicidal for any politician during the Restoration."

5. For a complete list of all the translations of Tracy's works in Italian, Spanish, German, Russian, and English, see the bibliography in Kennedy, *A Philosophe in the Age of Revolution.* Tracy was especially influential on Italian philosophy during this period, and "ideology" was the dominant school in Italy. See M. DeWulf, "Le sensualisme et l'eclecticisme en Belgique sous les régimes français et hollandais (1800–1830)," *Revue des sciences philosophiques et théologiques* 4(1910):257–70, for a discussion of "ideology" in Belgium. Daunou's *Essai sur les garanties* was translated into Spanish, Italian, and Greek.

6. See Guillermo Francovich, "La Filosofía de Destutt de Tracy en Bolivia," *Kollasuyo* (La Paz) 3 (January 1941):3–8. Tracy was always interested in Latin America, and wrote to Jefferson expressing his hope that the United States would support the Latin Americans against Spain. See Tracy to Jefferson (11 April 1818 and 10 March 1819), Chinard, *Jefferson et les idéologues,* pp. 178–80, 191–93. Bentham also met and thought highly of Rivadavia, who professed "utilitarian principles" and was for a time allegedly occupied in translating Bentham. See Bentham, *Works,* 10:500.

7. Ironically, the ideas of this friend of Sieyès, Cabanis, and Tracy became the only doctrine taught at the Sorbonne for a number of years, since Cousin had been removed from the Faculté des Lettres in 1820. Cousin gave no official lectures until 1828. See Prosper Alfaric, *Laromiguière et son école* (Paris: Les Belles Lettres. 1929), pp. 97–98. On Laromiguière, see also George Boas, *French Philosophies of the Romantic Period* (New York: Russell & Russell, 1964), pp. 34–35.

8. Despite some concessions to the possible independence of religious sentiment, Thurot was a thorough "ideologist" in his *De l'entendement et de la raison* (1830) and in his *Cours de philosophie.*

9. Alfaric, *Laromiguière,* p. 96.

10. Stendhal's *Souvenirs d'égotisme* remains the longest and most interesting account of the Tracy salon, which Stendhal frequented for about ten years. Undoubtedly, there is a strong connection between Stendhal's understanding of "ideology" and the psychological structure of his novels, and the subject has received a great deal of critical attention. For other contemporary accounts of the salon, see Sarah Newton Destutt de Tracy [Tracy's daughter-in-law], "Notice sur M. Destutt de Tracy," *Essais divers, lettres et pensées,* 3 vols. (Paris: Plon, 1852–

55), 1:306–404, and Lady Morgan [Sydney Owenson], *France in 1829–1830*, 2 vols., 2nd ed. (London: Saunders and Otley, 1831), 1:134–45.

11. See Charles Dunoyer, *Morale et l'industrie dans leurs rapports avec la liberté* (Paris: Sautelet, 1825) and Charles Comte, *Traité de législation, ou des conditions suivant lesquelles les nations prospèrent, dépérissent ou restent stationnaires*, 4 vols. (Paris: Chamerot, 1826).

12. *Memoirs of an Egotist*, trans. T.W. Earp (London: Turnstile Press, 1949), pp. 40–42.

13. Sarah . . . de Tracy, "Notice," p. 404. Cf. a characteristic pronouncement by Daunou: "Some more, some less, we are all born workers." *Cours d'études*, 2:130.

14. The writers of the *Censeur* were also much influenced by Constant's distinction between ancient and modern liberty, and by the work of Montlosier. See Ephraim Harpaz, " 'Le Censeur européen': histoire d'un journal industrialiste," *Revue d'histoire économique et sociale* 37 (1959), pp. 195–96.

15. Augustin Thierry, Review of *Commentaire sur l'Esprit des lois*, *Censeur européen* 7 (1818):258.

16. Ibid., p. 196.

17. *Censeur européen* 2:130.

18. See Elie Halévy, "Saint-Simonian Economic Doctrine," *The Era of Tyrannies*, trans. R.K. Webb (New York: New York University Press, 1966), pp. 22–35 passim. See also Harpaz, "Le Censeur," pp. 204–5. The *Censeur* used the term *industrieux*, which was also used by Say and Tracy. Saint-Simon used *industriel*.

19. See *Censeur européen* 9:1–107; 10:1–80.

20. See Augustin Thierry, *Dix ans d'études historiques* (Paris: Plon frères, 1846), pp. 1–24, 180–87. For a discussion of the difference between Thierry's approach to history and that of liberals like Guizot, see Shirley M. Gruner, *Economic Materialism and Social Moralism* (The Hague: Mouton, 1973), pp. 103–10. For Charles Comte's approach, see "De l'organisation sociale considerée dans ses rapports avec les moyens de subsistence des peuples," *Censeur européen*, 2:1 ff.

21. Georges Weill, *Histoire du parti républicain en France (1814–1870)* (Paris: Felix Alcan, 1928), p. 8.

22. The term *radical* was in fact first used in France in 1819 and 1820 by the conservative press to designate the "extreme" liberalism that was sweeping Germany, Italy, and Spain, as well as France. See Jacques Kayser, *Les grandes batailles du radicalisme, des origines aux portes du pouvoir 1820–1901* (Paris: Marcel Rivière, 1962), pp. 7–11. The term, explicitly borrowed from the English, was one of vague abuse. For example, the *Conservateur* 5 (October 1819):126, lumped together "visionaries, idéologues, reformers, radicals, fanatics." *Radical* failed to catch on in France until the early years of the July monarchy when it was adopted by republicans as a way of suggesting the need for a complete reform of the system of government without using the proscribed term *republic*.

23. Quoted in Henry Dumulard, "Joseph Rey de Grenoble et ses mémoires

politiques," *Annales de l'Université de Grenoble Section Lettres—Droits* 4 (1927):75. The following discussion is based on accounts of these memoirs in Dumulard, in C. Stryenski, "Un patron d'Autrefois: Le Comte Destutt de Tracy," *Revue des Alpes (1892)*, and in Richard Arthur Morris, "Joseph Rey of Grenoble, 1779–1855: Revolutionary—Educator—Humanitarian" (Ph.D. Dissertation, University of Iowa, 1966). Other contemporary sources are François de Corcelles, *Documens pour servir à l'histoire des conspirations* (Paris: Paulin, 1831) and *Paris Révolutionnaire*, 4 vols. (Paris: Gillaumin, 1833–34).

24. Freemasonry had by this time lost much of its revolutionary character, and was in fact criticized by many liberals for its elaborate rituals and symbolism. In this case it was apparently used as a respectable front. See François-André Isambert, *De la charbonnerie au Saint-Simonisme: étude sur la jeunesse de Buchez* (Paris: Edition de Minuit, 1966), p. 70.

25. See Alan Barrie Spitzer, *Old Hatreds and Young Hopes: the French Carbonari against the Bourbon Restoration* (Cambridge: Harvard University Press, 1971), pp. 39–50. Lafayette was titular head of the Haute Vente. With his usual caution, Tracy did not become a member, although he maintained links with the conspirators.

26. See, e.g., George Sencier, *La babouvisme après Babeuf; sociétés secrètes et conspirations communistes (1830–1848)* (Paris: M. Rivière, 1912), p. 37.

27. Georges Weill, "L'idée républicaine en France pendant la restauration," *Revue d'histoire moderne* 2 (1927):331. See also Sebastien Charléty, *La Restauration* (Paris: Hachette, 1921), pp. 176–77, and Stendhal's comments in the *New Monthly Magazine* (1 June 1825): "The *Commentaire sur l'Esprit des lois de Montesquieu* of the Comte de Tracy and the *Traités des garanties* [sic] of M. Daunou are in everyone's hands." *Courrier anglaise*, ed. Henri Martineau, 5 vols. (Paris: Le Divan, 1936), 2:367.

28. Trélat reported that every meeting began by cursing the memory of "the despot." "La Charbonnerie," *Paris Révolutionnaire*, 2:278.

29. Corcelles, *Documens*, p. 8. Bentham was not much known for his general moral and political theory, but rather for his theory of law and for his political economy. Generally, his work was seen as a complement to that of the Idéologues. See Isambert, *De la charbonnerie*, p. 121.

30. Corcelles, *Documens*, pp. 19–20. The theory of Kant was known mostly through the translation made by Villers and through Cousin's lectures at the Sorbonne in 1817. Part of the *Déclaration des principes* is reproduced in J.-T. Flottard, "Une nuit d'étudiant sous la restauration," *Paris Révolutionnaire*, 2:454–57. Other excerpts are given in Isambert, *De la charbonnerie*, pp. 127–30.

31. Quoted in Isambert, *De la charbonnerie*, p. 127.

32. Ibid., p. 128.

33. Cf. the fragment "De l'association en générale" written by Buchez at about this time, which clearly was based on the writings of Tracy and Daunou. See ibid., pp. 130–32.

34. Sainte-Beuve reported in the *Causeries de Lundi* that this review was sponsored by Lafayette and the "small republican church" in the Restoration. Quoted in Weill, "L'idée républicaine," p. 339.

35. "De l'institution du jury chez les américains du sud," *Revue américaine* (February 1827): 490–91.

36. The *Aide-toi* was a committee of liberals, founded in 1827 under the presidency of Guizot, for the purpose of aiding liberal candidates and electors to combat official efforts to keep them off the ballot and electoral lists. Young republicans tended to provide the leg work for this committee, although it was dominated by the established opposition. See Newman, "Republicanism," p. 252.

37. August Jean Raymond Fabre, *La Révolution de 1830, et le véritable parti républicain; exposé du plan de ce parti en juillet; mémorial historique de la Révolution, de ces causes et de ses suites, composés en partie de morceaux écrits au moment des événements,* 2 vols. (Paris: Thoisnier-Desplaces, 1833), 1:xxi.

38. *Tribune des départements,* 7 June 1829.

39. Three more journals appeared in the winter of 1829–30. See Daniel L. Rader, *The Journalists and the July Revolution in France* (The Hague: Martinus Nijhoff, 1973), pp. 107–10.

40. Fabre noted that it had been extremely difficult to get funds, "however, a few exceptions recalled France as she was before the invasion. Some day, they will be justified," *La Révolution de 1830,* 1:xxv.

41. Ibid., p. xxi.

42. *Tribune des départements,* 26 September 1829. Tracy was the acknowledged source for this distinction. Fabre argued that Tracy was the most illustrious political writer in France, that anyone with a political idea in his head could not fail to see the force of his arguments, that the commentary on Book Two of the *Esprit des lois* (the distinction between national and special governments) was one of the most remarkable pieces in the French language. See *La Révolution de 1830,* 1:xxx.

43. Ibid., pp. xciii–xcvii.

44. In general, Fabre called only for suffrage based on the qualifications set out in the 1791 Constitution, but, emboldened by the July Days, he apparently briefly endorsed universal suffrage. *Tribune des départements,* 5 August 1830.

45. Fabre also included demands for reclaiming national boundaries, reflecting the intense patriotism of the young republicans.

46. Fabre *La Révolution de 1830,* 1:cxxxi–ii. On the people's support of the Doctrinaires, see Edgar Leon Newman, "The Blouse and the Frock Coat: The Alliance of the Common People of Paris with the Liberal Leadership and the Middle Classes during the Last Years of the Bourbon Restoration," *Journal of Modern History* 46 (March 1974):26–59. Louis Blanc reports an incident in which a mob broke into the *Tribune*'s offices threatening to shoot the editors, and were dissuaded only by Auguste Fabre's calm demeanor. See *The History of Ten Years 1830–1840,* 2 vols. (London: Chapman and Hall, 1844), pp. 192–93.

47. Of "seditious incidents" reported to the police from 1825 to 1830, only two were republican, eighty-one were Bonapartist. See David H. Pinkney, *The French Revolution of 1830* (Princeton: Princeton University Press, 1972), p. 49.

48. Fabre, *La Révolution de 1830,* 1:xiv, attacked Napoleon's "blind ambition" and persecution of the Idéologues. The *Tribune des départements,* 1 May 1830, accused Bonaparte of suppressing true philosophy and supporting romanticism because the latter contributed to his arbitrary rule. The tactics of other liberal opponents of Charles X were more politic. Thus, Thiers wrote in the *National* shortly before the important June elections to the Chamber: "Napoleon was the greatest man of his century." Quoted in Jean-Lucas Dubréton, *Le culte de Napoléon 1815 –1848* (Paris: A. Michel, 1960), p. 269. The attitude toward resurgent Bonapartism was always a problem for the liberals. Hence, there was silence, even on the part of Constant, on the anti-Bonapartist themes of Madame de Staël's *Considérations sur les principaux événements de la Révolution française* when it appeared in 1818. See Cappadocia, "History of the Liberal Party," pp. 68 –69.

49. Fabre, *La Révolution de 1830,* 1:xcvii.

50. Ibid., pp. xlix –liii.

51. Ibid., p. lx.

52. Ibid., pp. liii, xcvi.

53. See *La Révolution de 1830,* 2:24.

54. In November of 1830, the *Globe* became a Saint-Simonian journal with the "conversion" of Pierre Leroux.

55. *Le Globe: Journal philosophique et littéraire.* 8 vols. (Paris, 1824 –30); 2 (24 May 1825): 565 –68.

56. See "De l'histoire de la philosophie en France au dix-neuvième siècle," ibid., 2 (26 May 1825): 571 –72.

57. See Alfaric, *Laromiguière,* p. 129.

58. For a list of the major articles pro and contra Broussais, see *Doctrine de Saint-Simon: Exposition Première Année,* ed. C. Bouglé and Elie Halévy (Paris: Marcel Rivière, 1924), p. 126n8.

59. "De nos sages modernes, M. Destutt de Tracy," *Gazette de France,* 8 August 1929, pp. 3 –4. Quoted in Kennedy, *A Philosophe in the Age of Revolution,* pp. 313 –14.

60. See Alfaric, *Laromiguière,* pp. 130 –32; Picavet, *Les idéologues,* p. 406, 413, 450 –52, 465. Armand Marrast, a faithful disciple of Laromiguière, published a prospectus in 1828 for an *Examen critique du cours de MM. Villemain, Guizot, et Cousin, leçon par leçon.* Marrast wrote his thesis under Laromiguière in 1825. He then became director of philosophical studies at a preparatory school in Paris, but was dismissed when he led the student demonstrations at Manuel's funeral. He also continued the philosophical orientation of Laromiguieère in the journal *Le Lycée,* founded with Guigniault, Patin, Quicherat, and Carpentier, and in the *Tribune,* edited with the Fabres. See also J.B. Say's fragment, "Essai sur l'utilité," *Oeuvres diverses,* pp. 717 –39, which he at one time planned to add to the final

volume of the *Cours complet*. Say wished to defend "utility" from the charge of egoism made by the "secte germanico-scholastique" and by those who opposed "le sentiment intime" to the useful. In this latter category he cited Mme. de Staël in *Corinne,* Constant in his writings on religion, and Cousin in his *Cours de philosophie.* See Say to Dumont, 10 May 1829, ibid., p. 558.

61. *New Monthly Magazine* (April 1823), *Courrier anglais,* 1:95–97. See also *New Monthly Magazine* (June 1825), ibid., 2:367.

62. The quote is from *New Monthly Magazine* (June 1824), *Courrier anglais,* 2:167. For other articles that defend "ideology," see *New Monthly Magazine* (March 1824, August 1824, January 1825, July 1826, September 1828, December 1828), *Courrier anglais* 2:143–45, 191, 246–47; 3:123, 409–11, 442–43; and *London Magazine* (March 1825, December 1825), *Courrier anglaise,* 4:339–403; 5:266.

63. *Documens,* pp. 44–55. See also ibid., p. 112: "In effect, public opinion will always be *idéologue* as long as humanity has need of justice and is susceptible to progress."

64. The lines were not absolute of course. The liberals of Coppet had been receptive to some of the new sensibility, while some old royalists were devoted to the classical literature of the seventeenth century.

65. After 1827, there was a certain realignment, with the defection of Chateaubriand to the liberal cause over the question of liberty of the press. See Guillaume de Bertier de Sauvigny, *The Bourbon Restoration,* trans. Lynn M. Case (Philadelphia: University of Pennsylvania Press, 1966), pp. 355–58.

66. *Tribune des départements,* 25 July 1829.

67. Ibid., 1 May 1830. For the articles on Damiron and Cousin, see ibid. 21, 26, 27, 31 July 1829. Cf. the favorable review of Thurot's *De l'entendement et de la raison,* ibid., 11 May 1830 and 7 June 1830.

68. Fabre, *La Révolution de 1830,* 1:cxx. The Fabres' relentless politicization of the romantic/classic antinomy becomes a permanent theme of part of the French left. Louis Blanc, for example, blames romanticism for falsifying French taste, killing all psychological insight, sacrificing classical unity to a barbarian mania for contrast, and dealing a serious blow to morality by glorifying egoism. See H.J. Hunt, *Le socialisme et le romanticisme: étude de la presse socialiste de 1830 à 1848* (Oxford: Clarendon Press, 1935), pp. 164–71, and Koenraad W. Swart, *The Sense of Decadence in Nineteenth Century France* (The Hague: Martinus Nijhoff, 1964), pp. 77–80.

69. Charléty, *La Restauration,* pp. 374–75; Rader, *The Journalists of the July Revolution,* pp. 231–32.

70. Pinkney, *Revolution of 1830,* pp. 269–73. The actual fighting had been done mostly by skilled craftsmen and veterans of the revolutionary armies.

71. Marrast was exiled in 1835. Corcelles, who remained aloof from the Jacobins, noted disdainfully: "C'est parodier une parodie." *Documens,* p. 99.

72. See John Eros, "The Positivist Generation of French Republicanism," *Sociological Review* 3 (December 1955):260.

73. Fabre, *La Révolution de 1830*, 1:xxxi. Fabre generally used *bourgeoisie* as a synonym for middle class. In the 1830s and 1840s *bourgeoisie* became a term of abuse among socialists for wealthy industrialists and bankers.

74. See, for example, Armand Carrel in the *National*, 18 February 1830, *Oeuvres politiques et littéraires d'Armand Carrel*, 3 vols., ed. M. Littré and M. Paul (Paris: F. Chamerot, 1857), 1:23: "[T]his untiring, active, numberless mass that is composed of ploughmen, workmen, shopkeepers, writers [and] artists is called *le peuple*." Cf. also Buchez: "We define the people as the poorest and most numerous class, [the class] that labors." "Du principe de la souveraineté," *Journal des sciences morales et politiques*, 10 December 1831, p. 18, quoted in François-André Isambert, *Politique, religion et science de l'homme chez Philippe Buchez (1796–1865)* (Paris: Cujas, 1967), p. 91.

75. Fabre, *La Révolution de 1830*, 1:xxxi–xxxiii; cii; see also 2:99, where Fabre argued that the people in France were superior to the masses of '89, but the majority of the *classe moyenne* were worse. The bourgeoisie had been generous; it was now corrupt. It had been enlightened; it was now ignorant. Instead of inspiring the people, it attempted to make them greedy, base, and servile like itself.

76. Fabre argued that the Revolution had been an example of a "union of all classes," and that the Doctrinaires had sold out for "self-interest." Ibid., p. 255.

77. Fabre believed that the triumph of the Doctrinaires would mean a triumph of Eclecticism, which would mean a general decline in the capacity to see enlightened self-interest. *La Révolution de 1830*, 1:cxv–cxxxiii.

78. Ibid., 1:lvi.

79. Ibid., pp. xlviii–xlix; see also 2:231 (on the striking printers): "[H]ow can they be dupes of that prejudice which sees machines as harmful to artisans? How is it that they do not see that by deserting the workshops they are liable to strike the last blow to the industry that provides them with a living?"

80. *La Révolution de 1830*, 1:xlviii–xlix.

81. Individuals still held these views, of course, but they were relatively isolated. See Gruner, *Economic Materialism*, p. 153: "[T]he Left after 1830 represented one big moral protest . . . against economics, 'ideology' and materialism—all classed together with aristocratism and oppression."

82. There was a new appreciation of DeMaistre, Bonald, and Chateaubriand, as well as a closer attention to history. According to Corcelles, the first appreciation of history came from the influence of Pelegrino Rossi. Rossi founded, with Sismondi and Dumont, the *Annales de législation et de jurisprudence*. He often translated excerpts from the German school of historical jurisprudence: Niebuhr and de Savigny. Corcelles, *Documens*, p. 65. There was also a new appreciation of the Scottish historians, especially Robertson. See *Le Producteur: journal de l'industrie, des sciences et des beaux arts*, 5 vols. (Paris: Sautelet, 1826), 4:410–13.

83. Enfantin also was a follower of "ideology" before his conversion to Saint-Simonianism. A note conserved in the Saint-Simonian archives indicates that Enfantin's "masters" were Destutt de Tracy and Laromiguière. Cited by V.H. d'Allemagne, *Les Saint Simoniens (1827–1837)* (Paris: Gründ, 1930), p. 28.

84. Those who were not discouraged often turned to the encouragement of revolution outside France. Philhellenism, e.g., was widespread during the Greek revolution. See Newman, "Republicanism," p. 225.

85. *Documens,* pp 67 –68. Cf. also Trélat, who claimed that the most valuable ideas of Saint-Simonianism were inherited from the Carbonari: philanthropy, equality, respect for work, and scorn of idleness. "La Charbonnerie," pp. 335 – 36.

86. From the Idéologues of the Institute, Saint-Simon picked up the notion of positive science, and especially the idea of the unity of all the sciences. Much of his physiology came from Cabanis and Burdin. The idea of religion as integrated with the scientific theory of an age he found in Dupuis and Tracy. See Frank Manuel, *The New World of Henri Saint-Simon* (Notre Dame, Indiana: University of Notre Dame Press, 1963), pp. 80 –81, 122 –38, 152 –54, 219 –20. On Saint-Simon's ideas of human evolution, Manuel notes: "The reflections of Saint-Simon are only simulacres of far more reasoned evolutionary hypotheses current among the *idéologues.* They are Saint-Simon in the rough" (p. 162).

87. *Doctrine de Saint-Simon,* ed. Bouglé and Halévy, p. 98.

88. For this interpretation, see Smith, "Tracy and the Bankruptcy of Sensationalism," pp. 195 –207. Gruner, *Economic Materialism,* pp. 137 –42, interprets Saint-Simonianism as a complete rejection of "ideology," but she considers only the stronger attack in the *Doctrine,* not the earlier *Producteur.*

89. "Considérations sur les tentatives qui ont été faites pour fonder la science sociale sur la physiologie et sur quelques autres sciences," *Revue occidentale philosophique, sociale et politique* 8 (1882):397.

90. Comte, *Cours de philosophie positive, Oeuvres d'Auguste Comte,* 12 vols. (Paris: Editions Anthropos, 1968), 3:617. In the *Discours sur l'ensemble du positivisme,* Comte defined *positive* as *relative, organic, precise, certain, useful,* and *real.* The last four terms were already comprised in the Idéologue use of the term. Especially important for Comte was the distinction between *conjectural* and *real,* i.e., between mysterious assumptions about causation and empirical laws based on observation. See Henri Gouhier, *La Jeunesse d'Auguste Comte et la formation du positivisme,* 3 vols. (Paris: J. Vrin, 1964), 2:4 –48, for a discussion of the "pre-positivists." In his *Auguste Comte and Positivism* (Ann Arbor, Michigan: The University of Michigan Press, Ann Arbor Paperbacks, 1968), p. 8, John Stuart Mill discusses the English precursors of positivism. Above all he cites Thomas Brown, on whom the influence of Tracy has already been noted (above, p. 214). "The writer who has best stated and defended Comte's fundamental doctrine is Dr. Thomas Brown. The doctrine and spirit of Brown's philosophy are entirely Positivist, and no better introduction to Positivism than the early part of his lectures has yet been produced."

91. *Oeuvres d'A.C.,* 3:617.

92. "Considérations sur les tentatives pour fonder la science sociale," p. 398.

93. *Oeuvres d'A.C.,* 3:618. See also ibid., p. 617, where Comte notes that the method necessarily led to "emptiness," and pp. 604 –30 passim.

94. *Producteur,* 3:466. The Saint-Simonians' criticisms of "ideology" became stronger as positivism itself lost favor. See Georg G. Iggers, Introduction to *The Doctrine of Saint-Simon: An Exposition, First Year, 1828–1829* (New York: Schocken Books, 1972), pp. xxxiii–xlvii.

95. See the series of articles entitled "Fragmens philosophiques par M. Cousin" by P.M.L. Laurent, *Producteur,* 3:325–38, 4:19–37.

96. *Producteur,* 4:21–27. Laurent notes that *idéologie physiologique* claimed to have limited its study to the "facts of consciousness"; therefore, Cousin's similar claim was not new. He also argues that Cousin left himself open to the criticism that Cabanis leveled at Condillac, i.e., he ignored instinct. *Producteur,* 3:335–38.

97. Ibid., pp. 273–74.

98. Ibid., p. 462; see also p. 466: "Thus two branches of the same science, founded until this time on conflicting explanations and studies, could be fused definitively only by the union of two men . . . equipped with the same general principle."

99. Ibid., pp. 469–72.

100. *Producteur,* 4:424.

101. See Isambert, *Buchez,* p. 223. Eventually, Buchez came to a religious understanding of this unifying impulse; this new perspective provided the grounds for a rather peculiar reconciliation with Catholicism. As Buchez's conception of the highest level of coordination of discrete psychic phenomena took on a more spiritual cast, the role of faith in society became more important.

102. See ibid., p. 229, for a discussion of freedom and necessity in Buchez.

103. Philippe Buchez, *Introduction à la science de l'histoire* (Paris: Paulin, 1833), p. 164. The second part of this work attempts to reconcile a view of history influenced by the Idéologues, Saint-Simon and Comte, with *Genesis.* See pp. 394–568.

104. *Producteur,* 2:159.

105. Ibid., p. 167.

106. Ibid., p. 164.

107. *Producteur,* 1:339.

108. The discussion of Tracy begins: "The most elevated minds do not escape such errors when, fighting against an outworn political system, they are not yet aware of the system that should replace it." *Doctrine de Saint-Simon,* ed. and trans. Iggers, p. 315.

109. *Doctrine de Saint-Simon,* ed. Bouglé and Halévy, pp. 310–16.

110. See the two articles by Rouen, entitled "De la classe ouvrière," *Producteur,* 3:304–18; 4:292–316.

111. The term *socialisme* was apparently first used by Pierre Leroux in 1833 as a synonym for collectivism. For the interaction between workers and republicans in the early 1830s, especially in the society *Amis du peuple,* see Bernard H. Moss, "Parisian Workers and the Origins of Republican Socialism," in *1830 in France,* pp. 203–21. See Lorenz von Stein, *The History of the Social Movement in France 1789–1850,* ed. and trans. Kaethe Mengelberg (Totowa, New Jersey: Bedminster

Press, 1965), pp. 278–301 for a still illuminating account of the disabused republicans' appeal to workers, and the gradual transformation of the content of republicanism. The dynamics of non-Marxist socialist movements, especially in relation to the growth of working-class movements, remain obscure. Certainly not until the 1840s, with the rise of Cabet's communism, was there a truly broad-based movement with worker-artisan support. On this point, see Christopher H. Johnson, *Utopian Communism in France: Cabet and the Icarians, 1839–1851* (Ithaca, N.Y.: Cornell University Press, 1974).

112. Rey constantly attempted to reconcile competing socialist theories. See, e.g., *Des bases de l'ordre social*, 2 vols. (Angers: Ernest le Sourd, 1836), 1:iv–ix. See also *Théorie et pratique de la science sociale; ou exposé des principes de morale, d'économie publique et politique et application à l'état actuel de la société de moyens généraux, immédiats, et successifs d'améliorer la condition des travailleurs et même des propriétaires,* 3 vols. (Paris: Jules Renouard, 1842), 1:x, where he notes that he is not an *homme à système* like Fourier, Owen, or Saint-Simon. The same note is struck in his *Appel au ralliement des socialistes* (Paris: Librairie phalansterienne, 1847) which attempts to mediate between Fourierists and Cabetistes. Among the socialists he considers are: the Saint Simonians, Fourier, Owen, Pierre Leroux, Louis Blanc, Theodore Dézamy, Jules Lechevalier, and William Thompson.

113. Published as *Des institutions judiciaires de l'Angleterre comparées avec celles de la France et de quelques autres états anciens et modernes,* 2 vols. (Paris: Nève, 1826). Bentham continued to recommend this work to his friends. He sent his own *Constitutional Code* to Rey, and asked him to translate it, if Dumont should die. Rey's response is unknown. See C. Stryenski, trans., "Lettres inédites de Jeremy Bentham," *Journal des économistes* (June 1890), pp. 368–72.

114. Rey wrote several letters to the *Producteur* that remained for many years the most important source for the French socialists' knowledge of Owen. See *Lettres au Redacteur du Producteur, sur le système de la cooperation mutuelle et de la communauté de tous les biens d'après le plan de M. Owen* (Paris: A. Sautelet, 1828). Rey became a propagandist for Owen's idea of community in France, and probably was responsible for introducing the term "cooperation" into France. See Morris, "Joseph Rey," p. 248. He was never wholly uncritical of Owen, however, and he became more critical as time went on. For Rey's popularization of Owen's ideas, see H. Desroche, "Images and Echoes of Owenism in Nineteenth Century France," in *Robert Owen: Prophet of the Poor,* ed. Sidney Pollard and John Salt (London: Macmillan Press, 1971), pp. 248; 260–61.

115. The *Traité des principes généraux,* published at the height of the attacks on "ideology," begins with a defense of "ideology" against Cousin, Jouffroy, and Auguste Comte. Rey noted that Tracy had ceased to write, because of his blindness, but that his disciple hoped to present, "with regard to moral science and to economics, some developments that the author was himself unable to include in his works," p. 79. See also the dedication to Tracy in the *Bases,* p. i: "I will have at least tried to grasp the thread of his great ideas, which form an immortal monument raised to genuine science, and which, properly developed, will forever

guarantee the triumph of truth while serving as an unshakeable foundation for the great structure of the fundamental principles of human society."

116. This method required: 1) an underlying canvass of physiological data, 2) a study of the laws of the understanding, 3) a study of the passions, and 4) a study of the will and its effects. See *Bases*, 1:3–30; *Théorie et pratique*, 1:vi–xiv, 1–10. In the *Bases*, Rey adopts a new terminology without a new structural conception. He calls the general study of man (called the science of man by Cabanis, and sometimes called "ideology" in a generic sense by Tracy), *anthropologie*. Physiology becomes *anthropobiologie*, the study of the rational faculties remains *idéologie*, the study of the passions becomes *phrénologie*, and the study of economics, *praxéologie*. See ibid., pp. 34–59. This new scheme, however, is dropped in the *Théorie et pratique*.

117. Rey includes data on anatomy, on the physiology of sleep, and on racial, sexual, and age differences. The material is culled from Cabanis, Roussel, Adelon, Bichat, Gall, Spurzeim, Rostan, Ribbes, Virey, Dutrochet, Fourcaut, and Pinel. See *Bases*, 1:53–332.

118. *Bases*, 1:101–2. See also ibid., pp. 270–96 for a discussion of Condorcet's view of progress versus that of Saint-Simon.

119. See *Traité des principes généraux*, pp. 184, 189; *Théorie et pratique*, 1:vii. Cf. Dunoyer, *L'industrie et la morale*, pp. 18–27.

120. *Traité des principes généraux*, pp. 128–29; see also *Bases*, 1:340, 352, 2:209; *Théorie et pratique*, 1:30. There was also some attempt at revision of Tracy's epistemology; thus, Rey reserves the term *sentir* for the passionate part of the human organization, and treats emotions and passions more fully. See *Bases*, 2:27–31.

121. *Bases*, 1:296.

122. *Théorie et pratique*, 1:160.

123. For Rey's criticisms of Fourier, see *Théorie et pratique*, 1:66 ff. Fourier himself was aware of the Idéologues, but only as the "respectable" elite that rejected his ideas. For his bitter denunciation of these "Obscurants," see *Oeuvres complètes de Charles Fourier*, 12 vols. (Paris: Editions anthropos, 1966–68), 3:117–23, 274–75; 10:13.

124. Rey entitled one of the chapters of the *Théorie et pratique*, "Is there room for everyone at the banquet of life?" He could not imagine a negative answer. See 1:191–228.

125. Ibid., pp. 67–82. Rey's attempt to use the concept of "synthesis" in a moral context shows the influence of the Saint-Simonians.

126. *Bases*, 2:394. Rey traces the "necessary" results of this movement in a logical thought experiment similar to Tracy's, moving man from a state of isolation to society in progressive steps. Ibid., pp. 176–98.

127. *Théorie et pratique*, 1:135–38.

128. Ibid., p. 256. See also *Bases*, 2:378–83; and *Traité des principes généraux*, p. 169, where Rey simply quotes from Tracy.

129. *Bases*, 2:385.

130. *Théorie et pratique,* 1:241. See also ibid., p. 247. Rey's moral understanding of the labor theory of value was similar to that of the Ricardian socialists. Rey, in fact, found his position confirmed in William Thompson, although he disputed some of the psychological premises behind Thompson's egalitarianism. See *Traité des principes généraux,* pp. 178–89.

131. I.e., society would be composed of spontaneously self-regulating individuals. See *Bases,* 2:460–71.

132. Without the introduction of competition as an organizing principle, state direction of industry would have to be introduced. This, Rey argued against the Saint-Simonians, would bring tyranny into the workplace. In his system, however, prices and wages are set, there is no land rent, ownership of large fixed capital is common, trade is regulated, and scarce luxuries are rationed. There is also some worker control in factories.

133. *Théorie et pratique,* 3:303.

134. Ibid., pp. 245–52.

135. Ibid., p. 302.

136. Ibid., p. 196.

137. Leroy, *Histoire des idées sociales,* 2:376.

138. Tracy, *Commentaire,* pp. 24, 125.

139. *Discours prononcé par M. Guizot, pour sa réception à l'Académie française,* reported on 23 December 1836 in *Le Moniteur universel; journal officiel de l'empire français,* 161 vols. (Paris: 1789 1868), 94:2261 63.

140. Charles Augustin Sainte-Beuve, *Premiers lundis,* 3 vols., 3rd ed. (Paris: Calmann-Levy, 1883), 3:313.

CONCLUSION

1. See, for example, Thomas Kaiser, "Politics and Political Economy in the Thought of the Idéologues," *History of Political Economy* 12 (1980): 148, 158.

2. For the traditional liberal interpretation, see A.D. Lindsay, *The Modern Democratic State* (London: Oxford University Press, 1951), pp. 136–40. Alan Ryan has persuasively argued that it is impossible to assess the influence of Bentham on nineteenth-century legislation and law. See *J.S. Mill* (London: Routledge & Kegan Paul, 1974), pp. 3–4.

3. Throughout his important historical and biographical study, *The Philosophic Radicals,* William Thomas deemphasizes the importance of the Philosophic Radicals' "shared doctrine." In explaining their political failures, he stresses both their "incorrigible individuality" (p. 440) and the fact that they lacked the sort of intellectual audience (a class of "disaffected intellectuals") that would have taken up their ideas (p. 451). But these factors were surely not enough to explain their lack of success; Thomas, therefore, also makes the more general arguments that their decline was due to a failure to find a following among working-class radicals, and a failure to win over their "natural" allies, the Whigs. I still find these latter arguments the most persuasive explanation for the Radicals' decline. And

the inability to make common cause either with other radicals or with Whigs was plainly in large part the effect of their doctrine, as Thomas acknowledges.

4. John Hermann Randall, Jr., *The Career of Philosophy,* vol. 2: *From the Enlightenment to the Age of Darwin* (New York: Columbia University Press, 1970), p. 533.

5. Bentham, *The Rationale of Reward, Works,* 2:266.

6. See Mill's critique of Bentham in *Comte and Positivism,* pp. 83–88, and also in *A System of Logic Ratiocinative and Inductive* (London: Longman's, Green, 1965), pp. 580–83.

7. David Hartley, *Observations on Man* (London: J. Johnson, 1801), p. 273.

8. Girarde, *Le Libéralisme en France,* p. 77.

9. Sheldon Wolin, *Politics and Vision* (Boston: Little, Brown, 1960), pp. 354ff.

10. Ibid., p. 392.

BIBLIOGRAPHY

The following is a selected bibliography of the most important works consulted for this study. Additional references will be found in the notes.

Selected Primary Sources

Archives parlementaires de 1787 à 1860, Recueil complet des débats législatifs et politiques de chambres françaises. Paris: Imprimerie administratif de Paul Dupont, 1875; Washington, D.C.: Microcard Editions, 1967.

Babeuf, Emile. *Procès de la conspiration dite républicaine de décembre 1830.* Paris: A. Hocquart Jeune, 1831.

Babeuf, Gracchus. *The Defense of Gracchus Babeuf before the High Court of Vendome.* Edited and translated by John A. Scott. Amherst, Mass.: University of Massachusetts Press, 1968.

Beccaria, Cesar Bonesana. *An Essay on Crimes and Punishments.* Dublin: John Exshaus, 1767.

Beik, Paul H., ed. and trans. *The French Revolution.* Documentary History of Western Civilization. New York: Harper & Row, 1970.

Bentham, Jeremy. *An Introduction to the Principles of Morals and Legislation.* Edited by J.H. Burns and H.L.A. Hart. London: Athlone Press, 1970.

—— *Jeremy Bentham's Economic Writings.* Edited by W. Stark. 3 vols. Leicester: Blackfriars Press, 1952.

—— *Of Laws in General.* Edited by H.L.A. Hart. London: Athlone Press, 1970.

—— *The Theory of Legislation.* Translated from the French of Etienne Dumont by Richard Hildreth. Edited by C.K. Ogden. London: Routledge & Kegan Paul, 1931.

—— *The Works of Jeremy Bentham.* Edited by John Bowring. 11 vols. Edinburgh: William Tait, 1843.

Bichat, Xavier-Marie-François. *Physiological Researches upon Life and Death.* Translated by Tobias Watkins. Philadelphia: Smith & Maxwell, 1809.

Blanc, Louis. *The History of Ten Years, 1830–1840.* 2 vols. London: Chapman & Hall, 1844.

Brown, Thomas. *Lectures on the Philosophy of the Human Mind.* 4 vols. Edinburgh: Adam & Charles Black, 1861.

Buchez, Philippe. *Introduction à la science de l'histoire ou science du développment de l'humanité.* Paris: Paulin, 1833.

Cabanis, Pierre-Jean-Georges. *Oeuvres philosophiques.* Paris: Presses Universitaires de France, 1956.

—— *Rapports du physique et du moral de l'homme.* 2 vols. Paris: Guiraudet, 1830.

Cahier de l'ordre de la noblesse du Bourbonnais. Et pouvoirs remis à MM. Denis-Michel-Philibert Dubuisson . . . Antoine-Louis-Claude, de Stutt . . . et Henry Coiffier . . . députés aux Etats-généraux. N.p., n.d.

Carrel, Armand. *Oeuvres politiques et littéraires d'Armand Carrel.* Edited by M. Littré and M. Paul. 3 vols. Paris: F. Chamerot, 1857.

Censeur européen; ou, Examen de diverses questions de droit public et de divers ouvrages littéraires et scientifiques. 12 vols. (February 1817–April 1819.)

Chill, Emanuel Stanley, ed. *Power, Property, and History: Barnave's Introduction to the French Revolution and Other Writings.* New York: Harper & Row, 1971.

Comte, Auguste. "Considérations sur les tentatives qui ont été faites pour fonder la science sociale sur la physiologie et sur quelques autres sciences (1819)." *Revue occidentale philosophique, sociale et politique* 8 (1882):368–99.

—— *Oeuvres d'Auguste Comte.* 12 vols. Paris: Editions Anthropos, 1968.

Comte, Charles. *Traité de législation, ou des conditions suivant lesquelles les nations prospèrent, dépérissent ou restent stationnaires.* 4 vols. Paris: Chamerot, 1826.

Condillac, abbé Etienne Bonnot de. *Oeuvres philosophiques de Condillac.* Edited by George Le Roy. 3 vols. Paris: Presses Universitaires de France, 1947–51.

Condorcet, Jean-Antoine-Nicolas Caritat, Marquis de. *Oeuvres de Condorcet.* Edited by A. Condorcet O'Connor and M.F. Arago. 12 vols. Paris: Firmin Didot Frères, 1847.

—— *Sketch for a Historical Picture of the Progress of the Human Mind.*

Translated by June Barraclough. London: Weidenfeld and Nicolson, 1955.

Constant, Benjamin. *Cours de politique constitutionelle ou collection des ouvrages publiés sur le gouvernement représentatif.* Edited by Eduoard Laboulaye. 2 vols. Paris: Guillamin, 1872.

Corcelles, François de. *Documents pour servir à l'histoire des conspirations des partis et des sectes.* Paris: Paulin, 1831.

Conservateur, Le. 6 vols. Paris, 1818–1820.

Conservateur, Le. Journal politique, philosophique et litteraire. Edited by Garat, Daunou, Chénier, etc. September 1797–January 1798.

Constitutionnel, Le. Journal politique et littéraire. Paris: October 1815–May 1819.

Cousin, Victor. *Philosophie sensualiste au 18e siècle.* Paris: Librairie Nouvelle, 1856.

Damiron, Jean. *Essai sur l'histoire de la philosophie en France au XIXième siècle.* 2 vols. Paris: Schubart et Heideloff, 1828.

Daunou, Pierre-Claude-François. *Analyse des opinions diverses sur l'origine de l'imprimerie.* Paris: Renouard, an XI (1803).

—— *Le contrat social des français.* N.p. [Paris]: 23 July 1789.

—— Convention Nationale. *Considérations sur le procès de Louis XVI.* N.p., n.d.

—— Convention Nationale. *Discours prononcé par le Cen Daunou, président de la Convention Nationale, 23 thermidor an III (1795), jour anniversaire du 10 aout.* N.p., n.d.

—— Convention Nationale. *Motion d'ordre sur le travail de la constitution.* Paris: Imprimerie Nationale, 1793.

—— Convention Nationale. *Observations sur la manière de discuter la constitution.* Paris: Imprimerie Nationale, n.d.

—— Convention Nationale. *Rapport sur les moyens de donner plus d'intensité au gouvernement actuel.* Paris: Imprimerie Nationale, floréal an III (1795).

—— Convention Nationale. *Rapports au nom des Comités de salut public et de sûreté générale.* Séances du 22 fructidor an III (7 September 1795) et 11 vendémiaire an IV (3 October 1795). Caen: Le Roy, 1795.

—— Convention Nationale. *Remarques sur le plan proposé par le Comité de salut public.* Paris: n.p., n.d.

—— *Cours d'études historiques.* Paris: Firmin Didot, 1842–1849.

—— *Discours au Conseils des cinq-cents pour l'anniversaire de la fondation de la République.* 1 vendémiaire an VII (1798).

—— *Discours prononcé aux funerailles de M. le Cte. Destutt de Tracy.* 12 March 1836. N.p., n.d.

—— *Essai sur la constitution.* Paris: Imprimerie Nationale, 1793.

—— *Essai sur les garanties individuelles que réclame l'état actuel de la société.* 3ième ed., revue, augmentée, et suivie de discours pronouncés à la Chambre des députés. Paris: A. Bobée, 1822.

—— *Essai sur la puissance temporelle des papes, et sur l'abus qu'ils ont fait de leur ministère spirituel.* Paris: Bureau Censeur européen, 1818.

—— *Mémoire sur les élections au scrutin.* Paris: Baudouin, pluviôse an XI (1803).

—— *Opinion de Daunou . . . contre un projet de loi tendant a établir des tribunaux spéciaux.* Paris: Imprimerie Nationale, an IX (1801).

—— *Opinion sur la proposition de déclarer la patrie en danger.* Paris: n.p., 27 fructidor an VII (1799).

—— *Rapport sur l'instruction publique.* Paris: Imprimerie Nationale, an IV (1796).

—— *Rapport sur l'organisation des écoles spéciales.* Paris: Imprimerie Nationale, an V (1797).

Décade philosophique, littéraire, et politique par une société de républicains. 42 vols. Paris: 1794–1807.

Destutt de Tracy, Antoine-Louis-Claude. *Analyse raisonné de l'Origine de tous les cultes ou religion universelle; Ouvrage publié en l'an III par Dupuis, citoyen français.* Paris: Courcier, 1804.

—— *Commentaire sur l'Esprit des lois de Montesquieu . . . suivi d'observations inédites de Condorcet sur le vingt neuvième livre du même ouvrage et d'un mémoire sur cette question: quelles sont les moyens de fonder la morale d'un people?* 1819. Reprint. Geneva: Slatkine, 1970.

—— *A Commentary and Review of Montesquieu's Spirit of Laws. Prepared for press from the original manuscript . . . To which are annexed, Observations on the thirty-first [sic] book by the late M. Condorcet; and two letters of Helvétius, on the merits of the same work.* [Translated by William Duane.] Philadelphia: Willliam Duane, 1811.

—— *De l'amour.* Translated with an introduction and notes by Gilbert Chinard. Paris: Société d'édition "Les Belles-Lettres," 1926.

—— "Les écoles centrales défendues par le philosophe Destutt de Tracy." *La Revolution française* 58 (1910):361–62.

—— *Elémens d'idéologie: Première partie, Idéologie proprement dite; Seconde partie, Grammaire; Troisième partie, Logique; Quatrième et cinquième parties, Traité de la volonté et de ses effets.* Paris: Courcier, 1817.

——— *Elémens d'idéologie: Première partie, Idéologie proprement dite; Second partie, Grammaire.* Edited with an introduction and notes by Henri Gouhier. Paris: J. Vrin, 1970.

——— *Observations sur le système actuel d'instruction publique.* Paris: Panckoucke, an IX (1801).

——— *Opinion de M. de Tracy sur les affaires de Saint-Domingue en septembre 1791.* Paris: Imprimerie de Laillet, 1791.

——— *Translation of a Letter from Monsieur de Tracy, Member of the French National Assembly, to Mr. Burke, in Answer to His Remarks on the French Revolution.* London: J. Johnson, 1790.

——— *A Treatise on Political Economy; to which is prefixed a supplement to a preceding work on the understanding, or Elements of Ideology, with an Analytical Table, and an Introduction on the Faculty of the Will.* [Translated by Thomas Jefferson.] Georgetown, D.C.: Joseph Milligan, 1817.

Destutt de Tracy, Sarah Newton. *Essais divers, lettres et pensées de Mme. de Tracy.* 3 vols. Paris: Plon, 1852–1855.

Dézamy, Theodore. *Code de la communauté.* Paris: Prevost, 1842.

——— *Organisation de la liberté et du bien-être universel.* Paris: Guerin, 1846.

Diderot, Denis. *Oeuvres politiques.* Edited by Paul Vernière. Paris: Garnier Frères, 1963.

Doctrine de Saint-Simon: Exposition, Première Année. Edited by C. Bouglé and Elie Halévy. Paris: Marcel Rivière, 1924.

Doctrine of Saint-Simon: An Exposition, The. Translated with an introduction by Georg G. Iggers. New York: Schocken Books, 1958.

Dumont, Etienne [Henry Frederic Groenvelt]. *Letters Containing an Account of the Late Revolution in France.* London: J. Johnson, 1792.

——— *Souvenirs sur Mirabeau et sur les deux premières assemblées législatives.* Paris: Librairie de Charles Gossalin, 1832.

Dunoyer, Barthélemy-Charles-Pierre-Joseph. *L'industrie et la morale considerées dans leurs rapports avec la liberté.* Paris: Sautelet, 1825.

Edinburgh Review, or Critical Journal. 250 vols. Edinburgh: A. and C. Black, 1802–1929.

Fabre, Auguste-Jean-Raymond. *La Révolution de 1830, et le véritable parti républicain, exposé du plan de ce parti en juillet; mémorial historique de la Révolution, de ces causes et de ces suites, composés en partie de morceaux écrits au moment des événements.* 2 vols. Paris: Thoisnier-Desplaces, 1833.

Fabre, Marie-Jacques-Joseph-Victorin. *Tableau littéraire du XVIIIième siècle, ou Essais sur les grands écrivains de ce siècle et les progrès de l'esprit humain en France. Suivi de l'Eloge de La Bruyère, avec des notes et des dissertations.* Paris: Michaud Frères, 1810.

Fourier, François-Marie-Charles. *Ouevres complètes de Charles Fourier.* 12 vols. Paris: Editions Anthropos, 1966–1968.

Garat, Dominique-Joseph. *Mémoire sur la Révolution, ou Exposé de ma conduite dans les affaires et dans les fonctions publiques.* Paris: J. Smits, 1795.

Globe, Le. Journal philosophique et littéraire. 8 vols. Paris: 1824–30.

Guizot, François. *Mélanges politiques et historiques.* Paris: M. Levy Frères, 1869.

—— *Mémoires pour servir a l'historie de mon temps.* Vol. 1. Paris: Michel Levy Frères, 1858.

Helvétius, Claude-Adrien. *De l'esprit.* 2 vols. Paris: Durand, 1958.

Jacquemont, Victor. *Letters to Achille Chaper; Intimate Sketches of Life among Stendhal's Coterie.* Philadelphia: American Philosophical Society, 1960.

Journal d'instruction sociale. Edited by Condorcet, Sieyès, and Duhamel. 6 nos. Paris: 1 June 1793–6 July 1793.

La Harpe, Jean-François. *Du fanatisme dans la langue révolutionnaire.* Liège: J.A. Latour, 1797.

Laromiguière, Pierre. *Leçons de philosophie ou Essai sur les facultés de l'âme.* 3d ed. 2 vols. Paris: Brunot-Labbe, 1823.

Mackintosh, James. *Vindiciae Gallicae.* London: G.G.J. and J. Robinson, 1791.

Maine de Biran, Marie-François-Pierre-Gonthier de. *Oeuvres.* 14 vols. Edited by Pierre Tisserand. Paris: Félix Alcan, 1920–1949.

Malthus, Thomas Robert. *On Population.* Edited by Gertrude Himmelfarb. New York: The Modern Library, 1960.

Marrast, Armand. *Les funérailles révolutionnaires.* Paris: Pagnerre, 1848.

Marrast, Armand, and J.-F. Dupont. *De l'organisation du suffrage universel.* Paris: Pagnerre, 1848.

Marx, Karl. *Capital.* Translated by Samuel Moore and Edward Aveling. Edited by Frederick Engels. 3 vols. New York: International Publishers, 1967.

Marx, Karl, and Frederick Engels. *Collected Works.* Vol. 5: *Marx and Engels: 1845–47.* Translated by Clemens Dutt, W. Lough, and C.P. Magill. London: Lawrence & Wishart, 1976.

Mémoires de l'Institut National. Classe des Sciences Morales et Politiques. 5 vols. Paris: Baudouin, 1798–1804.

Mill, James. *Analysis of the Phenomena of the Human Mind.* 2 vols. 1869. Reprint. New York: A.M. Kelley, 1967.

—— *Essays on Government, Jurisprudence, Liberty of the Press, and Law of Nations.* 1825. Reprint. New York: A.M. Kelley, 1967.

Mill, John Stuart. *Auguste Comte and Positivism.* Ann Arbor, Mich.: University of Michigan Press, Ann Arbor Paperbacks, 1968.

—— *A System of Logic Ratiocinative and Inductive.* London: Longmans, Green, 1965.

Moniteur universel. Journal officiel de l'empire français. 161 vols. Paris, 1789–1868.

Moniteur universel. Réimpression de l'ancien Moniteur; seule histoire authentique et inalterée de la Révolution française, depuis la réunion des Etats-généraux jusqu'au Consulat (mai 1789-novembre 1799). 32 vols. Paris: Plon frères, 1847–1850.

Montesquieu, Charles-Louis-Secondat, baron de. *Oeuvres complètes.* Paris: Editions du Seuil, 1964.

—— *The Spirit of the Laws.* Translated by Thomas Nugent. Introduction by Franz Neumann. New York: Hafner, 1949.

Morgan, Lady [Sydney Owenson]. *France in 1829–30.* 2d ed. 2 vols. London: Saunders & Otley, 1831.

Notices Biographiques et Bibliographiques. Institut de France, Académie des Sciences Morales et Politiques. Paris: Librairie d'Argences, 1960.

Paine, Thomas. *The Selected Work of Tom Paine.* Edited by Howard Fast. New York: Random House, The Modern Library, 1945.

Paris révolutionnaire. 4 vols. Paris: Guillaumin, 1833–34.

Price, Richard. *Additional Observations on the Nature and Value of Civil Liberty.* 2d ed. London: T. Cadell, 1776.

—— *Observations on the Importance of the American Revolution and the Means of Making it a Benefit to the World.* London: T. Cadell, 1785.

Priestley, Joseph. *An Essay on the First Principles of Government and on the Nature of Political, Civil, and Religious Liberty.* London: J. Johnson, 1781.

—— *Letters to the Right Honorable Edmund Burke Occasioned by His Reflections on the Revolution in France.* 3d. ed. Birmingham: n.p., 1791.

Procès verbal des séances de la Chambre de la noblesse aux Etats généraux de 1789. Paris, 1789.

Producteur, Le. Journal de l'industrie des sciences et des beaux arts. 5 vols. Paris: Sautelet, 1826.

Proudhon, Pierre-Joseph. *Qu'est-ce que la propriété?* Paris: Garnier-Flammarion, 1966.

Revue américaine: journal mensuel. Paris: July 1826–June 1827.

Rey, Joseph. *Addresse à l'empereur.* 2d ed. N.p., 1815.

—— *Appel au ralliement des socialistes; lettre de M. Rey de Grenoble, communiste, ancien conseiller à la cour royale, aux rédacteurs de la Démocratie pacifique.* Paris: Librairie phalanstèrienne, 1847.

—— *Des bases de l'ordre social.* 2 vols. Angers: Ernest le Sourd, 1836.

—— *Des institutions judiciaires de l'Angleterre comparées avec celles de la France et de quelques autres états anciens et modernes.* 2 vols. Paris: Nève, 826.

—— *Lettres au rédacteur du Producteur, sur le système de la cooperation mutuelle et de la communauté de tous les biens d'après le plan de M. Owen.* Paris: A. Sautelet, 1828.

—— *Théorie et pratique de la science sociale; ou Exposé des principes de morale, d'économie publique et politique et application à l'état actuel de la société de moyens généraux, immédiats et successifs d'améliorer la condition des travailleurs et même des propriétaires.* 3 vols. Paris: Jules Renouard, 1842.

—— *Traité des principes généraux du droit et de la législation.* Paris: Alex-Gobelet, 1828.

Ricardo, David. *Works and Correspondence.* Edited by Piero Sraffa. Cambridge: At the University Press, 1951–53.

Robespierre, Maximilien. *Discours et rapports à la Convention.* Paris: Union Générale d'Editions, 1965.

Roederer, Pierre-Louis. *Oeuvres.* Edited by A.M. Roederer. 8 vols. Paris: Firmin Didot, 1853–1859.

Saint-Beuve, Charles-Augustin, *Portraits contemporains.* 3 vols. Paris: Didier, 1846.

—— *Premiers lundis.* 3d ed. 3 vols. Paris: Calmann Levy, 1883.

Saint-Simon, Claude-Henri, comte de. *Oeuvres choisis.* 3 vols. Bruxelles: Van Meenen, 1859.

Say, Jean-Baptiste. *Cours complet d'économie politique pratique.* 2 vols. Paris: Guillaumin, 1852.

—— *Letters to Malthus; A Catechism of Political Economy.* Translated by John Richter. London: Sherwood, Nelly, & Jones, 1821.

—— *Oeuvres diverses de J.B. Say.* Edited by Ch. Comte, E. Daire, and Horace Say. Paris: Guillaumin, 1848.

—— *Traité d'économie politique.* Paris: Calmann-Levy, 1972.

—— *A Treatise on Political Economy.* Translated from the Fourth Edition by C.R. Prinsep. Introduction translated by Clement C. Biddle. Philadelphia: Grigg & Elliot, 1832.

Sieyès, Emmanuel-Joseph. *Discours dans les débats constitutionnels de l'an III (2 et 18 thermidor)*. Edited with an introduction by Paul Bastid. Paris: Hachette, 1939.

—— *Essai sur les privilèges*. Paris: n.p., 1789.

—— *Préliminaire de la constitution française: Reconnaissance et exposition raisonée de droits de l'homme et du citoyen*. Versailles: Bibliotèque Royale, 1789.

—— *Qu'est-ce que le Tiers Etat?* Edited with an introduction by Roberto Zapperi. Geneva: Librairie Droz, 1970.

—— *What is the Third Estate?* Translated by M. Blondel. Edited by S.E. Finer. Introduction by Peter Campbell. New York: Frederick A. Praeger, 1963.

Sismondi, Léonard Simonde de. *Nouveaux principes d'économie politique ou De la richesse dans ses rapports avec la population*. 2 vols. Paris: Delaunay, 1819.

Staël-Holstein, Anne-Louise-Germaine Necker, baronne de. *Considérations sur les principaux événements de la Révolution française*. 3 vols. Paris: Delaunay, 1820.

Stendhal [Marie-Henri Beyle]. *Courrier anglaise*. Edited by Henri Martineau. 5 vols. Paris: Le Divan, 1936.

—— *De l'Amour*. Edited by Henri Martineau. Paris: Garnier, 1959.

—— *The Life of Henry Brulard*. Translated by Jean Stewart and B.C.J.G. Knight. New York: Noonday Press, 1958.

—— *Memoirs of an Egotist*. Translated with an introduction by T.W. Earp. London: Turnstile Press, 1949.

—— *Oeuvres*. Edited by Henri Martineau. 46 vols. Paris: Le Divan, 1927–38. Reprint. Nendeln, Liechtenstein: Kraus, 1968.

Stryenski, C., trans. "Lettres inédites de Jeremy Bentham." *Journal des Economistes* (June 1890), pp. 367–74.

Taillandier, Alphonse H. *Documents biographiques sur P.-C.-F. Daunou*. 2d ed. Paris: Firmin Didot, 1847.

Thierry, Augustin. *Dix ans d'études historiques*. Paris: Plon Frères, 1846.

Thurot, J. François. *De l'entendement et de la raison, Introduction à l'étude de la philosophie*. 2 vols. Paris, 1830.

—— *Oeuvres posthumes*. Paris: Hachette, 1837.

Tribune des départements, La. Journal politique, commercial et littéraire. Paris: June 1829–January 1831.

Volney, Constantin-François Chasseboeuf. *An Abridgement of the Law of Nature, or Catechism of French Citizens*. London: n.p., 1796.

—— *Conditions nécessaires de la légalité des Etats généraux*. N.p., 1789.

—— *Lectures on History Delivered in the Normal School of Paris.* Philadelphia: J. Bioren, 1801.
—— *Oeuvres complètes.* 2d ed. 8 vols. Paris: Parmentier, 1826.
Westminster Review, The. London: Baldwin, Cradock & Joy, 1824–1914.

Selected Secondary Sources

Acton, H.B. "La philosophie du langage sous la Révolution française." *Archives de philosophie* (July-December 1961):426–29.
Alfaric, Prosper. *Laromiguière et son ecole.* Paris: Les Belles Lettres, 1929.
Allemagne, V.H.d'. *Les Saint Simoniens.* Paris: Gründ, 1930.
Allix, Edgard. "Destutt de Tracy, économiste." *Revue d'économie politique* 26 (1912):424–51.
Bagge, Dominique. *Les idées politiques en France sous la Restauration.* Paris: Presses Universitaires de France, 1952.
Baker, Keith Michael. *Condorcet: From Natural Philosophy to Social Mathematics.* Chicago: University of Chicago Press, 1975.
—— "The Early History of the Term 'Social Science'." *Annals of Science* 20 (1964):211–26.
—— "Politics and Social Science in Eighteenth-Century France: ▮▮▮▮▮ ciété de 1789." In *French Government and Society, 1500–1850: Essays in Honor of Alfred Cobban,* edited by J.F. Bosher, pp. 208–230. London: Athlone Press, 1973.
Barni, Jules. *Les moralistes français au 18e siècle.* Paris: G. Baillière, 1873.
Barny, Roger. "Les Aventures de la théorie de la souveraineté en 1789." In *La Revision de valeurs sociales dans la littérature européenne à la lumière des idées de la Révolution française.* Annales littéraires de l'Université de Besançon, vol. 109, pp. 65–93. Paris: Les Belles Lettres, 1970.
Bastid, Paul. *Benjamin Constant et sa doctrine.* 2 vols. Paris: Colin, 1966.
—— *Les institutions politiques de la monarchie parlementaire française, 1815 à 1848.* Paris: Editions du Recueil Sirey, 1954.
—— *Sieyès et sa pensée.* Paris: Hachette, 1970.
Beck, Thomas D. *French Legislators, 1800–1834.* Berkeley: University of California Press, 1974.
Becker, Carl L. *The Heavenly City of the Eighteenth-Century Philosophers.* New Haven: Yale University Press, 1970.
Belin, J.P. *La logique d'une idée-force: L'idée d'utilité sociale et la Révolution française (1789–1792).* Paris: Hermann & cie, 1939.

Berrian, Albert Harvey. "Stendhal and the Idéologues." Ph.D. dissertation, New York University, 1954.

Blount, Charles. "Bentham, Dumont and Mirabeau: An Historical Revision." *University of Birmingham Historical Journal* 3 (1952):153–67.

Boas, George. *French Philosophies of the Romantic Period.* New York: Russell & Russell, 1964.

Bourdon, Jean. "Le mécontentment public et les craintes des dirigeantes sous le Directoire." *Annales historiques de la Révolution française* 18 (1946):218–37.

Boutmy, Emile. *Etudes politiques.* Paris: A. Colin, 1907.

Bowley, Marian. *Studies in the History of Economic Theory Before 1870.* London: Macmillan, 1973.

Bréhier, Emile. *The History of Philosophy.* Vol. 6: *The Nineteenth Century: Period of Systems, 1800–1850.* Translated by Wade Baskin. Chicago: University of Chicago Press, 1968.

Brown, M. Gordon. *Les idées politiques et religieuses de Stendhal.* Paris: Jean-Renard, 1939.

Brussaly, Manuel. *The Political Ideas of Stendhal.* New York: Publications of the Institute of French Studies, Columbia University, 1933.

Burdeau, Georges. *Traité de science politique.* Vol. 6. Paris: R. Pichon et R. Durand-Auziat, 1971.

Caillet, Emile. *La tradition littéraire des Idéologues.* Philadelphia: The American Philosophical Society, 1943.

Cappadocia, Ezio. "The History of the Liberal Party in France, 1814–1826." Ph.D. dissertation, University of Chicago, 1957.

Carey, R.G. "The Liberals of France and their Relation to the Development of Bonaparte's Dictatorship 1799–1804." Ph.D. dissertation, University of Chicago, 1947.

Cassirer, Ernst. *The Philosophy of the Enlightenment.* Translated by Fritz C.A. Koelln and James P. Pettegrove. Boston: Beacon Press, 1965.

Chinard, Gilbert. *Jefferson et les idéologues d'après sa correspondance inédite avec Destutt de Tracy, Cabanis, J.B. Say et Auguste Comte.* Baltimore: Johns Hopkins Press, 1925.

—— *Volney et l'Amérique.* Baltimore: Johns Hopkins Press, 1923.

Church, William F., ed. *The Influence of the Enlightenment on the French Revolution.* Boston: D.C. Heath, 1964.

Cobb, R.C. *The Police and the People: French Popular Protest 1789–1820.* London: Oxford University Press, 1970.

Cobban, Alfred. "The 'Middle Class' in France, 1815–1848." *French Historical Studies* 5 (Spring 1967).

Collins, Irene. *Liberalism in Nineteenth-Century Europe.* London: Wyman & Sons, 1957.

Conchard, Vermeilde. "Cabanis homme politique (coups d'état du 18 fructidor an V et du 18 brumaire an VIII, d'après des lettres inédites)." *Société scientifique, historique et archéologique de la Carrèze Bulletin (Brive)* 35 (1913):678–98.

Cruet, Jean. *La philosophie morale et sociale de Destutt de Tracy.* Tours: P. Bousrez-J. Allard Succr, 1909.

Cumming, Robert Denoon. *Human Nature and History; a Study of the Development of Liberal Political Thought.* Chicago: University of Chicago Press, 1969.

Deslandres, Maurice. *Histoire constitutionelle de la France de 1789 à 1870.* Paris: A. Colin, Sirey, 1932.

Desroche, H. "Images and Echoes of Owenism in Nineteenth-Century France." In *Robert Owen: Prophet of the Poor,* edited by Sidney Pollard and John Salt, pp. 239–84. London: Macmillan Press, 1971.

Dictionnaire des sciences philosophiques (1844–1852). S.v. "Idéologie," "Destutt de Tracy."

Duguit, L.; H. Monnier; and R. Bonnard. *Les Constitutions et les principales lois politiques de la France depuis 1789.* 6th ed. Paris: Librairie générale de droit et de jurisprudence, 1943.

Dumulard, Henry. "Joseph Rey de Grenoble et ses mémoires politiques." *Annales de l'Université de Grenoble, Section Lettres-Droits* 4 (1927):71–111.

Dunham, Arthur Louis. *The Industrial Revolution in France 1815–1848.* New York: Exposition Press, 1955.

Duverger, Maurice. *Les Constitutions de la France.* Paris: Presses Universitaires, 1944.

Echeverria, Durand. *Mirage in the West: A History of the French Image of American Society to 1815.* Princeton: Princeton University Press, 1968.

El Shankakiri, Moh. "Jeremy Bentham: Critique des droits de l'homme." *Archives de philosophie du droit* 9 (1964):129–52.

Epsztein, Leon. *L'économie et la morale aux débuts du capitalisme industriel en France et en Grande-Bretagne.* Paris: Armand Colin, 1966.

Eros, John. "The Positivist Generation of French Republicanism." *Sociological Review* 3 (December 1955):255–77.

European Political History, 1815–1870: Aspects of Liberalism. Edited by Eugene C. Black. New York: Harper & Row, 1967.

Fargher, Richard. "The Retreat from Voltaireanism." In *The French Mind: Studies in Honor of Gustave Rudler,* pp. 220–38. Oxford: Clarendon Press, 1952.

Ferraz, Martin. *Histoire de la philosophie en France au XIX siècle.* Vol. 3: *Spiritualisme et libéralisme.* Paris: Perrin, 1887.

Foucault, Michel. *Les mots et les choses: une archéologie des sciences humaines.* Paris: Gallimard, 1966.

Fox-Genovese, Elizabeth. *The Origins of Physiocracy: Economic Revolution and Social Order in Eighteenth-Century France.* Ithaca: Cornell University Press, 1976.

Francovich, Guillermo. "La Filosofía de Destutt de Tracy en Bolivia." *Kollasuyo (La Paz)* 3 (January 1941):3–8.

Furet, François. *Penser la Revolution Française.* Paris: Gallimard, 1978.

Gallois, Leonard. *Histoire des journaux et des journalistes de la Révolution française (1789–1796).* Paris: Société de l'industrie fraternelle, 1845.

Gans, J. "The Relations between English and French Socialists at the Beginning of the Nineteenth Century." *Le Mouvement Social* 46 (January-March 1964):105–18.

Garnham, B.G. "The Social, Moral, and Political Thought of Destutt de Tracy." Ph.D. dissertation, University of Durham, 1974.

Gaulmier, Jean. *L'Idéologue Volney (1757–1820): Contribution à l'histoire de l'orientalisme en France.* Beyrouth: Impr. Catholique, 1951.

Gierke, Otto von. *Natural Law and the Theory of Society, 1500 to 1800.* Translated and introduced by Ernest Barker. Cambridge: The University Press, 1934.

Gillispie, Charles Coulston. *The Edge of Objectivity: An Essay in the History of Scientific Ideas.* Princeton: Princeton University Press, 1960.

Girard, M. *Le libéralisme en France de 1814 à 1848: doctrine et mouvement.* Paris: Centre de Documentation Universitaire, 1966.

Gobert, Adrienne. *L'Opposition des assemblées pendant le consulat, 1800–1804.* Paris: Sagot, 1925.

Godechot, Jacques. *Les Constitutions de France depuis 1789.* Paris: Garnier-Flammarion, 1970.

—— *Les institutions de la France sous la Révolution et l'Empire.* 2d ed. Paris: Presses Universitaires de France, 1968.

Goetz-Girey, Robert. *Croissance et progrès a l'origine des sociétés industrielles.* Paris: Editions Montchrestien, 1966.

Gordon, Barry. *Political Economy in Parliament, 1819–1823.* New York: Harper & Row, 1977.

Gouhier, Henri G. *La jeunesse d'Auguste Comte: la formation du positivisme.* 3 vols. Paris: J. Vrin, 1933–1941.

Greifer, Elisha. "Joseph de Maistre and the Reaction against the Eighteenth Century." *American Political Science Review* 55 (September 1961):591–98.

Groethuysen, Bernard. *Philosophie de la Révolution française*. Paris: Librairie Gallimard, 1956.

Grossman, Lionel. "Augustin Thierry and Liberal Historiography." *History and Theory*. Beiheft 15 (1976).

Grossman, Mordecai. *The Philosophy of Helvétius with Special Emphasis on the Ethical Implications of Sensationalism*. New York: Bureau of Publications, Teachers College, Columbia University, 1926.

Gruner, Shirley M. *Economic Materialism and Social Moralism*. The Hague: Mouton, 1973.

—— "The Revolution of July 1830 and the Expression 'Bourgeoisie.' " *The Historical Journal* 11 (1968).

Guerard, Benjamin Edme Charles. *Notice sur M. Daunou*. Paris: Dumoulin, 1855.

Guerlac, H. "Some Aspects of Science during the French Revolution." *The Scientific Monthly* 80 (1855):93–101.

Guillois, Antoine. *Le salon de Madame Helvétius: Cabanis et les idéologues*. Paris: Calmann Levy, 1894.

Gusdorf, Georges. *Les sciences humaines et la pensée occidentale*. Vol. 8: *La conscience révolutionnaire: Les Idéologues*. Paris: Payot, 1978.

Halévy, Elie. *The Era of Tyrannies*. Translated by R.K. Webb. New York: New York University Press, 1966.

—— *The Growth of Philosophical Radicalism*. Translated by Mary Morris. Boston: Beacon Press, 1960.

Hamburger, Joseph. *Intellectuals in Politics: John Stuart Mill and the Philosophical Radicals*. New Haven: Yale University Press, 1965.

—— *James Mill and the Art of Revolution*. New Haven: Yale University Press, 1963.

—— "James Mill on Universal Suffrage and the Middle Class." *Journal of Politics* 24 (1962):167–90.

Harnois, Guy. *Les théories du language en France de 1660 à 1821*. Paris: Société d'Edition "Les Belles Lettres," 1929.

Harpaz, Ephraim. "Le Censeur européen." *Revue d'histoire économique et sociale* 37 (1959):185–218, 328–57.

—— *L'école libérale sous la Restauration. Le "Mercure" et la "Minerve" 1817–1820*. Genève: Droz, 1968.

Hazard, Paul. *European Thought in the Eighteenth Century: From Montesquieu to Lessing*. New Haven: Yale University Press, 1954.

—— *La Révolution française et les lettres italiennes 1789–1815*. Paris: Hachette et Cie, 1910.

Herold, J. Christopher, ed. and trans. *The Mind of Napoleon: A Selection from His Written and Spoken Words.* New York: Columbia University Press, 1955.

Hill, Henry Bertram. "French Constitutionalism: Old Regime and Revolutionary." *Journal of Modern History* 21 (September 1949):222–27.

Hunt, H.J. *Le socialisme et le romanticisme en France: étude de la presse socialiste de 1830 à 1848.* Oxford: Clarendon Press, 1935.

Hunt, Lynn; David Lansky; and Paul Hanson. "The Failure of the Liberal Republic in France, 1795–1799: The Road to Brumaire." *Journal of Modern History* 51 (December 1979):734–59.

Imbert, Pierre Henri. *Destutt de Tracy: Critique de Montesquieu, de la liberté en matière politique.* Paris: A.G. Nizet, 1974.

Isambert, François-André. *De la Charbonnerie au Saint-Simonisme: étude sur la jeunesse de Buchez.* Paris: Editions de Minuit, 1966.

—— *Politique, religion et science de l'homme chez Phillipe Buchez (1796–1865).* Paris: Editions Cujas, 1967.

James, Michael. "Pierre-Louis Roederer, Jean-Baptiste Say, and the concept of *industrie.*" *History of Political Economy* 9 (Winter 1977):455–75.

Jellinek, Georg. *The Declaration of the Rights of Man and of Citizens; a Contribution to Modern Constitutional History.* Translated by Max Ferrand. New York: Holt, 1901.

Kaiser, Thomas E., "The Idéologues: From Enlightenment to Positivism." Ph.D. dissertation, Harvard University, 1976.

—— "Politics and political economy in the thought of the Idéologues." *History of Political Economy* 12, no. 2 (1980):141–60.

Kayser, Jacques. *Les grandes batailles du radicalisme, des origines aux portes du pouvoir 1820–1901.* Paris: Marcel Rivière, 1962.

Kelley, Daniel Kemp. "Ultra-Royalism: Ideology and Politics under the Bourbon Restoration." Ph.D. dissertation, University of Wisconsin, 1964.

Kelly, George Armstrong. "Liberalism and Aristocracy in the French Restoration." *Journal of the History of Ideas* 26 (1965):509–30.

Kennedy, Emmet. *A Philosophe in the Age of Revolution: Destutt de Tracy and the Origins of "Ideology."* Philadelphia: American Philosophical Society, 1978.

Keohane, Nannerl O. *Philosophy and the State in France: the Renaissance to the Enlightenment.* Princeton: Princeton University Press, 1980.

Kitchin, Joanna. *Un journal "philosophique": La Décade (1794–1807).* Paris: n.p., 1966.

Knight, Isabel F. *The Geometric Spirit: The Abbé de Condillac and the French Enlightenment*. New Haven: Yale University Press, 1968.

Koch, Adrienne. *The Philosophy of Thomas Jefferson*. New York: Columbia University Press, 1943.

Kohler, Oskar. *Die Logik des Destutt de Tracy*. Borna-Leipzig: n.p., 1931.

Kort, Fred. "The Issue of a Science of Politics in Utilitarian Thought." *American Political Science Review* 46 (1952):1140–52.

Lacroze, René. *Maine de Biran*. Paris: Presses Universitaires de France, 1970.

Leclercq, Jacques. *Du droit naturel à la sociologie*. 2 vols. Paris: Editions SPES, 1960.

Lefebvre, George. "La Révolution française et le rationalisme." *Annales historiques de la Révolution française* 19 (January–March 1947):4–34.

Lenoir, Raymond. "Psychologie et logique de Destutt de Tracy." *Revue philosophique* 84 (1917):527–56.

Leroy, Maxime. *Histoire des idées sociales en France*. 3 vols. Paris: Gallimard, 1962.

Letwin, Shirley Robin. *The Pursuit of Certainty*. Cambridge: At the University Press, 1965.

Levasseur, Emile. *Histoire des classes ouvrières et de l'industrie en France de 1789 à 1870*. 2d ed. New York: AMS Press, 1969.

Lichtheim, George. "The Concept of Ideology." *History and Theory* 3 (1963):164–95.

—— *A Short History of Socialism*. New York: Praeger, 1970.

Long, Douglas G. *Bentham on Liberty: Jeremy Bentham's Idea of Liberty in Relation to His Utilitarianism*. Toronto: University of Toronto Press, 1977.

Lucas, Colin. "The First Directory and the Rule of Law." French Historical Studies 10 (Spring 1977).

Lucas-Dubréton, Jean. *Le culte de Napoleon, 1815–1848*. Paris: A. Michel, 1960.

Lyons, David. *Forms and Limits of Utilitarianism*. Oxford: Clarendon Press, 1965.

—— *In the Interest of the Governed: A Study in Bentham's Philosophy of Utility and Law*. Oxford: Clarendon Press, 1973.

Macdonald, Margaret. "Natural Rights." In *Philosophy, Politics and Society*, First Series; edited by Peter Laslett, pp. 35–55. Oxford: Basil Blackwell, 1970.

Mack, Mary Peter. *Bentham: An Odyssey of Ideas 1748–1792*. New York: Columbia University Press, 1963.

Madinier, Gabriel. *Conscience et mouvement, étude sur la philosophie française de Condillac à Bergson.* 2d ed. Louvain: Nauwelaerts, 1967.

Manning, D.J. *The Mind of Jeremy Bentham.* New York: Barnes & Noble, 1968.

Manuel, Frank E. "From Equality to Organicism." *Journal of the History of Ideas* 17 (1956):54–69.

—— *The New World of Henri Saint-Simon.* Notre Dame, Indiana: University of Notre Dame Press, 1963.

Martin, Kingsley. *French Liberal Thought in the Eighteenth Century: A Study of Political Ideas from Bayle to Condorcet.* London: Phoenix House, 1962.

Mauzi, Robert. *L'idée du bonheur dans la littérature et la pensée françaises au XVIIIe siècle.* Paris: A. Colin, 1960.

Mayer, Jacob Peter. *Political Thought in France from the Revolution to the Fifth Republic.* London: Routledge & Kegan Paul, 1961.

McDonald, Joan. *Rousseau and the French Revolution, 1762–1791.* London: University of London, Athlone Press, 1965.

Meek, Ronald. "Smith, Turgot, and the 'Four Stages' Theory." *History of Political Economy* 3 (Spring 1971):9–27.

Mellon, Stanley. *The Political Uses of History: A Study of Historians in the French Restoration.* Stanford: Stanford University Press, 1958.

Merriam, Charles E. *History of the Theory of Sovereignty Since Rousseau.* Studies in History, Economics, and Public Law, no. 4. New York: Columbia University Press, 1900.

Mill, Anna Jean, ed. and intro. *John Mill's Boyhood Visit to France.* Toronto: University of Toronto Press, 1960.

Moore, F.C.T. *The Psychology of Maine de Biran.* Oxford: Clarendon Press, 1970.

Moore, James Maxwell. *The Roots of French Republicanism.* New York: American Press, 1962.

Moravia, Sergio. "Les Idéologues et l'âge des Lumières," *Studies on Voltaire and the Eighteenth Century* 154 (1976):1465–86.

—— *Il pensiero degli idéologues: scienza e filosofia in Francia* (1780–1815). Florence: La Nuova Italia, 1974.

—— "Philosophie et médicine en France à la fin du XVIIIe Siècle." *Studies on Voltaire and the Eighteenth Century* 89 (1972):1089–1151.

—— *Il tramonto dell'illuminismo: Filosofia e politica nella societate francese (1770–1810).* Bari: Laterza, 1968.

Mornet, Daniel. *Les origines intellectuelles de la Révolution française.* Paris: A. Colin, 1933.

Morris, Richard Arthur. "Joseph Rey of Grenoble, 1779–1855: Revolutionary-Educator-Humanitarian." Ph.D. dissertation, University of Iowa, 1966.

Mourant, John Arthur. *The Physiocratic Conception of Natural Law.* Chicago: University of Chicago Press, 1943.

Nesbitt, George Lyman. *Benthamite Reviewing: The First Twelve Years of the Westminster Review 1824–1836.* New York: AMS Press, 1966.

Newman, Edgar Leon. "The Blouse and the Frock Coat: The Alliance of the Common People of Paris with the Liberal Leadership during the Last Years of the Bourbon Restoration." *Journal of Modern History* 46 (March 1974):26–59.

—— "Republicanism during the Bourbon Restoration in France, 1814–1830." Ph.D. dissertation, University of Chicago, 1969.

Palmer, P.A. "Benthamism in England and America." *American Political Science Review* 35 (1941):855–71.

Parekh, Bhiku C., ed. *Jeremy Bentham: Ten Critical Essays.* London: Cass, 1974.

Parker, Harold T. *The Cult of Antiquity and the French Revolutionaries.* New York: Octagon Books, 1965.

Payne, Harry C. *"Pauvreté, Misère,* and the aims of enlightened economics." *Studies on Voltaire and the Eighteenth Century* 154 (1976):1581–92.

Perreux, Gabriel. *Au temps des sociétés secrètes: la propagande républicaine au début de la Monarchie de Juillet (1830–1835).* Paris: Hachette, 1931.

Picavet, François. *Les idéologues: essai sur l'histoire des idées et des théories scientifiques, philosophiques, religieuses, etc. en France depuis 1789.* Paris: Félix Alcan, 1891.

Piccirilli, Ricardo. *Rivadavia y su tiempo.* 3 vols. Buenos Aires: Ediciones Peuser, 1960.

Plamenatz, John. *The English Utilitarians.* Oxford: Basil Blackwell, 1958.

—— *Ideology.* London: Praeger, 1970.

—— *The Revolutionary Movement in France: 1815–71.* London: Longmans, Green, 1952.

Popkin, Richard H. *The History of Scepticism from Erasmus to Spinoza.* Berkeley: University of California Press, 1979.

Pratt, R. Cranford. "The Benthamite Theory of Democracy." *The Canadian Journal of Economics and Political Science* 21 (1955):20–29.

—— *Histoire des idées politiques.* Paris: Dalloz, 1966.

—— *Les institutions politiques françaises de 1789 à 1870.* Paris: Cours de droit, 1957.

Rader, Daniel L. *The Journalists and the July Revolution in France*. The Hague: Martinus Nijhoff, 1973.

Rastier, François. *Idéologie et théorie des signes: Analyse structurale des Eléments d'Idéologie d'Antoine-Louis-Claude Destutt de Tracy*. The Hague: Mouton, 1972.

Ritchie, David George. *Natural Rights: A Criticism of some Political and Ethical Conceptions*. London: Unwin Brothers, 1924.

Roels, Jean. *Le concept de représentation politique au dixhuitième siècle français*. Louvain: Nauwelaerts, 1969.

—— *La notion de représentation chez Roederer*. Heule: UGA, 1962.

Rosenblum, Nancy L. *Bentham's Theory of the Modern State*. Cambridge: Harvard University Press, 1978.

Rudé, Fernand. "A Forgotten Utopian Socialist: Joseph Rey, 1773–1855." *Annales des Lettres de l'Université de Grenoble* 20 (1944).

—— *Stendhal et la pensée sociale de son temps*. Paris: Plon, 1967.

Ruggiero, Guido de. *The History of European Liberalism*. Translated by R.G. Collingwood. London: Oxford University Press, 1927.

Ryan, Alan J. *J.S. Mill*. London: Routledge & Kegan Paul, 1974.

Ryan, Alan J., ed. *The Idea of Freedom*. Oxford: Oxford University Press, 1979.

—— "Two Concepts of Politics and Democracy: James and John Stuart Mill." In *Machiavelli and the Nature of Political Thought*, edited by Martin Fleisher, pp. 76–113. New York: Atheneum, 1972.

Salvadori, Massimo. *European Liberalism*. New York: Wiley-Interscience, 1972.

Samuels, W.J. "The Physiocratic Theory of Property and the State." *Quarterly Journal of Economics* 75 (February 1961):96–111.

Schapiro, Jacob Salwyn. *Condorcet and the Rise of Liberalism*. New York: Harcourt, Brace, 1934.

Schumpeter, Joseph A. *A History of Economic Analysis*. New York: Oxford University Press, 1974.

Sée, Henri. *L'évolution de la pensée politique en France au XVIIIe siècle*. Paris: Marcel Giard, 1923.

Seillière, Baron de. "Les sciences morales et politiques dans l'Institut de France à l'époque révolutionnaire." *Revue internationale de l'enseignement* 60 (January 1940):21–31.

Sencier, Georges. *Le babouvisme après Babeuf; sociétés secrètes et conspirations communistes (1830–1848)*. Paris: M. Rivière, 1912.

Sherman, Dennis, "The Meaning of Economic Liberalism in Mid-nineteenth-century France." *History of Political Economy* 6 (Summer 1974):171–99.

Sigmund, Paul. *Natural Law in Political Thought.* Cambridge, Mass.: Winthrop Publishers, 1971.

Simon, Jules. *Une Académie sous le Directoire.* Paris: Calmann Levy, 1885.

Simon, William, ed. *French Liberalism 1789–1848.* New York: John Wiley, 1972.

Smith, Colin. "Aspects of Destutt de Tracy's Linguistic Analysis as Adopted by Stendhal." *Modern Language Review* 51 (1956):512–21.

—— "Destutt de Tracy's Analysis of the Proposition." *Revue internationale de philosophie* 82 (1967):475–85.

—— "Destutt de Tracy and the Bankruptcy of Sensationalism." In *Balzac and the Nineteenth Century,* edited by D.G. Charlton, J. Goudon, and Anthony R. Pugh, pp. 195–207. Leicester: Leicester University Press, 1972.

Soltau, Roger Henry. *French Political Thought in the Nineteenth Century.* New York: Russell and Russell, 1959.

Sowell, Thomas. *Say's Law—An Historical Analysis.* Princeton: Princeton University Press, 1972.

Spengler, Joseph J. "French Population Theory since 1800." *Journal of Political Economy* 44 (1936):577–611.

Spitzer, Alan Barrie. *Old Hatreds and Young Hopes: The French Carbonari against the Bourbon Restoration.* Cambridge: Harvard University Press, 1971.

—— "Restoration Political Theory and the Law of the Double Vote." *Journal of Modern History* 55 (March 1983):54–70.

Starzinger, Vincent E. *Middlingness: Juste Milieu Political Theory in France and England, 1815–1848.* Charlottesville, Va.: University Press of Virginia, 1965.

Staum, Martin S. *Cabanis: Enlightenment and Medical Philosophy in the French Revolution.* Princeton: Princeton University Press, 1980.

—— "The Class of Moral and Political Sciences, 1795–1803." *French Historical Studies* 11 (Spring 1980).

Stein, Jay Wobith. "The Idéologues, their Theories and Politics; Intellectuals under the Governments of the French Revolution and Napoleonic Regime." Ph.D. dissertation, Columbia University, 1952.

—— *The Mind and the Sword.* New York: Twayne, 1961.

Stepanowa, Vera. *Destutt de Tracy: eine Historisch-Psychologische Untersuchung.* Zurich: Zurcher and Furrer, 1908.

Stephen, Leslie. *The English Utilitarians.* 3 vols. New York: Peter Smith, 1950.

Stryenski, C. "Un patron d'autrefois: Le Comte Destutt de Tracy." *Revue des Alpes* (1892).

Talmon, J. L. *The Origins of Totalitarian Democracy.* New York: Frederick A. Praeger, 1968.

Teilhac, Ernest. *L'oeuvre économique de Jean Baptiste Say.* Paris: Félix Alcan, 1927.

Thomas, William. *The Philosophic Radicals: Nine Studies in Theory and Practice 1817–1841.* Oxford: Clarendon Press, 1979.

Thompson, E.P. *The Making of the English Working Class.* New York: Vintage, 1963.

Van Duzer, Charles Hunter. "The Contribution of the Idéologues to French Revolutionary Thought." In *Johns Hopkins University, Studies in Historical and Political Science* 53 (1935).

Van Leeuwen, Henry G. *The Problem of Certainty in English Thought, 1630–1690.* The Hague: Martinus Nijhoff, 1963.

Vartanian, Aram. "Cabanis and LaMettrie." *Studies on Voltaire and the Eighteenth Century.* 155 (1976):2149–66.

Villefosse, Louis de. *The Scourge of the Eagle: Napoleon and the Liberal Opposition.* Translated and edited by Michael Ross. London: Sedgwick & Jackson, 1972.

Walzer, Michael, ed. and intro. *Regicide and Revolution: Speeches at the Trial of Louis XVI.* Translated by Marian Rothstein. London: Cambridge University Press, 1974.

Watt, E.D. "Locked in: De Maistre's Critique of French Lockeanism." *Journal of the History of Ideas* 32 (January–March 1971):129–33.

Waxman, Chaim I. *The End of Ideology Debate.* New York: Simon and Schuster, 1968.

Weill, Georges. *Histoire du parti républicain en France (1814–1870).* Paris: Félix Alcan, 1928.

——"L'idée républicaine en France pendant la restauration." *Revue d'histoire moderne* 2 (1927):321–48.

—— *Un précurseur du socialisme: Saint-Simon et son oeuvre.* Paris: Perrin et Cie, 1894.

Weulersse, George. *Le mouvement physiocratique en France (de 1756 à 1770).* 2 vols. Paris: Félix Alcan, 1910.

Willey, Basil. *The Eighteenth Century Background: Studies on the Idea of Nature in the Thought of the Period.* London: Chatto and Windus, 1940.

Woloch, Isser. *Jacobin Legacy: The Democratic Movement Under the Directory.* Princeton: Princeton University Press, 1970.

INDEX

Daunou, Pierre, 1, 3, 137, 147, 149, 155, 157, 158, 167, 190, 191, 194-95, 197n3, 206n92, 233nn122, 125, 239n45; archivist of the Empire, 41; arguments for representative government, 99-100, 102, 109-10, 114, 128-34; author of Constitution of 1795, 29-30; on Committee of Public Instruction, 34; constitutional organization of powers, 37; *Cours d'études historiques,* 211n140; critique of Declaration of Rights, 26-27; defense of property, 233n130; *Essai sur les garanties individuelles que réclame l'état actuel de la société,* 26-27, 97, 99, 128, 131, 151, 156, 158, 211n140; human nature, 97-98; and Idéologue interpretation of the *Charte,* 128-34; imprisoned, 27; influence of, 161, 162; lectured at Collège de France, 156; member of Independents, 155; and Napoleon, 38; new perspective on republican politics, 2, 42; on doubt, 66-67; on parliamentary factions, 238n37; on revolution, 110-11, 112-13, 114; supported Directory, 36

De Corpore (Hobbes), 213n31

"De la physiologie" (Buchez), 174-75

"De l'amour" (Tracy)", 118-19

De l'Angleterre et des Anglais (Say), 220n14

De l'esprit (Helvétius), 61

De l'influence de la Révolution d'Amérique sur l'Europe (Condorcet), 13-14

De l'irritation et de la folie (Broussais), 167

Décade philosophique (journal), 29, 30, 31, 39, 40, 219n12; attitude of, during Terror, 205n90; supported Directory, 36-37; suppressed, 41

Decazes ministry, 155

Declaration of rights, 58, 136; U.S. origin of, 7, 199n6

Declaration of Rights: Constitution of *1795,* 30, 32; prefacing Girondin constitution, 13; *1789,* 26-27, 32

Declaration of the Rights of Man and Citizen, 5, 6, 7-9

Defense of Usury (Bentham), 142

Dégerando, Joseph Marie, 206n91

Democracy(ies), 2, 100, 104, 105; direct, 103, 105-6, 107, 108, 228n44; representative, 183; utilitarian theories of, 145-51

Democratic clubs, 36

Des bases de l'ordre social (Rey), 178, 179

Desires, 56, 57, 58, 68, 182

Despotism(s), 33, 41, 108, 120

Destutt de Tracy, Antoine-Louis-Claude, 1, 2, 6, 35, 132, 135, 174, 181, 182, 191, 194-95, 197n3, 206nn91, 92, 210n137, 230n68, 239n45, 246n83; arguments for representative government, 99, 100-9, 113-28; attacks on, 167, 168, 173, 175, 214n42; battle over central schools, 40-41; civil equality, 140-45; *Commentaire sur L'Esprit des lois de Montesquieu,* 54-55, 97, 109, 111, 116, 119, 124, 127, 156, 157, 160, 162, 167, 211n139; correspondence with Burke, 20-22; "De L'amour," 118-19; defense of property, 177; did not join Carbonari, 242n45; disciples, 36; Elémens d'idéologie, 63, 73, 116, 118, 167, 175, 208n112, 211n139, 213n37; *Grammaire,* 63, 78, 217n94; "ideological" economics, 71, 73-96, 97; imprisoned, 27; inability to reconcile ideology and reality, 93, 119, 120, 125, 138; influence of, 29, 161, 162, 166, 179, 240n5, 247n86; liberty, 176; member of Independents, 155; *Mémoire sur la faculté de penser,* 53; mentioned in relation to other writers, 129, 131, 133; model republic, 114-28; moved Idéologue salon to Paris, 42; in Napoleonic Senate, 41; new perspective on republican politics, 42; *Observations sur le système actuel d'instruction publique,* 40-41, 124; on revolution, 110-12, 113-14; *Opinion sur Saint-Domingue,* 22-23; patron of Rey, 159; philosophy, 213n31; and question of certainty, 59-69; rational method, 50-52; reaction of, to use of words as weapons, 137; retirement to Auteuil, 28; salon, 156, 157, 240n10; skepticism, 194; social and political theory, 44, 50-59, 68-69, 138, 139-40, 147-51, 186, 187, 190; in Society of *1789,* 198n2; theoretical justification of Revolution, 20-23; *Traité sur la volonté et de ses effets* 55-56, 58, 73, 91; and *Tribune,* 163; use of "ideology" to clarify political concepts, 98, 117, 119, 128, utilitarian-

Reid, Thomas, 166
Religion, 101, 102, 115, 180, 194; integrated with science, 247n86
Religious liberty; *see* Freedom of religion
Representative assembly, 234n143
Representative government, 17-18, 19, 150, 158; destruction of, under Napoleon, 38-39; theory of, 114-34; Tracy's arguments for, 21, 99, 100-9, 113-28; U.S. as model of, 29
Representatives: election of, 32
Republic: enlightened, 107, 109-10; ideal vision of, 42; model (Tracy), 114-28
Republic (the), 6, 27, 30-31, 35, 42, 107-8; First, 109, 164; Second, 33
Republican virtue, 137
Republicanism, 158-60, 162-71
Resistance theory, 110-14, 168
Revolution, 110-14; legacy of, 5-43. *See also* French Revolution
Revolution of *1793-94* (France), 24
Revolution of *1830* (France), 164, 169, 186
Revolutionary terror, justification of, 24-26; *see also* Terror, the
Revue américaine, 162
Rey, Joseph, 160, 171, 178-85; *Des bases de l'ordre social,* 178, 179; *Mémoires,* 159; *Théorie et pratique de la science sociale,* 178; *Traité des principes généraux des droit et de la legislation,* 178
Ricardo, David, 72, 73, 77, 220n14, 222n39, 224n60; *Principles of Political Economy,* 70
Riches, 74, 76, 77, 95, 141
"Right reason," 16, 97, 114
Rights, 2, 189; come from needs, 55-56, 58, 65; consensus re, 133; equality of, 19, 31-32, 42; inalienable, 137; limits to, 17; mutable and relative nature of, 59; political, 146-50, 151, 183-84; to property, 10, 11, 25, 26, 76, 129, 171; scientific basis for, 161; sources of, 104
Rights of man (theory), 201n19; philosophical party and, 6-23; Tracy's analysis of, 55-59; *see also* Natural rights
Rights of Man (Paine), 70
Rivadavia, Bernadino, 156

Robespierre, Maximilien de, 24-26, 27, 29, 31, 204n76; legend of, 164, 165; republicanism, 107
Roche, Achille, 165
Rodrigues, Olinde, 172, 178
Roederer, Pierre-Louis, 6, 70, 206n91, 235n2; *Cours d'organisation sociale,* 202n35; views on women, 231n102
Romanticism, 166, 167-68, 170, 245n68
Rossi, Pelegrino, 246n82
Roucher, Jean Antoine, 27
Rouen, Pierre Isidore, 175-76
Rousseau, Jean-Jacques, 49, 70, 160, 161, 169, 222n33; dependency of poor, 79-80; general will (theory), 18
Roussel, Pierre, 49
Roux, Jacques, 25
Royal Society (England), 66
Royalists, 34, 35-36, 133, 154
Royer-Collard, Pierre Paul, 155, 166
Ruines, Les (Volney), 10

Saint-Pierre, Charles Irénee Castel, Abbé de, 2
Saint-Simon, Claude Henri, comte de, 102, 158, 172-73, 180
Saint-Simonians, 159, 171, 249n112, 250n125, 251n132
Saint-Simonianism, 172-78, 179, 180, 247n85
Sainte-Beuve, Charles Augustin, 187, 243n34
Sans-culottes, 24, 25, 35, 36
Santo Domingo, 22, 23
Sarrut, Germain, 169
Say, Horace, 37
Say, Jean-Baptiste, 1, 6, 29, 31, 87, 88, 92, 155, 157, 190, 198n3, 206n91, 210n137, 230n68; *De l'Angleterre et des Anglais,* 220n14; defense of utility, 245n60; definition of wealth, 76-77, 78; divisions in society, 121; influence on English radicals, 235n2; lectured at Athenée, 156; and Napoleon, 38; political economy, 71-73, 74, 94, 95; property, 89; supported Directory, 36-37; theory of production, 82-83; *Traité d'économie politique,* 71, 73, 82